BRITISH
AIRCRAFT
MANUFACTURERS
SINCE 1909

BRITISH AIRCRAFT
MANUFACTURERS
SINCE 1909

PETER G. DANCEY

FONTHILL

Fonthill Media Limited
Fonthill Media LLC
www.fonthillmedia.com
office@fonthillmedia.com

First published 2014

British Library Cataloguing in Publication Data:
A catalogue record for this book is available from the British Library

Typeset in 10/13 pt Sabon LT
Printed and bound in England

ISBN 978-1-78155-229-2

Contents

Acknowledgements

The photographs and illustrations in this work have been collected over several decades since the author began his career in aviation as a boy entrant with the RAF and many are from personal archives. To all contributors, I express my many thanks in particular to those persons I have been unable to contact. Should any material in this book be inadvertently unacknowledged and reproduced without permission or copyright infringed, the author offers his unreserved apologies.

I wish to dedicate this book to Mrs Cathy Starkey – my local NHS GP practice nurse at The Purbeck Health Centre, Stantonbury, Milton Keynes – as without her professional knowledge, diligence and care throughout 2012, this book might not have been possible.

Introduction

This book traces 100 years of British industrial aviation and its history, origins, mergers and takeovers. It details its evolution and is an epitaph to famous names such as Armstrong Whitworth, de Havilland, Chadwick, Claude-Graham White, Sopwith, A. V. Roe, Mitchell, Hawker, Handley Page, Petter and Fairey to name but a few. Also, designers from more recent times including Sidney Camm, Hooker and Hooper, all of whom made VTOL (vertical take-off and landing) more than just a dream, are covered in exhaustive detail. Of the major firms, most at some time or another have been absorbed, merged or reorganised to form a single conglomerate in what is now known as BAe Systems or in the aero-engine field Rolls-Royce. Only PBN-Britten Norman – who on several occasions escaped extinction due to financial difficulties – and Westland, now part of AgustaWestland, and Short Bros of Northern Ireland, remain independent although the latter are part of Canadian, Bombardier Co.

Chapter 1

Airframe Manufacturers' Mergers and Takeovers

Airco

George Holt Thomas established The Aircraft Manufacturing Co. Ltd (Airco) at The Hyde, Hendon, North London, in 1912. Airco concentrated on subcontract production until 1914 including ten Henri Farman biplanes, ninety Maurice Farman Shorthorn biplanes – Longhorn and Shorthorn reconnaissance and bomber aircraft and two prototypes – and the S.7 Longhorn No. 23 and S.11 Shorthorn No. 29 Series. Airco began producing its own designs in June 1914 when Geoffrey de Havilland, undoubtedly one of Britain's most outstanding pioneering aviators and designers, joined Thomas as his chief designer, de Havilland having previously designed the Royal Aircraft Factory Be series at Farnborough near Andover, Hampshire.

His first design for Airco was the DH.1, a two-seat, pusher-engined reconnaissance biplane, the prototype of which flew in the first week of January 1915. Developed at Farnborough, de Havilland used the 70-hp Renault pusher-engine, but the intention was to fit the more powerful British 120-hp Beardmore liquid-cooled inline engine. Once this enhanced powerplant became available soon after production of the DH.1, it was this engine that was fitted to all but seventy-two aircraft built. Aircraft powered with the Beardmore engine were designated as the DH.1A. As the need for more aircraft on the Western Front increased in 1915, an urgent requirement for a high-performance, single-seat fighter arose. As a result, Airco became heavily involved in the design and development of the DH.2 and production of the DH.1A passed to Savages Ltd of Kings Lynn, Norfolk. De Havilland realised that the DH.2 should be specifically designed for dogfighting and be reduced in size and weight from his and other designs at the time. Reasonably successful, the aircraft followed a 'gunbus' formula, mainly due to the lack of reliable gun interrupter mechanisms; however, these became available in due course for fitment to the DH.2. Four hundred DH.2 fighters were built before giving way to the twin-engine DH.3/3A bomber that was de Havilland's first twin-engine design. This was followed by the highly successful DH.4/4A two-seat, day-bomber that had its first flight in August 1916. Almost 6,300 DH.4 were built in over sixty variants using twenty-two different engine types and over 4,800 were manufactured under licence in America (USDH.4) by five different companies.

The first Airco (de Havilland) DH.4 two-seat bomber arrived at the Dayton-Wright Airplane Co. plant at Dayton, Ohio, on 15 August 1917. Fitted with an American Liberty engine, it was test flown for the first time on 29 October 1917. The Liberty Plane as it became known proved to be a reliable workhorse despite the unjustified 'Flying Coffin' nickname bestowed upon it by American pilots. The first American USDH.4 had a long and exemplary service life, logging over 1,080 hours of test and routine flying. It was the second machine to be powered by the Packard Liberty 12 engine – it made more than 4,000 flights and was involved in 2,500 experiments – flew more than 111,000 miles and US aviation pioneers Orville Wright and Glenn Martin made flights in it. Considering the average machines in service life at the time, the number of flying hours logged by the original USDH.4 is truly remarkable and is preserved as the 'Original No. 1 De Havilland' at the National Air and Space Museum, Washington DC. The civil British DH.4A that followed featured a cabin conversion behind the pilot to accommodate two passengers and many of these aircraft were used on cross Channel routes in 1919. Sixteen DH.4As were used by the Royal Air Force's Communication Flight in 1919.

The single-seat DH.5 scout and ground-attack fighter was designed in 1916 to replace the DH.2. It featured a staggered wing and was an attempt on de Havilland's part to maintain the same forward vision as was obtained with pusher aircraft, allowing the pilot's cockpit to be located directly below

Airco DH.4 day-bomber with a 375-hp Rolls-Royce Eagle VIII V12 liquid-cooled inline engine. (*V. Cosentino*)

Airco DH.4A civil transport with a 350-hp Rolls-Royce Eagle VIII V12 liquid-cooled inline engine. (*V. Cosentino*)

the leading edge of the upper wing. Unfortunately, this peculiar feature led to some unsavoury handling characteristics at low speeds. Nevertheless, the DH.5 was well suited to the ground-strafing role and at least 550 DH.5s were built by Airco and three subcontractors: Darracq Motor Engineering Co. Ltd, Fulham, London; British Caudron Co. Ltd, Cricklewood, London; and Marsh, Jones & Cribb Ltd, Leeds.

Although designed as a trainer, de Havilland's DH.6, many of which the RAF inherited from the RNAS, ended up as light-bombing, anti-submarine reconnaissance aircraft. When flown as a single-seater, a bomb of up to 100 lbs could be carried. At the end of 1918, the RAF had some 1,060 DH.6s on charge. Series production was undertaken by Airco and seven subcontractors: Grahame-White Aviation Co.; Gloucestershire Aircraft Co.; Harland & Wolff, Belfast; Kingsbury Aviation Co.; Morgan & Co.; Ransome Sims & Jeffries, Nacton, Ipswich, Suffolk; and Savages Ltd, Norfolk.

Designed in 1917, the Airco DH.9 bomber, the prototype of which flew for the first time in July 1917, was supposed to have been a superior version of the DH.4 it was intended to replace. However, numerous shortcomings of the Siddeley Deasey Puma engine had serious adverse effects on its performance. It was underpowered and although large numbers were used by the RAF and Hugh Montague Trenchard's Independent Force on the Western Front, it had a rather undistinguished service career. Although it had been intended that the 'Nine' should replace the 'Four', this never happened and production of the DH.4 recommenced in 1918 to provide a number of RAF day-bomber units with reliable aircraft. It had been planned that there would be over thirty DH.9 squadrons in operation, but this was never achieved, although the 'Nine' did see service in almost every theatre of war. Over 2,000 of these two-seat, day-bombers were built for the RAF, its airframe to be redesigned to be powered by the American 400-hp Liberty engine. It was developed into the DH.9A that proved to be one of the outstanding strategic bombers of the First World War. Commonly known as the 'Nine-Ack', the DH.9A was not built by Airco: the prime contractor was Westland Aircraft Ltd at Yeovil, Somerset, who built 423 out of the eventual total of 2,140 produced by twelve subcontractors. Deliveries to the RAF did not start until the last six months of the war, but the type remained in service until 1931. Initially, the RAF sustained heavy losses with the DH.9 as its Puma engine proved unreliable and underrated. Later aircraft, fitted with the excellent Packard Liberty 12 engine built by Westland, were redesignated as the DH.9A. British production was supplemented by 1,415 American-built USDH.9 aircraft. DH.9 and 9As were sold to no less than sixteen overseas countries. In the immediate post-war years, many were used on pioneering commercial air service routes.

Closely resembling the experimental DH.3 and DH.3A of 1916, the DH.10 Amiens three/four seat day-bomber just missed seeing action in the war and as a result, the original Air Ministry order of 1,300 was reduced to 220. With only two of the original ten delivered to the RAF at the end of October 1918, these saw service with Trenchard's Independent (Bomber) Force on the Western Front in France. After the war, a number were used by the Forces of Occupation and many others served with overseas squadrons in India and the Middle East on policing duties. Initial variants were fitted with the 375-hp Rolls-Royce Eagle VIII engine, although later variants fitted with 400-hp Packard Liberty 12 engines were designated Amiens IIIA. Later versions with the engines mounted directly on the lower main planes, dispensing with support struts, received the designation DH.10A. Production aircraft were built by Airco at Hendon and by Alliance Aero Co., Birmingham Carriage Co., Daimler Ltd, Mann Eggerton & Co., National Aircraft Factory (Stockport) and the Siddeley Deasey Car Co. The only other aircraft designed and built by Airco were the four-seat and eight-seat DH.16 and DH.18 airliners operated by Britain's first private airlines, Aircraft Transport and Travel Ltd, owned by Holt Thomas. Five series production DH.18s and a single prototype were built. The prototype aircraft was operated by Aircraft Transport and Travel from April to August 1920 when it was wrecked in a forced landing, the remaining five being operated by Instone Air Line. The British Government's failure to support the fledgling post-war civil aviation industry and drastic cuts in military orders saw Airco assets in the mid-1920s bought by the Birmingham Small Arms Co. (BSA) who had no intention of continuing with the company's aviation activities.

Airspeed Ltd – Airspeed (1934) Ltd

Airspeed Ltd was established by A. H. Tiltman (1897–1976) and Neville Shute Norway (the author who wrote under his first two names) in York in 1931 with just £5,000 of private capital. The first Airspeed aircraft was the AS.1 Tern glider that flew in August 1931 and on 24 August 1931, it established the first distance record for sailplanes in Great Britain. Airspeed's first powered design was the AS.4 Ferry built to a specification produced by Sir Alan Cobham (1894–1973), a pioneering aviator and founder of in-flight refuelling. Fitted with three DH Gipsy engines, the aircraft was a wooden biplane capable of carrying ten passengers. This was followed by the AS.5 Courier, a six-seat monoplane of which sixteen were built. This was the first British aircraft fitted with flaps and a hand-operated retractable undercarriage. The Courier had its first flight on 11 April 1933 at Portsmouth Airport to where Airspeed had moved into larger premises re-registering itself in August 1934 as Airspeed (1934) Ltd after becoming associated with the famous Tyneside shipbuilding firm of Swan Hunter & Wigham Richardson Ltd. A stretched twin-engine development of the Courier followed, designated the AS.6 Envoy, which saw service with a number of airlines and air forces after 1934. One example served in the Far East during the Second World War and was attached to SEAC headquarters Station Flight for communications duties.

Two types forever synonymous with Airspeed were the AS.10 Oxford advanced trainer and Horsa glider. The Oxford was designed to Air Ministry Specification T.23/26 and was the RAF's first twin-engine cantilevered monoplane trainer. The Oxford was a development of the Airspeed Envoy civil transport. The prototype (serial L4534) 'Ox-box' as it became known to aircrews flew on 19 June 1937 and an initial production contract for 136 aircraft was placed. Three Oxfords left Portsmouth in November 1937 entering service with the RAF's Central Flying School as an advanced trainer in January 1938. By the outbreak of war in September 1939, 400 or so had been delivered including seventy-five from the de Havilland factory at Hatfield, Hertfordshire, and in addition to the parent company, wartime contracts were placed with Standard and Percival as well as de Havilland. By 1945, a total of 8,586 Oxfords had been built including 4,411 by Airspeed at Portsmouth, 550 by Airspeed at Christchurch, Dorset, 1,515 by de Havilland Aircraft Co. Ltd, 750 by the Standard Motor Co. Ltd and 1,356 by Percival Aircraft Ltd.

Airspeed Oxfords were used by service flying training schools in the UK, Canada, Australia, New Zealand, Southern Rhodesia and the Middle East with a small number being made available under reverse Lend-Lease to the USAAF in Great Britain. In addition to training, the aircraft were used in the air ambulance role and on communications and radar calibration duties. The type was produced in five main versions for military use. From 1946 to

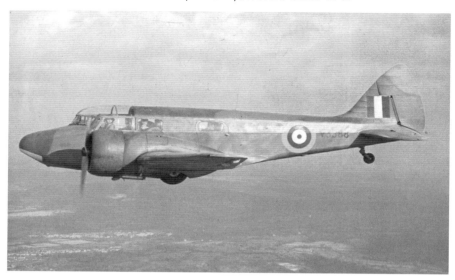

RAF Airspeed Oxford trainers from 1938 to 1954. The type was built in large numbers by Airspeed and under subcontract by de Havilland, Percival Aircraft and Standard Motors. *(Flight Colour)*

1948, Airspeed converted 160 surplus airframes into a commercial six-seat, light-transport aircraft that were redesignated as the AS.65 Consul. From the war's end, RAF Airspeed Oxfords were used mainly for communication duties although in 1951, they gained a new lease of life as trainers with the expansion of Flying Training Command to train National Service pilots. The aircraft was finally withdrawn from RAF use in 1954.

The Airspeed AS.51 Horsa I and AS.58 Horsa II military gliders designed by Hessell Tiltman were built to Air Ministry Specification X.26/40 and was the RAF's first troop-carrying glider. The prototype, serial DG597, first flew on 12 September 1941 and was followed by 3,792 series aircraft with 695 built by Airspeed at Christchurch and the rest by various subcontractors, mainly woodworking firms such as Harris Lebus. These gliders proved invaluable in the D-Day landings. Other wartime designs include the AS.39 Fleet Shadower – built to meet Air Ministry Specification S.23/37 for an aircraft to shadow enemy naval vessels during the hours of darkness – and the AS.45 Cambridge, an advanced training monoplane to meet Air Ministry Specification T.4/39 that remained in prototype form only. Airspeed was purchased by de Havilland in 1940 and in 1951, it became the Airspeed Division of de Havilland with eventual assimilation into the de Havilland organisation and loss of separate identity.

Sir W. G. Armstrong Whitworth & Co. Ltd – WGA – AWD

Sir W. G. Armstrong Whitworth & Co. Ltd, Newcastle-upon-Tyne, was founded in 1897 from the merger of two rival engineering and shipbuilding firms of Armstrong and Whitworth. As the onset of the First World War approached, the company moved into aircraft production building Royal Aircraft Factory Be.2a/b and Be.2c fighters at its Elswick Works at Gosforth, Newcastle-upon-Tyne. In early 1914, the aeroplane department of the company was established under its first works manager and chief designer, the Dutchman, Frederick Koolhoven. Koolhoven was a qualified pilot and had gained design experience working on French Deperdussin monoplanes. His first design for Armstrong Whitworth was intended as a small scout aircraft, the FK.1, to meet Royal Flying Corps (RFC) requirements. In the event on flying the prototype aircraft in September 1914, Koolhoven realised the aircraft had a number of shortcomings and that it was inferior to his competitors, the Sopwith and Bristol Scouts. As a result, its development was not pursued and it did not enter production. A number of other successful Frederick Koolhoven (FK) designs followed, namely the FK.3 two-seat reconnaissance aircraft and training biplane in 1915 and the larger FK.8 in 1916 with the two-seat FK.10 fighter-bomber following a year later. A total of three prototype FK.10s were built by Armstrong Whitworth after which five production aircraft were ordered from Angus Sanderson of Newcastle and three naval variants from the Phoenix Dynamo Company of Bradford with one aircraft configured as a bomber fitted with bomb racks for light bombs.

One of Koolhoven's most extraordinary designs was the FK.12 single-engine, three-seat triplane escort fighter. Four aircraft were ordered by the War Office but it is believed only two prototypes were completed. On leaving Armstrong Whitworth, Koolhoven returned to his native Holland establishing his manufacturing facility producing a multitude of his own successful designs. At this time, the company also built 250 Bristol Fighters and a number of airships at Barlow, Selby, South Yorkshire. Another early design from Armstrong Whitworth was the Ara, a small single-engine biplane fighter of conventional design using the infamous Dragonfly engine. The first prototype, serial F4971, designed by Fred Murphy flew in the spring of 1919. However, the aircraft was a victim of the problematic Dragonfly engine and the project was abandoned after completion of only three prototypes on the closure of the company's aircraft department prior to its move to the Midlands.

On purchasing the Siddeley Deasey Car Co. Ltd in February 1919, the company moved to Coventry with a subsequent reorganisation that gave rise to Armstrong Siddeley Motors Ltd. In 1921, Sir W. G. Armstrong Whitworth Aircraft Ltd was established with a factory at Whitley airfield and later at Baginton, Coventry. By this time, Koolhoven had left Armstrong Whitworth

Armstrong Whitworth FK.8 reconnaissance-bomber *c.* 1917 with a 160-hp Beardmore six-cylinder, liquid-cooled inline engine. (*V. Cosentino*)

having joined the British Aerial Transport Co. (BAT) – founded in 1917 by Samuel Waring (later Lord Waring of Foots Cray) at Willesden, London – before returning to his home country. The Siddeley Deasey Car Co. Ltd had entered into aeroplane production in the First World War building aircraft designs of other companies.

In 1917, Maj. F. M. Green, John Lloyd and S. D. Heron joined the firm as senior designers and all were formerly from the Royal Aircraft Factory, Farnborough, Hampshire. The company now began to build aircraft of its own design. After some early redesign work on an Re.8 (redesignated RT.1), Green began detailed work on the Siddeley SR.2 Siskin, a design he had started work on at Farnborough. It had been Green's intention to use the Royal Aircraft Factory's new 300-hp, fourteen-cylinder, two-row radial engine, but in the event all five prototypes were fitted with the infamous ABC Dragonfly I. Pending completion by Heron of his RAF 8 engine, he gained permission to take the design with him. However, disagreement over the cylinder design of the new engine led to Heron resigning to take up an appointment in the US leaving the engine design effort depleted until revived as the Jaguar I under the auspices of S. M. Viale. As a result, the SR.2 Siskin did not enter production but Green persevered with the design and by 20 March 1921, a much improved Armstrong Whitworth Siskin Mk II fighter (civil-registration G-EBHY) was flown fitted with a 325-hp Jaguar 1 engine. The company were pioneers in the development of all-metal aircraft and the use of high-tensile steel in aircraft construction, and in response to the Air Ministry's suggestion, Green redesigned the aircraft employing an all-steel structure providing the RAF with its first all-metal structured, fabric-covered aeroplane: the Siskin III, IIIA and the two-seat, dual-control Siskin III DC.

Armstrong Whitworth Atlas Army Co-operation airplane *c.* 1927 with a 450-hp Armstrong Siddeley Jaguar IVC fourteen-cylinder, air-cooled, radial piston engine. (*V. Cosentino*)

The Siskin III, serial J6583, flew on 7 May 1923 after having undergone structural tests at Martlesham Heath, Suffolk. Sixty-three Siskin IIIs were produced, six of which were built as Mk IIIDC two-seat, dual-control trainers with a further thirty-one converted from single-seaters. The Siskin IIIA was the most popular variant of which some 440 were produced with the much superior supercharged 420–450-hp Jaguar IVS engine. Production was also undertaken by Bristol who built eighty-four Siskins, Blackburn forty-two, Glosters seventy-four and Vickers forty-two. Armstrong Whitworth Siskins were followed by the larger Atlas two-seat army co-operation or dual-controlled advanced trainer. This was the first aircraft to enter RAF service that had been specifically designed for army co-operation work, the prototype having its first flight on 10 May 1925. It proved to be a rugged, reliable aircraft and highly suited to its role. Two other early 1920s designs, the twenty-five seat Awana troop-transport and the Wolf two-seat reconnaissance biplane, were unsuccessful and abandoned.

In the pre-1939 era, in parallel with its military Whitley AW.38 long-range night bombers and Abermarle AW.41 glider tug and troop carrier (the first British operational aircraft to be fitted with a tricycle undercarriage), the company produced a series of commercial airliners for Imperial Airways. Although produced in small numbers, these aircraft made a considerable impact on the establishment of the airline's Empire routes. The first of these aircraft was the Argosy, a twenty-seat passenger biplane fitted with three 385-hp Jaguar air-cooled radial engines, entering service on 16 July 1926. This was followed by the seventeen-passenger Atlanta AW.15 entering service on

Armstrong Whitworth series of Meteor night fighters included the NF.11, NF.12 and NF.14, all with British AI.10 radar. (*Warplane Collection, author and postcard*)

26 September 1932 and later by the four-engine, all-metal stressed-skin forty-passenger AW.27A (the first registration G-ADSR named Ensign), fourteen of which were built at Air Service Training (AST), Hamble, Hampshire. The AST was a member of the Hawker Siddeley Aircraft Co. Ltd of which Armstrong Whitworth Aircraft had become a founder member in 1935. The Ensign was the largest British pre-war airliner of which fourteen were built. It gave useful service with Imperial Airways but proved costly to operate and maintain.

Meanwhile, the factory at Whitley was working flat out on its namesake bomber for the RAF with its first flight, serial K4586, occurring on 17 March 1936 and entering service a year later. A second prototype, serial K4587, preceded production of eighty series aircraft, thirty-four of which were the Mk

Armstrong Whitworth (HS) Argosy 650/660 aircraft differed from their RAF military counterparts in not having the thimble-nose weather radar fit. (*Author*)

Hawker Siddeley Argosy of No. 105 Squadron operated from RAF Khormaksar Aden to 'up country' locations. Here, serial XP412 can be seen behind an oil drum revetment at Thumier in the north of Aden (now South Yemen). (*Aviation News*)

1 variant with Armstrong Siddeley Tiger IX engines and the remainder as Mk II with Tiger VIII engines. These were followed by eighty Mk.III and 120 Mk IVs which introduced the Rolls-Royce Merlin Mk IV engine and a Nash and Thompson power-operated tail turret with four .303-inch machine guns. The Merlin X-engined Mk V was in production from 1939 to 1942. Fifteen were converted in 1942 as freighters for BOAC, operating to the Middle East and on the perilous Leuchars-Stockholm diplomatic air run. In total, 1,824 Whitleys were built and most were the Mk V with a few Mk VIIs which continued in service until the end of the war. Production of the Whitley ceased in 1942, but it was still in service for glider towing and bomber training purposes when the war ended. Also in 1942, in addition to the Whitley Mk V converted for

use by BOAC as freight carriers, a number were also converted to Admiralty requirements for training flight engineers: this variant was designated as the Whitley VII (Naval).

The twin-engine AW.41 Albemarle, which started life as the Bristol Type 155, was designed to Air Ministry Specification B.17/38 (B.18/38) for bomber-reconnaissance duties, but was later produced as a glider tug and paratrooper carrier. It was designed at a time when it was feared there would be a shortage of light alloys and other specialised raw materials. Consequently, wood and steel were used in the structure of the aircraft and it is all credit to the design team that in spite of these severe design constraints, the aircraft had an all-up-weight close to other similar aircraft of its time. Armstrong Whitworth received an order for 200 Albemarles that included two prototypes. Armstrong Whitworth produced the two prototypes, serials P1360 and P1361, with P1360 having its first flight at Hamble, Hampshire, on 20 March 1940. All other aircraft were built by Armstrong Whitworth Hawkesley, a new company established in the Government No. 2 Shadow Factory at Brockworth, Gloucestershire, to undertake production of the Albemarle. Armstrong Whitworth Hawkesley, a contraction of Armstrong Whitworth/Hawker Siddeley, was set up as a joint production company.

Hawkesley received a further order for 780 aircraft from 1940. However, production was delayed as Hawkesley was busy building the urgently needed Hawker Hurricane fighter. As a result, the first three series aircraft were not completed until December 1941. Hawkesley had only built forty bombers due to the availability of the superior de Havilland Mosquito, and with the mediocre performance of the Albemarle in mind, Hawkesley were asked to concentrate on the production of transport ST (Special Transport) and glider-towing GT (Glider Tug) versions. Albemarle bombers were not used operationally. In total and including prototypes, some 610 Albemarles were built by the time production ceased in December 1944. A number were delivered to the Soviet Air Force (VVS).

In addition to its own designs, Armstrong Whitworth undertook large-scale wartime production of Avro Lancaster and Short Stirling bombers and Fairey Barracuda carrier-borne torpedo/dive bombers. Post-war, Armstrong Whitworth took over the development and manufacture of the Hawker Sea Hawk, (Gloster) Meteor night fighters (NF.11, NF.12 and NF.14) as well as building 133 Gloster Javelin all-weather night fighters.

The company's post-war designs included the unsuccessful AW 55 Apollo, a thirty-seat passenger transport powered by four Armstrong Siddeley Mamba turboprops, and the AW 650/660 Argosy. A civil and military twin-boom passenger and freight transport, it entered production as the Hawker Siddeley HS 650 Argosy, the first production aircraft flying in December 1958. Deliveries to the RAF (fifty-six) ceased in April 1964. Another Armstrong Whitworth design, the tailless AW.52 research aircraft, first flew on 13 November 1947.

A major reorganisation of the Hawker Siddeley Group, of which Armstrong Whitworth was now part of on 1 July 1963, resulted in the establishment of Avro Whitworth followed by the Whitworth Gloster Division with the original Armstrong Whitworth name disappearing on 1 April 1965.

Taylorcraft Aeroplanes (England) Ltd (Auster Aircraft Ltd) Beagle Aircraft

Auster Aircraft Ltd was the name of the company that succeeded Taylorcraft Aeroplanes (England) Ltd that had been formed in 1939 to manufacture designs under licence from the Taylorcraft Corporation of America. During the war, Taylor Aeroplanes (England) Ltd at its Thurmaston, Leicester, and Britannia Works had built 1,604 Taylorcraft Auster I, II, III, IV and V two/three-seat artillery spotters or AOPs for the Army Air Corp and the RAF, all seeing active service in the Second World War.

Auster Aircraft Ltd came into being on 7 March 1946 transferring its works to nearby Rearsby aerodrome, Leicestershire. The military Auster V formed the basis of the civil J-1 Autocrat. The J-1N Alpha and J-1U Workmaster aircraft were built in large numbers after the war as light two/three-seat private transports with upholstered interiors and other refinements. A number of other civil two and three-seat variants were built such as the J-2 Arrow and J-1B Aiglet of which most of the seventy built were exported. The J-4 Arrow fitted with a 90-hp Blackburn Cirrus Minor 1 engine, was followed by the

Taylorcraft Auster AOP. 9s equipped a myriad of RAF observation squadrons in the Second World War before serving post-war with the Army Air Corps. (*Warplane Collection*)

J-5F Aiglet Trainer. Auster's first four-seater aircraft was the J-5B Autocar that was built in several versions using a variety of powerplants. An interesting crop-spraying aircraft, the B-8 Agricola, was first flown on 8 December 1955; however, it did not sell and only two were built. Earlier in 1951, the B-4 was another interesting but unsuccessful aircraft and was designed as a rear-loading air ambulance. Post-war on the military front, Auster Aircraft Ltd produced 312 Auster AOP.6 Model K two-seat monoplanes for the RAF along with seventy-seven dual-controlled Auster T.7 trainer variants. The AOP.6 was flown in the Korean War and in Malaya operating against terrorists. The Auster AOP.9 was the last AOP aircraft produced by the company and was the only military type not derived from a civil variant being designed from the start as a military aircraft. The AOP.9 was designed to be used in a number of other roles such as casualty evacuation, cable laying and photographic and light transport duties. The aircraft had the unique feature that the rear cockpit floor could be easily removed by undoing six bolts so that the AOP.9 could suit another role in the field. One hundred and forty-five AOP.9s served with the RAF and Army Air Corps from 1955 until helicopters began to take over their role in the mid-1960s.

In June 1961, Auster Aircraft Ltd and F. G. Miles Ltd (formed in 1951) in association with an engineering firm merged to form Beagle-Miles, later reverting to Beagle Aircraft Ltd. The new company proceeded with development of the new D-Series that was continued by Beagle Aircraft. The last Auster-designed tail-dragger therefore entered production as the Beagle Husky.

Avro

Edwin Alliot Verdon Roe (1877–1958) has the distinction of achieving the first flight over British soil on 8 June 1908 in an all British-designed aircraft. Fitted with a British engine, the 9-hp JAP, it was designed and built by J. A. Prestwich with whom Roe had formed a brief business partnership before joining forces with his brother, Humphrey Verdon Roe, in 1909 forming A. V. Roe & Co. at Brownsfield Mills, Manchester. In 1912, Roe designed the world's first totally enclosed monoplane, the Avro Type F, which he personally flew on 1 May. However, it was the remarkable Type 504 Series, which first flew in July 1913 and developed from the Type 500 racing biplane, that established the company as a legend in its own right.

The Avro 504 biplane was produced in a proliferation of variants from A to N by A. V. Roe and a wide variety of subcontractors. A total of 8,340 were built in the First World War with a further 598 N-Types built from 1925 to 1932, although seventy-eight of these were 'K' conversions. The Avro 504K appeared in 1918 and differed from the many other versions that had preceded

This Avro Triplane, one of A. V. Roe's first designs, belongs to The Shuttleworth Trust at Old Warden, Bedfordshire. (*Author*)

it by having an open fronted 'horseshoe' cowling and engine mounts designed to accept a variety of different powerplants such as the 110-hp Rhone, 130-hp Clerget and 100-hp Monosoupape. A small number known as the Gosport was delivered to the Estonian Air Force in 1928.

While it is common knowledge that the Avro 504 was the most widely used trainer aircraft of the First World War, there has been little mention of the 274 J and K variants converted as makeshift single-seat, night fighters armed with a Lewis gun on a Foster-mounting above the wing for use by the RFC's Home Defence units. The aircraft were modified by A. V. Roe & Co. Ltd at Manchester and Hamble, Hampshire; The Grahame-White Aviation Co. Ltd, Hendon, London; and the Humber Motor Co. Ltd, Coventry.

The Avro 504 also claims a place in bombing history being the first British aircraft used on an organised bombing raid, the attack on Zeppelin sheds at Friedrichshafen on Lake Constance on 21 November 1914. Avro 504 production spanned twenty years and it was not until March 1933 that the type was finally declared obsolete by the RAF. At the end of the First World War, many 504Ns were sold on the civil market and used by private fliers and flying clubs for joy rides, banner towing and charter work. A number of ex-RAF Avro 504s were fitted with five-cylinder Mongoose engines. In anticipation of further orders for Home Defence fighters, Avro at Miles Platting, Manchester, designed and produced a single Type 531 Spider, so called because of its Warren girder strut arrangement. The type did not enter production as by mid-1918, the German night attacks on England had almost ceased and more

The Avro Anson Mk 1 was used by RAF Coastal Command for coastal patrol and observation duties. (*Wings*)

suitable types such as the Sopwith Snipe were becoming available.

To meet First World War demand for the 504, Avro built new factories at Miles Platting, Failsworth, Hamble and Newton Heath. With the advent of peace, Avro were forced into the manufacture of toys and sports goods to keep the factories gainfully employed. However, in spite of very difficult times between the wars, Avro built some thirty-five different types starting with Britain's first post-war practical light aircraft, the Avro Baby, fitted with a 35-hp Green engine designed by Gustavus Green (1865–1964) builder of the first British Aero Engines. Eight Avro Baby were built. An early post-war all wooden single-seat fighter designed by Roy Chadwick, the Avro Type 566, did not enter production as the Air Ministry did not favour aircraft using Napier Lion or Condor engines. Another Chadwick design, the Type 584 Avocet, which was his first design using metal stressed-skin construction, was designed to Air Ministry Specification 17/25. However, like the Baby, not one Avocet entered production. The Avro Type 549 Aldershot, a single-engine heavy-bomber, was produced to Air Ministry Specification 2/20. Eventually after competitive trials against the de Havilland Derby, fifteen aircraft were ordered, enough to equip No. 99 Squadron on a twin-flight basis at RAF Bircham Newton. The type only remained in service for about two years when they were replaced by the Handley Page H.P.24 Hyderabad as the Air Ministry abandoned its large single-engine heavy-bomber programme. Three ambulance transport versions of the Aldershot bomber were supplied to RAF Halton, Buckinghamshire, for use by the RAF hospital and the aircraft were renamed Andover.

After three years of comparative trials against other elementary trainers, the Avro Type 621 Tutor was chosen to succeed the ubiquitous 504 as the RAF's standard trainer. Prior to full-scale production, a trial batch were flown

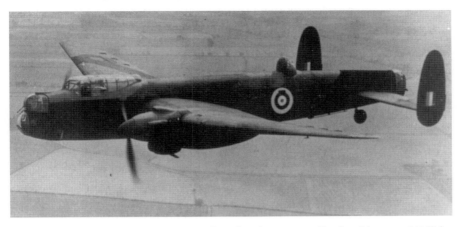

RAF Avro Manchester seven-seat medium-bombers were fitted with two 1,760-hp Rolls-Royce Vulture 1 inline piston engines. (*Warplane Collection*)

fitted with five-cylinder Siddeley Mongoose engines instead of the Armstrong Siddeley seven-cylinder Lynx IV C fitted to later production aircraft. Seven navigator training variants were supplied to the RAF from January to July 1935 named Prefect in addition to fourteen twin-float Avro Sea Tutors that were delivered to the RAF from February 1934 until April 1936 for use by the Seaplane Training Flight at Calshot, Hampshire.

The Avro factory at Newton Heath had been built during the First World War and specifically designed for large-scale aircraft production. In 1920, Newton Heath became the company's head office. Some fifteen miles away in 1924, A. V. Roe purchased land at New Hall Farm at Woodford, Cheshire, where it started manufacturing and has continued to do so to this day. (The plant under the auspices of BAe Systems was where all manufacturing of the Avro 146 (formerly BAe 146) and RJ regional airliners took place, following closure of BAe's Hatfield (Commercial Aircraft) Plant in the early 1990s.)

In 1928, Edwin Alliot Verdon Roe sold his interest in A. V. Roe & Co. Ltd to J. D. Siddeley of Sir Armstrong Whitworth Aircraft, then forming a new company with Samuel Saunders to form SARO (Saunders-Roe Ltd) involved in the design, manufacture and repair of marine and amphibious types. In 1935, Avro became a founder member of the Hawker Siddeley Aircraft Co. Ltd and in 1938, all operations were moved to Woodford and a large new factory of one million square feet at Chadderton, near Oldham, north of Manchester, and a new shadow factory at Yeadon. In 1928, Roy Chadwick, who had joined the company in 1911, was appointed chief designer. Another young man who had joined the company in 1914 and worked for Chadwick during the war was Roy Dobson. By the end of the war, Dobson had become works manager and in 1934 was appointed general manager. The two men

Avro Lancaster B.1 of No. 419 'Moose' Squadron of the RCAF in 1943. On 12 June 1944, P/O A. C. Mynarski was awarded the Victoria Cross. (*Flypast Calender*)

worked together in great harmony with Chadwick looking after design and Dobson production. It is not without doubt that much of the Avro company's success can be accredited to these two men. It is also significant that by 1936, the company had fully established new mass-production methods involving extensive jigging, tooling and the utilisation of modern precision machine tools. The Air Ministry at the time described the company 'as the best organised manufacturing unit we have, extremely efficient and with a well-equipped tool room, drawing office and machine shops'.

One of Avro's most famous designs that served the RAF for more than thirty-two years was the Avro 625A Anson named after Lord George Anson (1697-1762), British Admiral of the Fleet and circumnavigator. The Anson was a military development of the six-passenger commercial aircraft, the Avro 652, two of which were ordered by Imperial Airways in 1934 (G-ACRM Avalon and G-ACRN Ava).

Initial military aircraft differed very little from their civil counterparts except in the fitment of Armstrong Siddeley Cheetah VI engines in place of the Cheetah V. The Anson served the military in a variety of roles and variants from trainer and transport to bomber and reconnaissance. After a continuous production run of seventeen years with a peak output of 130 a month at the Avro Yeadon factory in 1943-1944, the last Anson, T.21, WJ561, was delivered to the RAF at the end of May 1952. This was the 8,138th Anson built in Britain at Avro's, Newton Heath, Chadderton and Yeadon factories and 2,882 were also built in Canada by Federal Aircraft Ltd. Most Canadian-built Ansons were fitted with engines of American origin. In Canadian service, however, the Anson was known as the Blowpipe. The last flying Anson was in Australia in 1987, fifty years after the type's first flight.

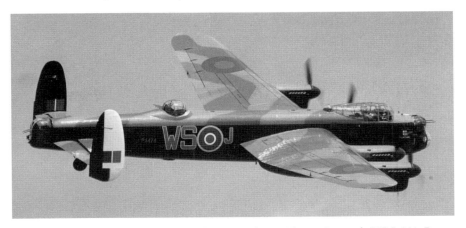

Avro Lancaster B.1 of No. 9 'Bat' (Bomber) Squadron with wartime code WS J. (*Air Power International*)

Avro's entry into heavy-bomber design and production started rather inauspiciously with the disappointing twin-engine Avro Type 679 Manchester. Development centred on the new Rolls-Royce 1,760-hp Vulture engines. The Manchester's brief and unfortunate service life was not in any way the fault of the design, but more the fault of the underdeveloped and unreliable Vulture engines. The prototype, serial L7246, first flew on 25 July 1939. Deliveries to the RAF commenced in mid-1940 with the type declared operational from November 1940 until July 1942 when, due to frequent engine failures, the RAF was forced to withdraw it from use.

Luckily, the Avro Type 683 Lancaster heavy bomber had already successfully completed service and acceptance trials at RAE Boscombe Down in 1941. The Lancaster (Manchester II) evolved as a result of chief designer Roy Chadwick's persistence strictly against official policy – all Rolls-Royce Merlin engines were needed for fitment to Supermarine Spitfire fighters – in acquiring four 1,130-hp Merlin X water-cooled inline engines to prove that the basic design of the heavy bomber was sound and that the main problem with the Manchester were its underpowered Vulture engines. The first prototype Lancaster I, serial BT308, was at one time known as the Manchester III and within nine months, Lancaster Is were being delivered to RAF Bomber Command fitted with four Merlin XX engines. A total of 7,377 Avro Lancasters were built throughout the war with production centred at Avro, Manchester and Yeadon, who built three prototypes, followed by 3,670 Mk I/IIIs. Armstrong Whitworth at Baginton, Bitteswell and South Marston produced 1,029 Mk I/IIIs and 300 Mk IIs; Austin Motors 150 Mk Is and 180 Mk VIIs; Metropolitan-Vickers 1,081 Mk I/IIIs; Vickers Armstrong at Chester and Castle Bromwich 535 Mk Is; and Victory Aircraft of Canada, who were appointed as major subcontractors, built 430 Mk Xs.

At the peak of production from August to October 1944, the combined 'Production Group' manufactured more than 300 aircraft a month. At Newton Heath alone, output peaked 100 bombers a month. It has been estimated that to make one Lancaster, it took in the region of 35,000 man hours requiring half a million separate manufacturing processes to bring together some 50,000 parts for each aircraft. As a safeguard against Merlin engine shortages, 300 Lancaster IIs built by Armstrong Whitworth were powered with 1,725-hp Bristol Hercules VI or XVI radial engines. These aircraft were designated as the Lancaster II. In the event, there were no shortages of Merlin engines and all subsequent variants were fitted with either Rolls-Royce or American Packard Liberty engines. The Lancaster has the distinction of being the first British heavy bomber to carry navigational airborne bombing radar: 'Gee-H'. In total during the Second World War, Lancaster bombers had flown some 156,000 sorties and dropped 608,612 tons of bombs. The Lancaster was the only wartime bomber capable of carrying the 10-ton Grand Slam bomb.

Some modified Lancasters assumed the role of maritime reconnaissance (ASR GR.3 Lancaster MR.3) until superseded by the Lockheed Neptune and Avro Shackleton. Lancasters were also converted for civil use under the designation Type 691 Lancastrian and of the eighty-two built, early variants were built in Canada by Victory Aircraft Ltd at Malton, Ontario, for Trans-Canada Air Lines. Victory Aircraft also manufactured bomber variants (Mk X) at a rate of about four aircraft a week which were then shipped or flown to the UK for use by Lancaster squadrons of the RCAF.

Sixty-seven, thirteen-passenger Lancastrian transports were British registered and several RAF aircraft were later used as flying test beds for jet engines which were mounted in place of the outer Merlins. With the war ended, Lancaster bombers remained in service until supplanted by the scaled-up version, the Avro Type 694 Lincoln (originally designated as the Lancaster IV and V). The first prototype Avro Lincoln flew from Woodford in June 1944, but in spite of utilising many left over Lancaster components, production slipped so that it was not until the war had ended in August 1945 that the Lincoln entered RAF service. Even so, deliveries were delayed and it was well into 1946 when RAF squadrons were fully equipped with the type. Production of the Lincoln in the UK amounted to 532 aircraft with Avro producing 168 (plus three prototypes), Armstrong Whitworth 281 and seventy-nine by Metropolitan-Vickers. Canada built one, a B. Mk XV, and Australia built forty-three B. Mk 30s and thirty B. Mk 30As of which twenty were later modified to Mk 31 standard with a longer nose to accommodate search radar and two operators. Production aircraft were fitted with a variety of powerplants: eighty-two Mk Is used Rolls-Royce Merlin 85 or 85A engines and 447 Mk IIs used Merlin 66, 68 or 300 variants. As the last British piston-engine heavy bomber flown by the RAF, the Lincoln B.2 from 1947 was prepared for operational frontline service in two different standards according to its electronics fit:

Lincoln B.2 (IIIG) with H2S Mk IIIG, Gee II and Rebecca II

Lincoln B.2 (IVA) with H2S IVA, Gee-H Mk II and Rebecca II or IV.

In 1948, all RAF Avro Lincolns were 'tropicalised' and various squadrons served for periods in Singapore against communist terrorists in Malaya and Kenya against the Mau Mau. The aircraft could carry up to 14,000 lbs of bombs, although in the Far East and African operations, the 1,000-lb GP bomb did little damage, having more of a psychological effect on target areas. The Lincoln remained in RAF frontline service until the mid-1950s although a number were used for signals training in 1963. Twelve ex-RAF aircraft went to the Argentine Air Force, supplemented by eighteen specially-built new aircraft by Armstrong Whitworth.

Other immediate post-war types were the Avro Type 688 Tudor I (Avro XX), Type 689 Tudor II (Avro XXI) and the Avro Type 685 York, which although designed and flown in 1942, did not enter large-scale service with RAF Transport Command until after the war. The York, of which 257 were built, was the only British transport aircraft produced (albeit in small numbers) during the Second World War as the majority of military transports were of American origin and supplied under the Lend-Lease agreement. The York was another Lancaster derivative with an entirely new fuselage designed to accommodate twenty-four passengers. Of the small number produced in

Avro 107A, serial WZ736, can be seen at the Manchester Aerospace Museum in Lancashire. (*Author*)

Avro Type 698 Vulcan bomber prototype, serial VX770. (*Author*)

Second Avro prototype Type 698, serial VX777, at the end of a long development career, seen at rest at A&AEE Farnborough. (*Author*)

the war, most were VIP variants including serial LV633 for Sir (then Mr) Winston Churchill, serial MW102 for Lord Louis Mountbatten C-in-C South East Asia Command, MW107 for General Smuts and MW140 for HRH the Duke of Gloucester, Governor-General of Australia. In May 1943, serial LV633 was delivered to No. 24 Squadron at RAF Northolt and furnished as a flying conference room. The aircraft was named Ascalon and took Prime Minister Churchill, senior Allied commanders and King George VI on their many tours of troops and war zones in the Mediterranean and North Africa. The Avro York is most noted for its part in the Berlin Airlift when the type flew some 29,000 flights and carried in excess of 230,000 tons of badly needed supplies to the city. Of the total of 257 built, 208 were built for the RAF with five for BOAC in 1944. Of the remainder, three were VIP aircraft and three freighters and a combined passenger-freighter was produced.

Avro Vulcan B.2 fitted with an electronic countermeasures rear radome. (*Author*)

No. 617 'Dambuster' Squadron Avro Vulcan B.2 at RAF Scampton prior to flying a deterrent mission *c.* 1961. (*Author*)

The next Lancaster derivative from Avro was the Type 696 Shackleton long-range maritime-reconnaissance and anti-submarine aircraft of all metal stressed-skin construction with a crew of ten. Developed from the Lincoln GR III, the Shackleton retained the Lincoln's wings and undercarriage, but introduced a revised shortened fuselage with four Rolls-Royce Griffon engines each driving a six-blade contra-rotating propeller. The aircraft was named by Avro's chief designer Roy Chadwick after his grandmother's son, Sir Ernest Shackleton, the Arctic explorer. The prototype MR.1, serial VW126, first flew on 9 March 1949. Seventy-seven MR.1s and MR.1As were built followed by seventy MR.2s featuring a longer streamlined nose increasing the fuselage length to 87 feet 3 inches from 77 feet 6 inches and a semi-retractable 'dustbin' radome for the ASV radar aft of the wings.

In 1957, seventeen T.4s converted from MR.1s and ten T.2s converted

Above and left: Avro Vulcan B.2 Douglas Skybolt trials aircraft. (*Author/Take-off*)

Below: Avro Vulcan B.2BB, serial XM607, at RAF Waddington proudly showing its three successful bombing missions insignia after the Falklands conflict. (*Author*)

Avro Vulcan B.2A
MRR of No. 27
Squadron. (*Take-off*)

An Avro Vulcan B.2BB
at Avro's Manchester
factory on completion
of 'Shrike' missile
modifications (supplied
by the US). (*Author*)

from MR.2s as crew trainers were produced. These trainers had all their defensive armament deleted; however, additional radar positions for pupils and instructors were supplied.

In 1954, a new and updated variant evolved designated as the MR.3. The aircraft featured much new and improved equipment as well as auxiliary wingtip fuel tanks increasing its all up capacity to 4,248 gallons. Another feature that initially proved to be the variant's Achilles' heel was the introduction of a tricycle undercarriage. Unfortunately, the nose wheel appeared to be too weak for the airframe and there were innumerable accidents caused by the nose wheel collapsing. Eight MR.3 variants were exported to South Africa for use as a maritime-patrol aircraft by the SAAF. It is thought their patrols in the region helped to arrest the spread of communism in the area. The other Shackleton variant was the AEW.2, twelve of which were derived from rebuilt MR.2 airframes. The aircraft were specifically configured in the airborne early warning (AEW) role with a large chin radome to accommodate the American APS-20 radar removed from Fairey Gannet aircraft on their withdrawal from use after the demise of the Royal Navy's fixed-wing aircraft carriers.

Six Avro Vulcan B.2s were modified as B (K).2 in-flight refuelling tankers by BAe at Woodford near Manchester. (*Take-off*)

Avro Vulcan B.2A, serial XL426, lands at Southend Airport following its final flight. (*Aviation News*)

With the cancellation of the Hawker Siddeley Nimrod AEW.3 project, the AEW.2 Shackleton – which were all named after characters in the BBC's children's television programme *Magic Roundabout* – were destined to remain the UK's only AEW aircraft until the introduction of the Boeing AWACS E.3 Sentry in the early 1990s. Unfortunately, almost as the type was due to be withdrawn from use, one aircraft was lost along with its crew while on a routine patrol. A total of 180 Shackletons were eventually produced by Avro.

The final military type produced by Avro was the massive Type 698 Vulcan bomber. The large delta was designed as a high-altitude bomber to deliver freefall nuclear bombs over long distances. The aircraft, serial VX770, made its first flight on 30 August 1952 and was powered by four Rolls-Royce Avon turbojets. Series production aircraft were powered by four Bristol Olympus turbojets of the spool type developing 12-13,000 lbs of static thrust. Five Avro 707 research aircraft had been built to test the behaviour of delta wings, especially at low speeds. The first, serial VX784, made its first flight at Boscombe Down on 4 September 1949.

All modern combat types in service or under development in the new millennium feature the delta-wing principle with forward canards for greater stability. Forty-five Avro Vulcan B.1s were delivered followed by eighty-nine re-winged B.2 and B.2A variants with provision to carry the Blue Steel supersonic cruise-type missile. In 1966, the Vulcan B.2 was developed as a low-level penetration bomber using the specially developed terrain-following radar or Navigational Bombing System (NBS).

In 1982, an Avro Vulcan B.2 made the longest bombing raid in history (a record now held by a USAF ACC Boeing B2 Spirit) when it bombed an airfield runway at Port Stanley in the Falkland Islands. The aircraft was supported by sixteen Handley Page Victor in-flight refuelling tankers operating from Ascension Island in the mid-South Atlantic.

Nine Avro Vulcan B.2s were converted into long-range strategic-reconnaissance aircraft and redesignated as the B.2 (MRR). In 1982, this was followed by six aircraft which were converted into tankers and designated as the B (K).2.

At one time, it was thought that the medium-range Avro 748 civil airliner and its military counterpart, the Type 780 Andover manufactured by Hawker Siddeley Aviation Ltd in Manchester, would be the last aircraft to emerge from the Avro stable. This was suggested when the company lost its identity in July 1963 when it merged into Hawker Siddeley. However, in 1993, the famous Avro name re-emerged when BAe at Woodford created a new Avro division and branded its BAe 146 regional airliners as the Avro 146 RJ.

British Aircraft Corporation (BAC)

The British Aircraft Corporation (BAC) was formed on 1 July 1960 with the amalgamation of Bristol Aircraft, English Electric Aviation Ltd, Hunting Aircraft Ltd and Vickers Armstrong based at Weybridge, Surrey, and Preston, Lancashire. The first aircraft to be produced by the company was the BAC 1-11 (One Eleven), originally conceived in March 1961 as the Hunting H.107 fifty-nine passenger, short-range airliner. However, airlines displayed little interest in an airplane with such a small passenger payload and the BAC 1-11 was enlarged to become the BAC 107. Able to accommodate seventy-nine passengers, the airplane was redesignated as the BAC 1-11.

The prototype first flew on 20 August 1963 at Bournemouth, Hurn Airport, powered by two Rolls-Royce Spey engines. Two months later, the prototype was lost in a fatal crash as a result of a 'deep stall' caused by failure of the aft engines fitted on the T-tail configuration. After the problem was resolved, a number of sales were secured and the type entered service with British United Airways and Braniff in April 1965. Two hundred and twenty BAC 1-11s were built in the UK and twelve in Romania as the ROMBAC 1-11. A small

An RAF No. 101 Squadron BAC VC 10K refuelling a French Air Force Mirage and a HARM-equipped RAF Tornado IDS aircraft. (*Aviation News*)

The RNZAF ordered two BAC 1-11-217s with two 12,550-lb thrust Rolls-Royce Spey Mk 512 DW turbofans. (*Warplane Collection*)

number are still in use to this day with a number of overseas operators and air arms more than fifty years after the prototype's first flight. Attempts to build a modernised variant, the ROMBAC 2000, were abandoned.

Starting life as the Vickers Type 1100, the BAC VC 10 was produced as a result of a requirement issued by BOAC in 1957 for an airliner capable of carrying a 15,422-kg (34,000-lb) payload over a range of 6,437 km (4,000 miles). The first BAC VC 10 flew at Weybridge, Surrey, in June 1962 and entered service with BOAC in April 1964. In spite of further development as the Type 1150, Super VC 10, the aircraft created little interest with airlines and only fifty-four were built, fourteen of which were supplied to the RAF as long-range strategic transports. Subsequently, the RAF purchased further VC 10s with low airframe hours for conversion by BAe at Filton, Bristol, into in-flight refuelling tankers designated K.2, K.3 and K.4, some of which remain in use today with No. 101 Squadron based at RAF Brize Norton in West Oxfordshire. In September 2013 RAF BAC VC 10K in-flight refuellers made their final flight.

One of the world's most famous airliners is without doubt the Aerospatiale/ BAC *Concorde* supersonic passenger jet. Built jointly by Aerospatiale and BAC, much has been written about this superb SST that served British Airways and Air France for more than thirty years until it was finally retired in 2004. In structural design, BAC was made responsible for the front fuselage including the flight deck, engine nacelles, air intakes and engine mountings, rear fuselage, fin and rudder. It also had design responsibility for the following systems: electrics, oxygen, fuel, engine instrumentation, engine controls, fire safety, air conditioning distribution and de-icing.

Following extensive multi-million pound modifications (which mainly entailed the fitment of 'puncture proof' wing fuel cells following the fatal crash of Air France registration F-WTSC on 25 July 2000 near Charles de Gaulle Airport, Paris, caused by debris that had fallen onto the taxiway from another airliner) a limited number of *Concordes* of both airlines re-entered service in November 2001. Enjoying a brief renaissance until a repeat of the mysterious missing tailplanes, a number of forced diversions due to engine problems and unprecedented projected routine maintenance costs presented by Airbus – who had assumed responsibility for the airplanes from BAe Systems – forced both operators in 2004 to withdraw all *Concorde* SSTs from use. Most examples were dispersed to various locations and aviation museums in France, the UK and US for posterity. One was donated to the Air and Space Museum, New York, and another returned to its ancestral home at Filton aerodrome, Bristol, in the UK.

The creation of BAC meant the company inherited a number of military projects and aircraft types. The most notorious of these being the TRS.2 multi-role aircraft conceived by English Electric and Vickers Armstrong in 1959 with BAC awarded the production contract. The controversial cancellation of the project brought BAC close to collapse, but orders for the BAC 1-11-500, the Super VC-10, and orders for the BAC (English Electric) Lightning supersonic air defence fighter and joint venture SEPECAT Jaguar kept the company going. The BAC Lightning was the first truly supersonic British fighter aircraft. The aircraft was conceived by W. E. 'Teddy' Petter, designer of the English Electric Canberra B.2 light bomber. The Lightning presented such complex aerodynamic problems that a special wind tunnel was constructed to carry out airframe tests, the first of its kind in the UK. The prototype Lightning, serial WG760, first took to the skies on 4 August 1954 at RAE Boscombe Down, near Salisbury, Wiltshire, in the West of England.

From 1954 to 1964, tests of cutting-edge military aircraft provided a wealth of data for Concorde's designers

HP115

Short 5B5

English Electric
Pl Lightning

TSR2

AVRO Vulcan

BAC 223

Bristol
B

BAC 221

Fairey FD2

Concorde

Dassault
Mirage IIIc

Nord-SFEC MAS
1502 Griffon

Super Caravelle

Sud-Est SE212
Durandal

Dassault
Mirage IV-01

SO 9050
Trident

Cold-war competitiveness was crucial i
creating the world's first — and only
supersonic people carrier. Its wings' lea
edge emerged from tests on delta-wing
aircraft. Data from the Fairey FD2 — th
to fly level at 1,000mph — led to its spe

COMPONENT	PIECE	PRODUCTION REALISATION	DESIGN ETUDE
FUSELAGE NOSE	POINTE AVANT	BAC WEYBRIDGE	BAC FILTON
FORWARD FUSELAGE	FUSELAGE AVANT	BAC FILTON	'' ''
INTERMEDIATE FUSELAGE	FUSELAGE INTERMED!º	SUD MARIGNANE	'' ''
FORWARD WING	ONGLETS DE VOILURE	SUD BOUGUENAIS	DTA UC
CENTRE WING	PARTIE CENTRALE 46 a 54 fus.	SUD MARIGNANE	'' ''
'' ''	'' '' 46 a 50 voil.	'' ''	'' ''
'' ''	'' '' 50 a 54 voil.	SUD TOULOUSE	'' ''
'' ''	'' '' 54 a 60	'' ''	DTA UT
'' ''	'' '' 60 a 63 voil.	'' ''	SILAT
'' ''	'' '' 60 a 69 fus.	'' ''	''
'' ''	'' '' 63 a 66 voil.	'' ''	''
'' ''	'' '' 66 a 69 voil.	'' ''	FIAT
'' ''	'' '' 69 a 72	SUD St NAZAIRE	''
OUTER WINGS	VOILURE EXTREME	GAM DASSAULT	GAMD
ELEVONS	ELEVONS	ROHR	DTA UC
REAR FUSELAGE	FUSELAGE ARRIERE	BAC PRESTON	BAC PRESTON
NACELLES	NACELLES	BAC FILTON & ROHR	BAC FILTON
NOZZLE	TUYERES	SNECMA	SNECMA
FIN	DERIVE	BAC WEYBRIDGE	BAC PRESTON
RUDDER	GOUVERNAIL	'' ''	'' ''
LANDING GEAR MAIN	TRAIN PRINCIPAL	HISPANO SUIZA	'HISPANO SUIZA
NOSE	TRAIN AVANT	MESSIER	MESSIER

B A C	FILTON Division
ELECTRICS	ELECTRICITE
OXYGEN	OXYGENE
FUEL	CARBURANT
ENGINE INSTRUMENTATION	INSTRUMENT REACTEURS
ENGINE CONTROLS	COMMANDES
FIRE	FEU
AIR CONDITIONING DISTRⁿ	DISTRIBUTION AIR CONDITIONNE
DE-ICING	DEGIVRAGE

SUD	TOULOUSE
RAULICS	HYDRAULIQUE
NG CONTROLS	COMMANDES DE VOL
IGATION	NAVIGATION
IO	RADIO
CONDITIONING SUPPLY	ALIMENTATION CONDIT!. D'AIR

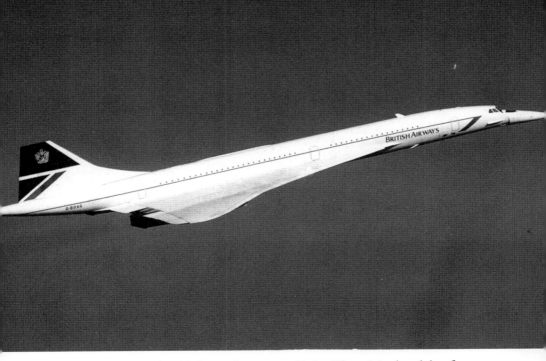

The British Aerospatiale/BAC Concorde was assembled at Filton, Bristol, and then flown to nearby RAF Fairford, Gloucestershire, for test flying. This was due to the long runway at Fairford that allowed a greater margin of safety. (*Air Power International*)

Opposite: The birth of an aviation icon. (*Wings*)

After a lengthy development phase with twenty pre-production aircraft produced, the Lightning began to enter RAF frontline service in 1960 as the Lightning F.1 armed with two 30-mm cannon and two Firestreak air-to-air missiles. A unique feature of the aircraft was that its two Rolls-Royce Avon 300 turbojets with reheat were mounted in the fuselage one above the other. It is rumoured that specification limits for fitment of the engines to the airframe were so tight that one airframe produced had to be scrapped as it was impossible to fit the lower engine. In total, 258 production Lightnings were delivered to the RAF by the time the final F.6 left the production line in August 1967 with production totalling 388 aircraft. The aircraft achieved some limited export success being used by the Royal Saudi Air Force and the Kuwaiti Air Force for a number of years, although neither of these air arms operated the type to its full potential. It is interesting to note that the Lightning remains the only RAF combat aircraft never to have been involved in hostilities or fired its missiles in anger throughout its service life of thirty years. Also, it was the only all-British produced fighter capable of attaining well over Mach 2.0.

The SEPECAT (Sociétè Europèenne de Production de l' Avion Ecole de Combat et d' Appui Tactique) Jaguar was a collaborative venture between

'Raspberry Ripple' BAC Canberra B.2 was based at RAE Bedford for GEC/Marconi AI.24 Foxhunter A-model radar trials with the equipment (LRUs) fitted in the bomb bay. (*Author*)

A unique and all-over orange BAC Canberra B.2 as used by the Luftwaffe during the Cold War for survey duties. (*Author*)

The ogival intake of the English Electric P.1A prototype was made circular in series production Lightnings to accommodate the Ferranti AI.23 Airpass radar. (*Wings*)

A mirror image of a BAC (EE) Lighting F.6 at a Farnborough SBAC Show is testament that Britain's rains are not just a phenomena of the new millennium. (*Air Power International*)

BAC and Dassault/Breguet to manufacture some 400 low-level strike fighters. A similar collaborative agreement was reached by Rolls-Royce and Turboméca for design and production of Adour 811 turbofan engines with reheat. Many French and British designs were studied before the Breguet Br.121 was selected as the basis for the new warplane. It has since become a classic ground-attack aircraft and achieved success in the export markets with the Jaguar International variant used by Ecuador, Nigeria, the Royal Omani Air Force and the Indian Air Force who initially acquired thirty-five single-seaters and five dual-seat trainers, later manufacturing in excess of 100 under licence by HAL (Hindustan Aeronautics Ltd).

Series production of British Jaguars was undertaken at the BAC plants at Preston and Warton, Lancashire. Five hundred and seventy-three SEPECAT Jaguars were built in total. Amongst the trials aircraft, one is of particular importance. Serial XX765, allocated by the Ministry of Defence RAE (later DERA, now QinetiQ) for ACT or Active Control Technology evaluation, is

Supersonic BAC F.3 Lightning with ventral tank, Red Top air-to-air missiles and crew access ladder. (*Author*)

RAF No. 74 'Tiger' Squadron BAC (EE) F.1 Air Defence Fighter, serial XM135, as seen at the Imperial War Museum in Duxford. (*Author*)

Two BAC F.6 Lightnings fitted with over-wing tanks were retained by BAe at Warton for development and were also used as chase planes. (*Author*)

in effect fly-by-wire. Much useful knowledge was gained over a number of years, much of which had practical applications in the Eurofighter Typhoon's fly-by-wire control systems. Another military design inherited by BAC was the H.145 (BAC Jet Provost T.5), a private venture development by Hunting Aircraft of Luton to provide the RAF with a pressurised version of the proven variant of the earlier Jet Provost T.3 and T.4 trainers. The T.5 was intended to meet the RAF's requirement for a high-altitude jet trainer needed by modern air forces. When Hunting became the Luton division of the BAC, the type was redesignated as the BAC.145. The prototype T.5, a converted T.4, serial XS230, made its maiden flight at Warton aerodrome on 28 February 1967. The closure of the Luton plant meant production of the 110 T.5s was carried out at the company's Preston plant. The company secured export orders for some 150 Jet Provost aircraft, notably for Saudi Arabia, Kuwait, New Zealand and at least six other countries for the trainer ground-attack BAC 167 Strikemaster derivative.

BAC was a founder member of Panavia GmbH (Gesellschaft mit beschränkter Haftung), a company set up to manage the development and production of the Tornado multi-role combat aircraft. Originally known as the MRCA multi-role combat aircraft, the variable-geometry wing IDS interdictor strike Tornado made its first flight on 14 August 1974. Two hundred and twenty-eight GR.1s were ordered by the RAF including fourteen reconnaissance aircraft. The German Luftwaffe received 212 IDS variants and the Marineflieger received 112. Italy received 100 IDS aircraft and Saudi Arabia forty-eight with a further

RAF Sepecat Jaguar GR.1 single-seat, tactical support airplanes were fitted with two 7,305-lb reheated thrust Rolls-Royce/Turboméca Adour Mk 102 turbofans. These similar Jaguar aircraft are from the French Air Force's 11e Escadre de Chasse. (*Warplane Collection*)

A dual-seat Sepecat (BAC) Jaguar T.2 was operated by the Defence Research Agency (DRA) at Boscombe Down. (*Author*)

Due to its small wing area, the diminutive Sepecat Jaguar carried its air-to-air missiles on over-wing pylons. (*Aviation News*)

order placed in 1993 at the al-Yamamah II arms deal for a further forty-eight and twenty-four of the F.3 air defence variant. Britain also purchased 144 F.3 ADVs, the first of which flew in November 1985, minus their GEC/Marconi AI 24 Foxhunter radars on operational training duties at RAF Coningsby, Lincolnshire, until January 1988.

The British Government first proposed that BAC and Hawker Siddeley should merge as one on 21 November 1966 and just over a decade later, BAC became British Aerospace (BAe) on 1 January 1978 due to further rationalisation of the British aviation industry. BAe took control of the assets of BAC, Hawker Siddeley and Scottish Aviation, the latter company based at Prestwick Airport, Scotland.

British Aerospace – New British Aerospace – BAe Systems

BAe Systems, formerly British Aerospace (BAe), was comprised of BAe Commercial Aircraft Ltd and based at Woodford, Cheshire, and BAe Defence Ltd at Warton in Lancashire. The commercial aircraft division included BAe Airbus Ltd with responsibility for the design and manufacture of Airbus wing sets at Filton, Bristol, and Broughton, North Wales, and Avro International Aerospace to market, lease and support the four-engine 146/RJ regional jet series of aircraft under the Avro banner. Scottish Aviation also took part in the venture with the twin turboprop series of aircraft, most of which remain operational with regional carriers in the US. Subsequently in 2006, BAe Systems announced it was to sell its 20 per cent stake in Airbus to its European

Hunting Jet Provost T.3 of No. 1 FTS RAF Linton-on-Ouse and Yorkshire. The Jet Provost derived from the earlier piston-engined Percival (Hunting) Provost and introduced the RAF's 'all-through' jet training in the late 1950s. (*Aviation News*)

The BAe Jet Provost T.5 was the only high-altitude pressurised variant of the Jet Provost series to enter RAF service. (*Author*)

BAe Strikemasters of the Royal Saudi Air Force remain in use in the new millennium. (*Aviation News*)

A line of Panavia Tornado GR1 swing-wing IDS interdictor strike bombers with fighter-type flash on the forward fuselage surrounding the roundel. (*Aviation News*)

No. 617 'Dambusters' Squadron Tornado GR.1 fitted with Tornado F.3 ADV external drop tanks. (*Aviation News*)

parent EADS. A proposed BAe Systems EADS merger was abandoned in 2012 mainly due to the intervention of governments with regards to political and defence constraints.

Meanwhile in December 2001, BAe Systems announced all civil aircraft production was to cease on completion of the twelve Avro RJ 146 variants on the production line at their Woodford plant. As a result of the formation of British Aerospace in 1977, the new company was left with a number of ongoing projects to complete. On the civil side, not least the delivery of the last few BAC/Aerospatiale *Concorde* supersonic airliners along with the outstanding

One of eighteen interim Panavia Tornado F.2A ADV aircraft delivered without AI 24 Foxhunter radar that was replaced by ballast to maintain its centre of gravity. (*Author*)

Opposite top: Desert camouflaged GR.1 Tornado on a low-level practice bombing mission *c.* 1990 prior to its assignment in the Persian Gulf during the first Gulf War to remove Saddam Hussein's forces from Kuwait.

Opposite middle: Panavia Tornado GR.4s had their baptism of fire during the second Gulf War in 2003 when they were equipped with BAe Dynamics' 'Storm Shadow' cruise missiles. (*Aviation News*)

Opposite bottom: Upgraded Panavia GR.4 on a low-level test flight over the Lake District in the North West of England. This particular aircraft was based at BAe Systems' Warton Aerodrome near Preston, Lancashire. (*Aviation News*)

orders for the BAC 1-11 twin-jet airliners. Also, the introduction of the new BAe 146 regional airliner came into production where design and development had commenced some thirty years prior under the auspices of de Havilland at Hatfield. It also inherited development and support of the highly successful DH.125 series of biz-jets including manufacture at Chester of the Series 800 and Series 1000 which made its first flight on 16 June 1990. Another aircraft was the fifty-seat HS 748 turboprop airliner, production of which ceased in 1989 after 379 had been built including thirty-one HS Andover C1s for the RAF fitted with a unique ramp with the rear of the aircraft capable of being lowered to provide easier access for loading. A completely new sixty-four-seat ATP Advanced Turbo-Prop regional transport based on the original HS.748 was introduced in 1986 when the first prototype flew on 6 August that year.

BAe Systems at Broughton, North Wales, is contracted to supply wing sets for the EADS Airbus and A380 'Super Jumbo'. (*Air Power International*)

The long-range BAC VC 10 passenger-transport was optimised for BOAC's route network that included many 'hot-and-high' locations with short runways. It had a large 'clean' wing with four 9,525-kg (21,000-lb) static thrust Rolls-Royce Conway RCo.42 turbofans fitted in paired pods on the sides of the rear fuselage below the distinctive T-tail. Initial deliveries comprised of twelve airplanes to BOAC; two to Ghana Airways; three to British United Airways; and fourteen to the RAF as C.1 military transports with a revised wing, greater fuel capacity and up-rated Rolls-Royce RCo.43 engines. In addition, the prototype airplane was brought up to production standard and sold to Laker Airways.

Subsequently, the RAF purchased a number of aircraft with low airframe hours for conversion by BAe at Filton into in-flight refuelling tankers. As an increasing number of RAF overseas bases and staging posts closed, it was realised in order to support future overseas deployments an adequate long-range tanker force was becoming a necessity. With this in mind, the RAF searched for a suitable airframe to meet its needs. Having operated the BAC VC 10 as a strategic-transport since the mid-1960s, it is not surprising with a large number of VC 10s on the second-hand market at the time, it was this airplane that was decided on. Finally, in the House of Commons during March 1978, it was announced an order was to be placed for the purchase of nine ex-civil VC 10 and Super VC 10 airplanes to fulfil

The RAF Andover C.1 was used for 'Open Skies' monitoring. This aircraft is shown in its RAF seventy-fifth anniversary livery. (*Author*)

RAF Hawker Siddeley Andovers and light transports were used by Signals Command on airfield calibration duties. (*Warplane Collection*)

the RAF's in-flight tanker requirements. Just over a year later in April-May 1979, British Aerospace was awarded a nine-million pound contract to cover the design work for aircraft preparation, pending a decision as to whether the conversion work should be given the go ahead. By this time, four Super VC 10s, civil registered 5H-MMT, 5H-MOG, 5H-UVJ and 5Y-ADA from the defunct East African Airways, had been repossessed by British Aerospace and gathered at its Filton airfield while five retired Gulf Air VC 10s were lying unused at Stansted Airport. These airplanes were later prepared for a single flight to Filton to join the others. With registrations A40-V1 and A40-VK, they departed on 28 March 1978 and were followed by A40-VC and A40-VG on 30 March and A40-V following on 3 April.

The contract to proceed was subsequently awarded with design work to be undertaken by BAe and conversions by BAe and Marshalls Engineering of Cambridge. The initial plan called for the five standard Type 1101 airplanes to become K.2 tankers – serials ZA140-144 and the four Super VC 10s Type 1153 to become K.3 serials ZA147-150 – with both variants as three-point hose and drogue tankers with two underwing FRL Mk 32/2800 pods and FR Mk 17 internal hose reel in the rear fuselage. Conversion of the former airliners for their new role involved a complete strip down of the fuselage with removal of all airline cabin fitments being replaced by fuel tanks built at Hurn in Bournemouth. Five were fitted in the standard airframe and six in the Super VC 10s. Installation of the cylindrical tanks in the K.2 was achieved by removing a section of the fuselage roof and lowering them in while those of the K.3 were loaded through the wide forward cargo door (which although disabled and sealed for normal operations, can be opened for servicing purposes). Not all of the space available was taken up by fuel tanks and eighteen passenger seats in the K.2 and seventeen in the K.3 could be fitted in the forward fuselage compartment. The six tanks in the K.3 produced a total fuel load of approximately 80,000 lbs, that of the K.2 being some 10,000 lbs lower. Other changes to the fuselage included deletion of the left hand crew door and its replacement by an emergency slide ramp. Most of the windows were blanked off and the baggage racks were removed from the tank bay. Further forward, an in-flight nose-mounted refuelling probe and associated piping was installed, permitting the tanker to dispense and receive fuel. Other changes were embodied to afford a degree of commonality with the VC 10 C.1 transports. These included avionics, auxiliary power unit (APU) and deletion of the inboard engine thrust reversers. Once the tanking modifications had been completed, a small crew rest area galley was fitted. To dispense its fuel, the tankers were fitted with a FRA Mk 17B Hose Drogue Unit (HDU) in the rear freight bay and two Mk 32 pods on the wingtips. Refuelling is achieved under the control of the flight engineer who can monitor all three refuelling points by means of a monitor linked to an under fuselage closed circuit television system. Normal procedure for combat types refuelling is for two airplanes to make contact with the wing drogues, one after another so that successive link-ups can be monitored on television. The Mk 17 centreline hose reel provides 600 imperial gallons per minute for large receivers with an 81-foot hose compared with the Mk 32 wing pods capable of delivering 350 imperial gallons per minute with a 53-foot hose.

Reformed at RAF Brize Norton on 1 May 1984, No. 101 Squadron received its first VC 10K tanker the same day with deliveries continuing until the last of the four K.3s were received on 24 September 1985. In January 1985, a further House of Commons statement indicated the intention to convert a further six of the fourteen serials ZD230-243 ex-British Airways Super VC 10s placed in open storage at RAF Abingdon in 1984 to aerial refuellers. However, when funding became available, it was only for five airplanes as a sixth aircraft was moved from Abingdon to Filton for spares. Meanwhile, the demise of the Victor tanker fleet prompted the decision to convert the VC 10 C.1 transports to two-point tanker-transports as part of ASR Air Staff Requirement 416. Originally, this only covered eight airplanes although the contract was later extended to cover all thirteen Type 1106 airplanes then current with No. 10 Squadron also based at RAF Brize Norton. For its new dual role, the C (K).1 would be fitted with a FRL Mk 32 pod under each wing and a refuel control panel on the flight deck. The modification programme was managed by British Aerospace although most of the work was carried out by FRL at Hurn Airport, Bournemouth.

The first aircraft, serial XV101, was received for conversion on 28 February 1991 being followed by XV103 on 25 October the same year. XV101 was expected to be completed by October 1991 but was delayed as a certain amount of anti-corrosion work was necessary with new wiring and interior trim panels to be fitted. The replacement wiring work was undertaken at East Midlands Airport by Hunting Aircraft. Following conversion, all C (K).1s were delivered to Boscombe Down for service validation before rejoining the squadron. Unlike the tanker fleet, no extra tanks were installed with the airplanes retaining their full passenger and cargo capabilities, original paint scheme and markings. The first K.2, serial ZA141, was painted in grey-green camouflage and ready for ground runs on 17 June 1982 and taxi trials on 21 June. The first flight with Roy Radford and John Lewis at the controls took place on 26 June. Following their first flights, all aircraft were flown to Hurn for installation of emergency escape chutes in the lower forward fuselage. Once initial company trials had been completed, ZA141 was delivered to A&AEE Boscombe Down for testing and evaluation. These tests were completed by 25 July 1983 although ZA141 suffered fin and rudder damage by an out of control drogue and these were replaced by items removed from the redundant serial XX914 airframe at Farnborough. Meanwhile, the second conversion to emerge from the Filton line was another K.2, serial ZA143, which undertook its first flight on 22 December 1982, this time in the new hemp colour scheme. It was quickly followed by the third airframe, serial ZA140, delivered to No. 241 OCU on 25 July 1983. The designated RAF tanker unit was No. 101 Squadron, a former Second World War and post-war bomber unit that had relinquished its Avro Vulcan B.2s in August 1982. Reformed at RAF Brize Norton on 1 May 1984, the squadron received its first VC 10K tanker the same day with deliveries continuing until the last of the four K.3s were received on 24 September 1985.

The world's most famous supersonic passenger airliner was the BAC/ Aerospatiale *Concorde* that originated from separate French and British projects which were considered too costly for single nation development. As a result in 1962, a French and British inter-governmental agreement was made to build the aircraft. Sud-Aviation, later Aerospatiale, and BAC, later British Aerospace, were appointed as airframe contractors. The French were responsible for the wings, rear cabin section, flying controls, air conditioning, hydraulics and the navigation and radio systems. BAC were responsible for the three forward fuselage sections, rear fuselage and vertical tail, engine nacelles and ducts, engine installations, electrical, fuel and oxygen systems, and noise and thermal insulation. Similar collaboration and work was shared between Rolls-Royce and Snecma for design and construction of the engines which were redesigned and up-rated Bristol Siddeley Olympus engines similar to those used to power the Avro Vulcan bomber. The Olympus was the only engine available at the time that was capable of powering the aircraft supersonic.

Concorde was an outstanding technical success, but political and environmental constraints, and the ever-escalating cost of jet A1 aviation fuel – which from July 1971 increased from $25.60 for 1,000 litres to $188.20 in July 1979 – eventually led to the aircraft's untimely demise. The tremendous escalation in the cost of aviation fuel prompted all foreign countries to cancel their orders for the aircraft realising that operating costs would be prohibitive. The French Government halted the programme while they assessed the situation and it was finally decided that only two prototypes, two pre-production and sixteen series aircraft should be produced, eight for Air France and eight for British Airways. This drastic cut to the programme was a terrific blow for the British aviation industry; however, this was less so for the French who were enamelled with the success of Airbus. Britain had retired from the Airbus programme on 1 March 1969 arguing that it would be 'impossible to sell such an aircraft'. The UK was replaced by Germany and subsequently both France and Germany were to enjoy huge benefits from the Airbus success story. Later, Britain, under the auspices of British Aerospace, was to re-enter Airbus Industries utilising its expertise to design and manufacture the wings for the consortium – however, this time with only a 20 per cent shareholding as opposed to the 50 per cent initial participation. The following are the *Concorde* production, constructors' numbers, suffix and allocation details:

Previous Registration	Final Registration	Status prior to withdrawal in 2004
001 Prototype F-WTSS	f/f 20/03/1969	Preserved at Le Bourget, Paris
002 Prototype G-BSST	f/f 0 9 /04/1969	FAA Museum, Yeovilton
01 PP Model G-AXDN	f/f 17/12/1971	IWM Duxford, Air Museum
02 PP Model F-WTSA	f/f 10/01/1973	Preserved Paris/ Orly Airport
001 Series F-WTSB		Retained Airbus, Toulouse, France
002 Series G-BBGD		Retained BAe, Filton, UK
003 Series F-WTSC	F-BTSC	Air France, crashed Paris 25/07/00
004 Series G-BOAC	G-N81AC	British Airways
005 Series F-BVFA	N94FA, F-BVFA	Air France
006 Series G-BOAA	G-N94FA, G-BOAA	British Airways
007 Series F-BVFB	N94FB, F-BVFB	Air France
008 Series G-BOAB	G-N94AB, G-BOAB	British Airways
009 Series F-BVFC	N94FC, F-BVFC	Air France
010 Series G-BOAD	G-N94AD, G-BOAD	British Airways
011 Series F-BVFD	N94FD, F-BVFD	Air France
012 Series G-BOAE	G-N94AE, G-BOAE	British Airways
013 Series F-WJAM	F-BTSD, N94SD	Air France
014 Series G-BFKW	G-BOAG	British Airways
015 Series F-WJAN	F-BVFF	Air France
016 Series G-BFKX	G-BOAF	British Airways

In 2001, six *Concorde* SSTs were stored at the 'idle fleet' facility in the Mojave Desert in California, US. But following extensive multi-million pound modifications such as the fitment of 'puncture proof' wing fuel tanks after

A Handley Page Victor K2 returning to a wintry RAF Marham in Norfolk. It had previously been on an in-flight refuelling sortie with an Avro Vulcan B.2 prior to the 'Black Buck' missions during the Falklands conflict in 1982. (*Aviation News*)

the tragic crash of Air France F-WTSC and a limited number of new and efficient aircraft to both airlines, *Concorde*'s fate was sealed. Enjoying a brief renaissance until a repeat of mysterious missing tailplanes, a number of forced diversions due to engine problems and unprecedented projected routine maintenance costs by Airbus, both operators were forced to withdraw the *Concorde* from use in 2004.

British Aerospace came into being on 29 April 1977 when nationalisation of the industry was ordered by the socialist government under the powers afforded them by the Aircraft and Shipbuilding Industries Act. BAC, Hawker Siddeley Aviation, Hawker Siddeley Dynamics and Scottish Aviation were all transferred to the new corporation although they did retain their separate identities until 1980 when BAe was partially privatised with full privatisation following in May 1985. BAe Defence Ltd formed in 1992 with its headquarters based at Warton in Lancashire to combine the former BAe Military Aircraft Ltd with BAe Dynamics.

Establishment of BAe from the amalgamation of all other existing British

The Bloodhound SAM 1 and 2 were designed and manufactured by Ferranti Ltd, now part of BAe Systems. (*Author*)

aircraft companies meant the new corporation faced a considerable task in managing the successful completion of existing and outstanding orders, and the rationalisation and restructuring of the company to ensure it remained a competitive and viable organisation on the world stage. On reflection – except for the company's brief sojourn into motor manufacturing and property development which was offloaded with its early 1990s reorganisation – it can be said without any doubt that after more than three decades at the helm, BAe's management had gone some way to restoring the UK to its rightful place amongst the world's leading aircraft manufacturers. Reorganisation and restructuring of the company was not achieved without some considerable pain as many dedicated scientists, designers and engineers were throw on the scrapheap. Another bitter pill to swallow was the closure of a number of sites at Weybridge, Kingston and Hatfield. This move resulted in Corporate Jets Ltd with responsibilities for the BAe 125 series being sold to the Raytheon Aircraft Corporation with all manufacturing activities transferred to a new facility at Wichita, Kansas. Raytheon Corporate Jets operated as a

The Hawker Siddeley (DH) Domine T.1 replaced RAF Vickers Varsity piston-engined navigation trainers in the early 1960s and continues to do so in its upgraded T.2 form. (*Author*)

UK subsidiary to maintain a service facility for 125s at BAe in Chester.

A successful commuter airliner for BAe was the re-launched Garrett TPE331-powered Jetstream 31 and Super 31 that was certified in October 1988 and derived from the Handley Page HP.137 Jetstream. The prototype made its first flight on 28 March 1980 and delivery of production aircraft commenced in 1982. By mid-1990, no fewer than 250 Jetstream 31s were serving with fifteen US commuter airlines. Over 400 Jetstream 31 airliners were eventually produced and the more powerful and better performing Super 41 followed with some 161 examples sold, many to the US. The RAF purchased twenty-six Jetstreams to replace the Vickers Varsity as multi-engine trainers which served until March 2004 when they were supplanted by seven leased civil-registered Beech Super King Air 200s. The larger twenty-nine seat Jetstream 41 (first flown at Prestwick Airport, Scotland, on 25 September 1991) was not so successful as its predecessors with only 104 aircraft sold following the types initial rollout on 27 March 1991. The first flight commenced in June that year and a larger Jetstream 61 attracted little interest from the airlines although the ATP that followed fared slightly better. The ATP was technically a stretched development of the Avro 748 with new engines, systems and equipment, a slightly sweptback fin and rudder, and redesigned nose. It incorporated an advanced flight deck with EFIS (Electronic Flight Instrument

Two BAe (HS) 125-700Bs were sold to Russian company Air Limousine Services. They were the first foreign executive jets to be sold in the former Soviet Union. (*Aviation News*)

BAe's final 125 design before Corporate Jets was sold to Raytheon in the US was the BAe 125-800 series. (*Author*)

Scottish Aviation Jetstream T.1s were flown by No. 45 (R) Squadron at RAF Finningley, Yorkshire, from July 1992 until they moved to RAF Cranwell in Lincolnshire where the type was supplanted by leased Raytheon Beech Super King Air 200s. (*Aviation News*)

System) and an extensively modernised and improved interior. However, as orders for the ATP had not reached expectations when only sixty examples had been delivered, production of the type ceased in early 1995.

BAe claim to have lost one million pounds on each aircraft sold and all Jetstream production ceased in 1997. Cessation of production meant that the Avro RJ series was the only airliner still in production in the UK in 2001. Unfortunately unbeknown at the time, this too was to meet its demise. The new Avro RJ family of Regional airliners – the RJ 70, RJ 85, RJ 100 and RJ 115 (the number indicates seats) – differed from the early BAe 146 mainly in the fitment of up-rated Textron Lycoming LF507 turbofans in place of the ALF502s offering increased thrust at higher temperatures and increased fuel economy. Subsequently, all RJ series production ceased and the only civil airliner production in the UK is that associated with the EADS Airbus subassemblies and wing sets.

On the military front, BAe inherited a number of excellent designs already on the production lines which at the time had not realised their full sales potential. Aircraft such as the dual-seat HS.1182 Hawk jet trainer had been extremely successful with some 775 examples sold to twenty air forces worldwide by mid-1977. This also included the T-45 Goshawk navalised advanced trainer for the US Navy that was developed in a joint venture with McDonnell Douglas.

The HS Hawk is a tandem two-seat advanced trainer that replaced the Folland Gnat and Hawker Hunter in RAF service. The prototype first flew

Royal Navy Jetstream 31s were used to train Sea Harrier pilots in the use of the Sea Harrier FRS.1 and F/A.2 radar. (*Author*)

during August 1974 as the P.1182. One hundred and seventy-five aircraft were ordered 'off the drawing board' and the first Hawk T. Mk 1 was delivered to No. 4 Flying Training School (RAF) in November 1976. Later, fifty-one (originally intended to be seventy-one) were converted to Mk 1A standard to carry AIM-9 Sidewinder air-to-air missiles to supplement the Panavia F.3 ADV Tornado in the air defence role. The type also flies as an ambassador for Britain by way of its use by the famous Red Arrows aerobatic team, thrilling crowds at all major air shows around the world.

An upgraded development of the Hawk Mk 60 with a slightly

Above: Avro RJ regional jets which replaced the BAe 146 series were sold to a number of overseas operators including Ansett Western Australia. (*Aviation News*)

Left: Upgraded 'glass-cockpit' Boeing Goshawks provide the US Navy with onboard carrier LIFT training for its MDC/Boeing F/A-18 Hornet pilots. (*Aviation News*)

lengthened fuselage and 2,463-kg (5,340-lb) static thrust Rolls-Royce Turboméca Adour Mk 851 engine has been undertaken by BAe, namely the Hawk 100. A tandem two-seat advanced systems trainer and light ground-attack aircraft featuring a 'combat wing', the Hawk 100 secured a number of orders mainly in Asia, the Far East and Australia.

In addition, BAe as a private venture undertook the development of a single-seat lightweight fighter designated as the Hawk 200. The aircraft has an 80 per cent commonality with the Hawk 100. The 'combat wing' is similar and both aircraft have a similar avionics fit except the 200 variant carries a Westinghouse APG-66H multi-mode radar, a modified version of the General Dynamics F-16 Fighting Falcon radar. However, only sixty-eight Hawk 200s had been sold by 2012.

In the late 1980s, BAe initiated the independent development of an advanced Harrier although this was subsequently abandoned and the McDonnell Douglas AV-8B Harrier II was licence-built and designated as the Harrier GR.5. Sixty Harrier GR.5s were ordered for the RAF, the aircraft being jointly

Above: No. 6 FTS at RAF Finningley, Yorkshire, flew BAe Hawk T.1s on low-level navigator training missions. (*Take-off*)

Right: Representatives of the three BAe Hawk T.1A units that form No. 4 FTS at RAF Valley consists of Nos 19, 74 'Tiger' and 208 Reserve Squadrons. (*Take-off*)

produced by Baez and McDonnell Douglas with final assembly and flight testing being undertaken at Dunsfold Aerodrome in Surrey. Forty-two GR.5s and eighteen GR.5As, the latter an interim upgraded GR.5, were upgraded to GR.7 (MDC AV-8B) standard in parallel with the production of thirty-four 'new builds'. As a result with the GR.7, the MDC/BAe Harrier II came of age as a true combat aircraft with full capabilities for night flying with a NVG-compatible cockpit and all-weather operations and a truly awesome payload of weaponry. To help with the demanding conversion flying, thirteen combat-capable two-seat T.10 trainers powered by a Rolls-Royce Pegasus Mk 105 vectored thrust turbofan were built.

The Royal Navy BAe Sea Harrier FRS.1 was developed from the RAF Harrier GR.3, the STOVL (short take-off and vertical landing) strike aircraft providing the British FAA with a ship-borne multi-role fighter. In total, the Royal Navy received fifty-seven Sea Harrier FRS 1s including attrition replacements during the Falklands conflict and four trainers including three T4Ns. A midlife update initiated in 1985 refined the Sea Harrier into a

All black Royal Navy BAe Hawk T.1s were used by the Fleet Requirements Air Direction Unit (FRADU) to simulate incoming 'sea-skimming' missiles such as the French-built Exocet to train the crews of surface ships employed on missile detection and tracking equipment. (*Take-off*)

SAAF BAe Hawk 120 conducting flight trials over Cape Town. (*Take-off*)

BAe's Hawk 200 single-seat fighter is fitted with a 'combat wing' and sanitised APG-66 radar. (*Aviation News*)

BAe Systems Hawk 100 Lead-in Fighter Trainer (LIFT) demonstration aircraft. (*Aviation News*)

AIM-9 Sidewinder-equipped BAe Systems single-seat Hawk 200. (*Aviation News*)

RAF BAe Harrier GR.5 of No. 1 (F) Squadron based at RAF Wittering, 'Home of the Harrier'. These were soon replaced by interim GR.5As that were of a similar standard as the MDC/BAe GR.7 Harrier II. (*Author*)

more capable interceptor designated as the F/A 2 (initially FRS 2). The most significant visual difference was the re-contoured nose radome to house the Ferranti Blue Vixen intercept radar. Fifty FRS 1s were converted to F/A 2 standard along with the conversion of four Mk 4N to T.Mk 8N for conversion training. In 1975, the Indian Navy ordered twenty-four FRS 1s (FRS 51) and four T.60 trainers. Nine remained in use in 2012 pending delivery of the new Mikoyan MiG-29K from Russia to equip the Indian Navy's new aircraft carrier.

The Panavia Tornado swing-wing bomber mentioned earlier is the product of

The MDC/BAe Harrier II with its redesigned composite wing gave rise to the USMC, AV 8B and RAF GR.7 which replaced the interim BAe GR.5A in RAF service. (*Aviation News*)

The Royal Navy's Harrier Jump Jet heritage: the original Sea Harrier FRS.1 and F/A-2 in the foreground. Both types were equipped with Ferranti airborne intercept radar, a feature the RAF GR types lacked. (*Aviation News*)

the collaboration of BAe (formerly BAC), MBB of Germany and Aeritalia in Italy and all participating countries were entitled by agreement to a proportionate share of the work. However, BAe ended up with the lion's share of the 992 aircraft produced, by virtue that 197 of the total were of the air defence variant developed solely for British use and seventy-two aircraft ordered by Saudi Arabia (forty-eight IDS and twenty-four F.3 ADVs) were manufactured at Warton. BAe also upgraded large number of RAF Tornado IDS GR.1 variants to GR.4 standard by way of a phased modification programme over a number of years and twenty ADVs to Tornado 2000 (F.3) standard.

Above: Royal Navy BAe Sea Harrier FRS.1 of 899 NAS with stylised 'winged fist' insignia in celebration of the unit's fiftieth anniversary. (*Warplane Collection*)

Left: A Royal Navy Sea Harrier F/A-2 was lost over the Adriatic while returning from flying CAP over the Balkans in the 1990s. (*Aviation News*)

Amongst a number of other British aircraft that BAe assumed responsibility for were the forty-six Nimrod MR.1, MR.2 and four Elint Nimrod R1.P aircraft derived from the de Havilland Comet jet transport, but fitted with an additional fuselage 'bubble' below the pressurised cabin to house the cavernous weapons bay. In addition on 31 March 1977, the then Defence Secretary, Fred Mulley, announced that eleven surplus Nimrod MR.1 airframes were to be converted for the AEW role fitted with British Marconi Avionics AEW radar and associated computers. BAe at Warton inherited the task of completing the airframe conversions and all eleven Nimrod AEW.3 airframes were delivered on time. However, severe cost escalations and seemingly insurmountable development problems with the GEC/Marconi radar led to the cancellation of the project in 1986 in preference to the Boeing AWACS E 3 Sentry to fulfil the RAF's AEW requirements. It is believed that seven remaining Nimrod AEW.3 airframes are currently stored at Warton intact (minus radar) never having flown since the day they were delivered.

BAe also has a major stake in the Eurofighter Typhoon, having laid the groundwork as long as 1982 when the three Panavia companies agreed to co-

The Hawker Siddeley Nimrod MR.1 was the first jet-propelled, maritime-patrol and ASW airplane in the world. It achieved its extended endurance and ability to remain on station at range by shutting down two of its four Rolls-Royce Avon engines to conserve fuel. (*Aviation News*)

The original GEC/Marconi AEW 3 trials airplane resplendent in DRA Farnborough colours before the addition of the tail scanner at the rear of the fuselage to ensure 360 degree coverage. (*Wings*)

A Hawker Siddeley AEW2 Nimrod produced by BAe to fulfil the MoD requirement for eighteen series airplanes of which all were delivered. However, eight never flew and were placed in storage where they remain to this day. (*Aviation News*)

A Hawker Siddeley (BAe) AEW 3 development airframe ended its last flight before cancellation at Newcastle Airport having been forced to land due to severe overheating of the GEC/Marconi AEW radar. (*Wings*)

operate on the development of an Agile Combat Aircraft (ACA) derived from BAe designs, the P.110 and MBB TKF90 projects. In the event, both Germany and Italy decided to withdraw from the project leaving BAe with the difficult decision whether to go ahead on their own or abandon the project completely. It is credit to their tenacity and foresight that they decided to continue with the project that was to lead to the privately-funded technology demonstrator, the EAP, military serial ZF534. The fighter first flew on 8 August 1986, only three months after the agreed date when all three nations first muted the project. The aims of the EAP were to provide detailed information on the new composites to be used and provide a means of investigating the full flight parameters of fly-by-wire with an aircraft fitted with canards. It says much for the concept of the EAP and the Eurofighter that the demonstrator exceeded Mach 1.1 on its first flight and flew a further nine times within a week. Unfortunately, due mainly to the prevarication on the part of the Germans that the in-service date of the Eurofighter – later after initial hesitation by the Germans due to the Typhoon's Second World War heritage as a famous piston-engine ground-attack

The Eurofighter Typhoon F.3 multirole airplane assembled by BAe Systems at BAe Warton has replaced the Panavia Tornado F.3 and is deployed at RAF Mount Pleasant in the Falklands as defence of the islands. (*Postcard*)

fighter – was considerably delayed, a full production agreement was eventually signed in mid-1997 by all the participating nations. Germany agreed to take their full quota of 140 aircraft with the last forty to be multi-role configured. Seven Eurofighter prototypes were produced and firm series production orders existed for 620 aircraft with options on a further 128. In addition, seven P-P (pre-production) models for development purposes were built and are flying although one Spanish Casa-built P-P development model crashed early in the development flying programme.

Early in 1999 with the merger of GEC's defence businesses, the company assumed the trading title of New British Aerospace. This was revised in December 1999 to BAe Systems that in the new millennium after many years of negotiations finally secured the order to supply the Indian Air Force with sixty-six Hawk trainers, the majority to be assembled in India by HAL. On 21 December 2012, it announced that it had secured an order for twelve Eurofighter Typhoons and eight Hawk advanced lead-in fighter trainers from Oman. Saudi Arabia placed an order for seventy-two Typhoon aircraft, eighteen single-seat and six two-seaters. Twenty-four having been delivered by 2012.

Beagle Aircraft Ltd

Beagle (British Executive & General Aircraft Ltd) was formed in 1960 by Sir Peter Masefield with the intention of securing a share for Britain in the world markets for 'light' executive twins. Auster Aircraft Ltd merged with F. G. Miles Ltd to form Beagle-Miles in June 1961, the company then assuming the title of Beagle-Auster Aircraft Ltd. A year later, it was renamed Beagle Aircraft Ltd. The first aircraft from the company to carry the Beagle Aircraft name was the D5/180 Husky and A61 Terrier. A single example of the Husky, serial XW635, entered service with the RAF in January 1969 and it remained on charge for almost seventeen years providing air experience flights for ATC cadets flying over 5,000 hours with No. 5 Air Experience Flight at Cambridge. The A61 was a rework of the Army Air Corps Auster 6 and was converted into a three-seat touring and training aircraft. A heavier four-seat variant was redesignated as the A109 Airedale, having its first flight at Rearsby Aerodrome in Leicestershire on 16 April 1961. It was the first Beagle aircraft to be fitted with a nose wheel and variable-pitch propeller, and it is believed close to eighty examples were built.

The light executive twin, Beagle B.206X, was the first original design produced by the company. The second and enlarged prototype, the B.206Y, first flew on 12 August 1962. The original military variant was the B.206Z and two

Scottish Aviation (Beagle) Bulldog elementary trainers were used by University Air Squadrons before the advent of Grob-powered gliders. (*Author*)

were ordered by the Ministry of Aviation, serials XS742 and XS743. Twenty B.206R Bassett CC 1 five to eight-seat communications aircraft were also built for the RAF. Originally intended for transport of RAF Bomber Command V-bomber crews, its payload and range obviated its use in this capacity and most aircraft ended up as squadron communications aircraft. However, due to its poor serviceability and reliability, the aircraft were withdrawn from use after only nine years in RAF service and most were sold for civil use.

The company's most successful type was the B.121 Pup, an all-metal aerobatic aircraft. Three versions of the Pup were produced at Rearsby and Shoreham aerodrome in Sussex. These were the two-seat Series 1 with a 100-hp Rolls-Royce Continental engine; the Series 2 Pup 150 with an optional third seat and a 150-hp Lycoming engine; and the three-seat Series 3 Pup 160 with a 160-hp Lycoming. The company's final design produced the B.125 Bulldog 100 trainer that had its maiden flight on 19 May 1969 and was a Pup fitted with a 200-hp Lycoming engine. With the sudden closure of the company that went into voluntary liquidation in 1970, production of 120 Bulldogs for the RAF was taken over by Scottish Aviation at Prestwick Airport, Scotland. At the time of its closure, Beagle Aircraft had produced 127 B.121 Pups and had orders for a further 267 on its books.

Beardmore

Scottish shipbuilding and engineering firm William Beardmore became involved in aircraft manufacturing shortly after the outbreak of the First World War in 1914 when it acquired a licence to produce Austro-Daimler engines. It was also a major subcontractor for the production of RAF Be.2c and Sopwith Pup biplane fighters. In 1916, most major subcontractors were encouraged to submit their own designs and Lt G. Tiltman-Richards was appointed Beardmore's chief designer. Richards' first two designs, the Beardmore WB.I (bomber) and WB.II reconnaissance aircraft, failed to secure substantial orders. However, the WB.III, a development of the Sopwith Pup for the Admiralty for ship-borne use, distinguished by its folding wings and strengthened landing gear, was more successful with fifty-five ordered by the Royal Navy. Tiltman-Richards then produced the WB.IV, a single-seat biplane naval fighter. Many considered the WB.IV to have been one of the most advanced designs of the First World War, it being an unusual design at the time in which the propeller was driven from a rear-mounted engine by means of an extension shaft that went between the pilot's feet. The fuselage was built entirely from plywood and a large flotation chamber projected from each side of the nose to form a large lateral buoyancy surface in the event of ditching the aircraft at sea. Unfortunately, its top speed was way below that of contemporary scouts of the day and only one prototype was built.

William Stancliffe Shackleton, the company's newly appointed chief designer in 1925, was tasked with producing a tandem two-seat fighter for Latvia. The only aircraft built was flown in 1925 and no records exist of its subsequent history. The company next received an Air Ministry contract for two Inverness flying boats and a giant landplane bomber, the Inflexible. The Inflexible was the largest British landplane built before the Second World War, but its all-metal construction meant it was grossly overweight and seriously underpowered by its three 650-hp Rolls-Royce Condor engines. Unfairly chastised as the world's worst aircraft, the Inflexible was subsequently decommissioned at Martlesham Heath in 1930 where it was used for investigations into metal airframe corrosion problems.

Beardmore bought the licence of the highly advanced German Rohrbach metal airplane building technique. The two Inverness aircraft were built in Denmark by Rohrbach Metal Airplane Company. Designed by Kurt Tank of the infamous Focke-Wulf Fw 190 fighter, only the Inflexible, serial J7557, was constructed in Britain. Registered as G-EBNG, it made its first flight on 5 March 1928. The Inflexible was a highly ambitious project with great expectations, but the British air budget was too small for series production of such an advanced, complicated and expensive airplane. Later, the Inflexible was the main spectacle of the famous 'Flying Circus' of Sir Alan Cobham at RAE Martlesham Heath near Ipswich, Suffolk. In contrast, Beardmore's final design was the two-seat Wee Bee 1 fitted with a single 32-hp Bristol Cherub engine. Flown by Maurice Pearcy, it won the 1924 Lympe Light Aircraft Trials and only one aircraft was built. It was later sold to an investor in Australia in 1933.

Blackburn Aeroplane and Motor Co. – Blackburn & General Aircraft Ltd – Blackburn

The Blackburn Aeroplane and Motor Co. in Leeds was founded in 1914 by civil engineer Robert Blackburn who started designing monoplanes in 1909 and produced his first aircraft in 1910. The Blackburn Monoplane 1 was followed by the Mercury, powered by a 50-hp Isaacson radial engine. As with other fledgling aircraft manufacturers of the time, the company became a subcontractor undertaking the manufacture of RAF Be.2cs, Sopwith Baby fighters and Sopwith Cuckoo torpedo-bombers at its Olympia Leeds Works and at Sherburn-in-Elmet. Blackburn eventually concentrated on naval types and specialised in torpedo-carrying carrier-based bombers. They also produced multi-engined civil and military flying boats starting with the RT.1 Kangaroo. After the November 1918 armistice, of the twenty RT.1s built, eleven were later converted into civil freighters and pleasure flight aircraft. The RT.1 was followed by the T1 Swift, T2 Dart, T3 Velos and T5 Ripon torpedo-bomber of 1926. The Ripon's water-cooled engine was later replaced with a 545-hp Bristol Pegasus radial with the type renamed as Baffin in 1932 of which there were fifteen new builds with sixty-two Ripons converted to Baffins. The B6 Shark followed in 1933 and were all single-seat or twin-seat biplanes, and with the exception of the Baffin, all used the Napier Lion water-cooled engine.

Following an Admiralty requirement set out in specification N.1B for a long-range escort fighter capable of accompanying the Navy's large patrol flying boats, Blackburn produced the Blackburn N.1B Nib and was designed by Harris Booth and Maj. Linton Hope. Unfortunately, the Admiralty changed its requirements after work on the three airplanes had started. Only the hull of one aircraft, serial N56, was completed before work on the project was halted. The N56 hull was later incorporated in the Blackburn Pellet. Amongst the experimental bombers of the 1920s was the Blackburn T4 Cubaroo, one of the largest single-engined bombers ever built powered by a 1,000-hp Napier Cub engine that had previously powered the Armstrong Whitworth Aldershot Mk II. Only two prototypes were built, serials N166 and N167, both designed as torpedo bombers. The all-metal Blackburn Iris general-reconnaissance flying boat which equipped one RAF squadron from 1930-1934 was Blackburn's first large flying boat design. The Blackburn Perth that followed was a massive machine powered by three 825-hp Rolls-Royce Buzzard IIMS engines. Four Perth flying boats were operated by the RAF's No. 209 Squadron for flying mainly over the Irish Sea and operating closely with the Royal Navy. The Blackburn Bluebird, of which seventy-nine were built, was the first side-by-side two-seat floatplane to enter series production.

Landplanes designed by the company between the wars commenced with the F.1 Turcock, a single-seat biplane fighter. Designed by Maj. Frank Arnold Bumpus and B. A. Duncan, it was the company's first attempt at producing a land-based aircraft for eight years. Only one F.1 was built. The next landplane designed by Bumpus and G. E. Petty was the F.2 Lincock lightweight single-seat biplane fighter. Five Mk IIIs were built, one demonstrator and two each for Japan and China. Other landplane designs were the B1 Seagrave and the B2 side-by-side all-metal biplane trainer. These aircraft were built at Leeds or the new factory at Brough to the west of Hull. In 1936, Blackburn arranged with the Scottish shipbuilders William Denny & Bros Ltd of Dumbarton to organise and jointly operate a factory at Dumbarton on the Clyde, primarily to manufacture flying boats and the Blackburn Botha torpedo bomber. Wartime production included large numbers of Fairey Swordfish and Fairey Barracuda torpedo-bombers and the company's own types.

Designed in 1937, 192 Blackburn B.24 Skua dive-bombers were built and delivered by March 1940. The Skua was the first monoplane to enter FAA service. The Blackburn Roe turret-fighter developed from the Skua was not very successful and the land-based reconnaissance torpedo-bomber was a complete failure. The RAF's B.26 Botha was seriously underpowered and could not be used operationally, although it was used quite successfully on operational training duties. An alarming feature associated with the Botha design was the sitting of the wing-mounted engines. They were so close to the fuselage that any pilot daring to look out of the cabin side windows was likely to be beheaded so close were the tips of the revolving propellers!

The Botha was followed by the B.27 Firebrand torpedo-bomber that only saw limited service after the war when 225 Firebrands of all variants were built. Blackburn's main contribution to the Second World War effort was the licensed-production of aircraft that originated from other companies and the modification of American naval warplanes arriving at Liverpool Docks to meet British operational requirements.

In January 1949, Blackburn Aircraft Co. Ltd as it was now known acquired General Aircraft Ltd of Hanworth, Feltham and Middlesex. The acquisition brought with it the four-engine GAL 60 Universal Freighter that was redesignated as the B.101 Beverley, forty-seven of which were built for the RAF as the Beverly C.1 tactical-transport, serving from 1956 until 1968. The company also undertook subcontract work which included licensed-production of the Boulton Paul Balliol and Percival Prentice trainers.

Following another name change to Blackburn and General Aircraft Ltd, the company produced the iconic Blackburn B.103 Buccaneer carrier-borne, low-level transonic warplane to meet the Air Ministry's Naval NA.39 requirement. An initial order for forty S Mk 1s was received followed by an order for eighty-four S Mk 2s, seventy of which were later transferred to the RAF to add to their new-build S Mk 2B standard aircraft. Sixteen Buccaneer S Mk 50s were delivered – flown out by SAAF pilots trained in the UK when en route one was lost – to South Africa and were operated by No. 24 Squadron SAAF in the maritime strike reconnaissance role, although it was also used in the notorious African 'Bush Wars'. The Buccaneer was destined to assume the Hawker Siddeley mantle when Hawker Siddeley Aviation took over Blackburn in 1960.

In the twilight of its career, the 'Bucc' had a brief moment of glory in the first Gulf War in 1991 during Operation Desert Storm when the maritime strike aircraft of Nos 12 and 208 Squadrons (RAF) acted as laser designators for Panavia GR.1 IDS Tornados. A number of Buccaneer aircraft were subsequently used as trials aircraft for the Panavia Tornado F.3 ADV development, especially the GEC/Marconi AI 24 Foxhunter radar with one aircraft permanently wired for instrumentation purposes operating from RAE Bedford, close to the GEC/

The Blackburn NA.39 prototype (later named by the FAA as the Hawker Siddeley Buccaneer S.1) is proudly displayed at the entrance of the Fleet Air Arm Museum at Yeovilton, Somerset. (*Author*)

RAF sea-grey Hawker Siddeley Buccaneer maritime strike-bombers were hastily repainted 'desert pink' in 1991 for use in Operation Desert Storm with RAF Panavia Tornado GR.1 IDS aircraft as laser designators. (*Aviation News*)

Marconi design and development site at Milton Keynes. Radar trials were undertaken with Buccaneer aircraft fitted with modified Panavia Tornado F.3 radomes fitted to accommodate the GEC/Marconi AI 24 Foxhunter radar.

After operating briefly as the Hawker Blackburn Division, the company finally lost its identity on 1 April 1965. The last design to emanate from the Blackburn Aircraft Company was the Buccaneer maritime strike-bomber for the Royal Navy. Prototype Blackburn NA 39, serial XK488, is displayed at the entrance to the Fleet Air Arm Museum, RNAS Yeovilton, near Yeovil, Somerset.

Boulton Aircraft Ltd – Boulton Paul

Established in 1873 as a wood-working firm, Boulton Paul of Norwich set up an aircraft department in 1915 at Mousehold Aerodrome, Norwich, when it obtained a contract to manufacture 100 Sopwith Camels and the Royal Aircraft Factory's Fe.2b under the management of Leslie Frise (1897-1979).

In 1917, the company obtained the services of John D. North from the Austin Motor Co. whose first design was the P3 Hawk fighter, later renamed Bobolink. Only one prototype was built. Having produced three wooden biplanes, the P6, P9 and P7 Bourges, a twin-engine, two-seat day-bomber, North then designed a series of all-metal high- performance biplane day-bombers. The first of these was the P 29 Sidestrand, which was a descendant of the Bourges and Bugle twin-engine bombers, neither of which entered series production. Eighteen Sidestrand Is were delivered to the RAF's No. 101 Squadron in 1928. The 101 Squadron aircraft were re-engined with two 480-hp Bristol Jupiter VIIIF engines in place of the original 465-hp Jupiter VI. These aircraft were redesignated as the Sidestrand III. Subsequently, No. 101 Squadron was the only squadron to operate the much improved P.75 Overstrand medium-bomber.

It was the first RAF bomber to feature a power-operated, enclosed gun turret mounted in the nose that increased the gunnery strike rate from fifteen to eighty-five. Such a defensive capability for a bomber hastened the development of multi-gun turrets which became a notable feature on British Second World War bombers such as the Avro Lancaster. The pilot had an enclosed transparent canopy with a sliding cover and the rear upper gunner's position was protected by a large windshield. Two 635-hp Bristol Pegasus IIM engines gave increased performance and the cockpit was heated and fitted with an automatic pilot.

Of the subsequent Boulton Paul designs – the P 31 Bittern and the P 33 Partridge fighters, and the P 41 Phoenix and P 64 Mailplane – none entered series production. Designated as the P 71A, two triple-finned models of the P 64 Mailplane fitted with the Armstrong Siddeley Jaguar VIA radials were delivered to Imperial Airways in February 1935 for use as light transports and VIP aircraft. In 1935, Boulton Paul Aircraft Ltd was re-established as Boulton Paul (name change in 1936) at Wolverhampton where some 1,065 day/night fighter and target tug Defiants were produced. The first prototype, serial K8310, first flew on 11 August 1937 and initially went on to some early successes against the Luftwaffe. However, the Defiant proved unsuited to daylight operations and was relegated to the night-fighter role, being officially retired from frontline RAF service in 1942.

After the Second World War, the company produced an excellent advanced three-seat trainer, the P 108 Balliol prototype, serial VL917. The second prototype aircraft, which flew on 24 March 1948, was the first Balliol to fly powered by a single turboprop engine (an Armstrong Siddeley Mamba). As the trials of the P 108 proceeded, the Air Ministry revised its requirements to that of a more conventional piston-engine two-seat trainer. Four prototypes were ordered along with seventeen pre-production models. The new variant designated Balliol T.2 was intended to replace the RAF's ageing North American Harvard trainers.

Initially, large orders were placed, but in 1951, a further change in Air Ministry policy favouring a jet type for advanced flying training led to only

Boulton Paul Balliol T.2 piston-engine trainers were used alongside the similar looking piston-engined Percival Provost in the 1950s by RAF Flying Training Command. (*Author*)

200 Balliols/Sea Balliols being ordered, thirty of which were subcontracted to Blackburn Aircraft Ltd. A number of Balliols were produced for export to Ceylon (now Sri Lanka).

The last aircraft to be built by Boulton Paul before their withdrawal from aircraft manufacturing in 1954 were their first jets: the P 111 and P 120 delta-wing research aircraft. These flew on 10 October 1950 and 6 August 1952 respectively. In 1961, Boulton Paul leased out its designs and joined the Dowty Group. Boulton Paul built a total of 4,826 aircraft, 1,341 of which were of its own design. This is not a large number for more than seventy-five years of aeroplane production. In fact, at their Norwich plant, Boulton Paul only built fifty aircraft of its own design in seventeen years. Defiant production represented 77 per cent of all Boulton Paul aircraft built, the Balliol trainer a further 27 per cent and there were a number of subcontracts. Nevertheless, Boulton Paul realised many significant milestones in technical development such as the P-15 Bolton, a three-crew experimental bomber and the RAF's first all-metal aircraft. It also undertook work on the R.101 airship, Britain's largest flying object, and the R.75 Overstrand was the first aircraft with an enclosed power-operated gun turret. The P.108 Balliol was the world's first aircraft powered by a single propeller turbine engine and Boulton Paul's power-operated gun turrets assured the firm a leading position in the British aviation armaments market for many years.

British & Colonial Aeroplane Co. Ltd (Bristol) – Bristol Aeroplane Co. Ltd

Founded on 19 February 1910 by Sir George White at Filton, Bristol, the British & Colonial Aeroplane Co. Ltd (Bristol) made an inconspicuous start building the French Zodiac biplane. The first Bristol type heralding a long line of truly famous British military aircraft from the company was the Bristol Boxkite or Standard Biplane trainer flown on 31 July 1910. The aircraft was an adaption of the Henri Farman biplane and fitted with a French 50-hp Gnome engine. A total of sixteen were built. Eight were sold to Russia while the remainder went to the British Army for co-operation duties and a single aircraft was sold to a Belgian pilot.

Extensive recruitment both at home and abroad brought the company a number of distinguished designers, including Frank Barnwell and Henri Coanda from Romania who joined Bristol in December 1911 and January 1912 respectively. Three semi-autonomous design offices were set up under Coanda's general control while he also pursued his own ideas. His pusher biplane design, the PB.8, never flew as at the outbreak of war the War Office requisitioned the engine. In 1913, Coanda commenced design work on a

The Bristol Boxkite was a French-designed Farman airplane. The example shown is owned by The Shuttleworth Trust near Biggleswade, Bedfordshire. (*Author*)

single-seat monoplane, the SB.5, for the Italian Government. However, work had only started on construction of the fuselage before the project was abandoned. At this time, there was considerable interest in single-seat military scouts and Barnwell was given permission to redesign the SB.5 as a scout biplane using the wing and tailplane designs of the PB.8 and much of the unfinished fuselage of the original SB.5. The aircraft was affectionately dubbed the 'Baby Biplane', but was officially designated the Bristol Scout.

In March 1916, Barnwell began work on designing a new two-seat fighter embodying many features of the Royal Aircraft Factory's Be.2, many of which Bristol had produced. The initial design, the R.2A (later F.2A), was intended to use the 120-hp Beardmore engine until it was realised that the aircraft would be underpowered, therefore the design was changed to accommodate the 150-hp Hispano-Suiza. However, two months later, Rolls-Royce offered its 190-hp Falcon I. Barnwell immediately set about redesigning the aircraft around the Rolls-Royce engine and the famous Type 96 Bristol Fighter F.2b 'Biff' or 'Brisfit' was born. By September 1919, 4,747 examples had been built. The F.2b continued in service use for some fifteen years with many being subsequently reconditioned after the war along with 378 upgraded new builds. A total of 5,329 Bristol F.2b fighters were built with exports to eleven countries.

An early Bristol design was the M 1C Monoplane. An excellent machine

The Bristol Bulldog Mk II fighter with a 490-hp Jupiter VIIF radial piston engine was from 1929 to the mid-1930s the backbone of the RAF's fighter force for the ADGB that became Fighter Command in 1936. (*Warplane Collection*)

with many superior qualities to its contemporaries, it failed to overcome the deep-seated prejudice against monoplane designs from officialdom that went back to 1912. Due to the number of accidents involving monoplane designs at the time, the Air Ministry opted to continue with biplane designs; however, during the First World War, the Bristol M 1C did see limited service in the Middle East. They also became popular with instructors at various home-based training schools. During the post-war period, many M 1Cs were used privately as racing aeroplanes. Despite the economic difficulties of the inter-war years, the British & Colonial Aeroplane Co. Ltd (Bristol) produced around 2,600 new and reconditioned aircraft. Although various new fighter designs were produced, none were as successful as the Type 105 Bristol Bulldog interceptor fighter. Produced as a private venture, it first flew on 17 May 1927. In total, 312 were built including five for Latvia and a Bulldog II was sent to the US for evaluation, followed by a second aircraft in February 1930 after the initial airplane had crashed. Two went to Siam followed by eight to Australia for use by the RAAF. Towards the end of 1930, three were sold to Sweden and a further seven to Latvia with the final seventeen aircraft going to the Danish Army in 1932. This made a total of 443 examples of which sixty-nine were TM Bulldog Type 124 two-seat, dual-control trainers for the RAF.

The Bristol 130, later named Bombay, was a bomber-transport with a crew

Bristol Bombay troop transports were mainly used in the interwar period in the Middle East where the RAF was employed on peacetime 'policing' duties. (*Warplane Collection*)

of three and capable of carrying twenty-four troops. Although the prototype, serial K3583, made its maiden flight on 23 June 1935, production was delayed by priority work on the Blenheim. Bombay production was therefore transferred to the Short & Harland factory in Belfast where fifty were built to Air Ministry Specification 47/36 that called for a bomber troop-transport.

An unusual Bristol venture in the mid-1930s was the Bristol Type 138A, a single-seat, high-altitude research aircraft built to Air Ministry Specification 2/34 that called for a research airplane capable of attaining 50,000 feet. In the event, this was exceeded by Flt Lt M. J. Adam (RAF) on 30 June 1937 when in a flight lasting 2 hours and 15 minutes, he reached an altitude of 53,937 feet. At this altitude, the canopy cracked, but Adam escaped injury thanks to his special pressure suit and sealed helmet.

In 1934, newspaper tycoon Lord Rothermere commissioned Bristol to produce a light personal transport. The aircraft appeared in April 1935 as the Type 142 and its high performance at 285 mph outpaced many biplane fighters of the day. The Air Ministry asked Rothermere's permission to evaluate the aircraft as a light bomber. In the event, air-minded Rothermere presented the aircraft as 'Britain First', serial K7557, to the nation. After extensive redesign, the prototype Bristol Blenheim bomber, serial K7033, flew on 25 June 1936 with the wing raised to mid-position to make room for an enclosed bomb bay. A retractable turret mounting a single machine gun was provided on the

Bristol Blenheim IV with wartime code WM Z indicates a No. 68 Squadron airplane. (*Flypast Calendar*)

upper fuselage decking and the glazing in the nose was extended to provide a bomb-aiming position. The Blenheim I was the first in a long line of Bristol light monoplane bombers and became the first British aircraft to make use of the new Airborne Interceptor (AI) radar. The need for extra range and better accommodation for the navigator led to the 'long-nosed' Blenheim IV with more powerful Bristol Mercury XV radial engines. It was a Blenheim IVL of No. 139 Squadron RAF that made the first British operational flight of the Second World War, taking off on 3 September 1939 on a 4 hour and 49 minute flight to photograph the German fleet at Kiel. Blenheims were often mistaken for the Junkers Ju 88 and on no less than sixteen occasions in 1940, Blenheims were attacked by British air defences. Some 4,544 Blenheims were built in a number of variants, including under licence in Finland and Yugoslavia with others going to Greece and Romania. In the UK, Blenheims were built by Bristol, Avro and the Rootes Motor Car Co. Six hundred and seventy-six Blenheim Mk IVs were built in Canada by Fairchild as the Type 149 Bolingbroke I coastal reconnaissance and light bomber.

Designed in 1937, production of the Bristol Type 152 Beaufort torpedo-bomber, a development of the Blenheim, reached 2,129 aircraft of which 700 were built in Australia. Production in the UK was centred at Bristol's Filton and Banwell plants. Frank Barnwell was killed on 2 August 1938 in a flying accident leaving Roy Fedden and Leslie Frise to complete designs of the private venture Bristol Type 156 Beaufighter. In its original concept, it incorporated around 75 per cent of the Beaufort's airframe and only the main fuselage and engine mountings were of a new design. The use of Beaufort subassemblies and parts made it possible for the prototype Beaufighter, serial R2052, with its two Bristol Hercules III engines to fly on 17 July 1939, only eight months after the design began. Over 5,600 production variants of the Beaufighter entered service with the RAF (Mks I, II, VI, X and XI). The Beaufighter was manufactured by The Bristol Aeroplane Co. Ltd at Filton and Whitchurch; Fairey Aviation Co. Ltd at Stockport, Cheshire; the MAP Shadow Factory, Old Mixon, Weston-super-Mare; and Rootes Securities Ltd, Blyth Bridge, Staffordshire. A further 364 were built in Australia at the Beaufort Division, DAP, Fisherman's Bend, Melbourne, Victoria, for use by the RAAF.

Originally planned in 1942 as a day bomber to replace the Blenheim, the Type 163 Buckingham was not available in quantity until 1944 by which time it had been made obsolete by the excellent performance of its de Havilland counterpart, the stunning Mosquito. This resulted in the original order for 400 Buckinghams to be reduced to 119 with the last sixty-five built as high-speed transports. Even those originally delivered as bombers were converted retrospectively to transports. As a transport, the aircraft could carry four passengers and three crew 2,360 miles at an average speed of 294 mph. With the reduced orders for the Buckingham, sufficient components remained to fit out 110 airframes as advanced high-speed trainers with side-by-side seating and provision for an air signaller. This variant was given the designation Type 166 Buckmaster, some of which were used to train radar navigators.

The Type 164 Bristol Brigand was originally conceived as a torpedo bomber. Initially named as the Buccaneer, it was to supersede the Beaufighter. However, with the diminished requirement in the post-war RAF, the type was re-roled as a light ground-attack bomber for overseas squadrons. The Brigand utilised the wings, tail unit and twin Bristol Centaurus engines of the Buckingham with a new and smaller cross-section fuselage, but with the power-operated turret deleted. An interesting feature of the design was the close grouping of the three crew members in a single compartment with the navigator and radio operator sitting side-by-side facing to starboard. The navigator could also move to a small seat on the front spar behind the pilot where he could direct the intricate operations involving torpedo firing at high speed. Only eleven TF.1 torpedo-fighters were built, the main production model being the B Mk 1 light-attack bomber. The RAF received 142 Brigands of which sixteen were Met.3 weather reconnaissance variants for use by No. 1301 Flight in Ceylon and nine T.4 radar navigator trainers. About thirty new

All marks of Bristol Sycamore helicopters served the RAF well on resupply and transport duties in Malaya during Operation *Firedog*. (*Author*)

Twin-rotor Westland (Bristol) Belvederes based at RAF Khormaksar in the early 1960s and deployed on 'up-country' resupply duties were often shot at by dissident tribesman in the Radfan Valley as were Hunter FGA 9s and Avro Shackleton MR.2s. (*Author*)

build radar navigator trainers were designated as the T.5.

Bristol has the distinction of having built the largest British aircraft to fly: the Bristol Brabazon transatlantic airliner. The massive eight-engine aircraft had its flight trials in September 1949; however, it did not go into series production as jet airliners such as the de Havilland Comet rendered the design as obsolete. The first prototype and two partially completed airframes were eventually scrapped in 1953, the remains and few parts donated to the Bristol Industrial Museum and Scotland's National Museum of Flight.

The twin-engine, light utility Bristol Wayfarer/Freighter was developed into the highly successful Bristol 170 Freighter of which some 200 were produced in many different variants. The cargo hold had been specially designed to facilitate rapid loading through the nose with large doors opening sideways to give unobstructed access to the full width of the hold. To this end, the aircraft was extremely popular in the 1950s with cross-channel car ferry operators. The aircraft was also popular with a number of overseas air forces as a military transport, namely Australia, Canada, New Zealand and Pakistan. The Type 175 Britannia was probably the company's most popular post-war design and although the aircraft had a number of teething troubles, it was the first British turboprop airliner to fly the Atlantic on 19 December 1957. However, with the advent of the jet age, only eighty-five Britannias were built with some production subcontracted to Short Brothers & Harland Ltd, Queens Island, and Belfast. Twenty-one aircraft were exported and twenty-three military variants designated as the Type 253 delivered to the RAF. Also at this time, Bristol were engaged in a number of design studies for high-speed research aircraft and supersonic transports.

In 1945, Bristol had formed a helicopter department at Weston-super-Mare, Somerset, which produced two successful designs before it was taken over by Westland in 1960. The Type 171 Sycamore piston-engine SAR helicopter was the first British designed helicopter to go into service with the RAF. One hundred and seventy-eight Sycamores were produced and it played an important part in the development of the RAF's operational use of helicopters such as undertaking night flying and troop drops in mountainous regions in Malaya during Operation Firedog with No. 194 Squadron.

Although the Type 192 Belvedere HC.1 was built by Westland Aircraft Ltd who had taken over Bristol's helicopter interests on 23 March 1960, the helicopter was commonly known as the Bristol Belvedere when in RAF service. Only twenty-six examples were built, a number seeing service in the Middle East and Far East RAF Commands in the mid-1960s.

In 1960, Bristol Aircraft Ltd became part of the newly established British Aircraft Corporation and the name disappeared completely in December 1963 when the Filton plant was reorganised as BAC's Filton Division working on the Anglo-French *Concorde* SST.

Britten-Norman Ltd – Pilatus Britten-Norman

Britten-Norman Ltd was formed by John Britten and Desmond Norman at Bembridge on the Isle of Wight. The two men had met while attending the de Havilland apprenticeship Technical School at Hatfield. The company's first project was the BN-1F Finibee, an ultralight of which only one was built. For a short period, Britten-Norman concentrated on agricultural types and conversions, but later produced a low cost, ten-seat, high-wing STOL aircraft for utility and short haul operations designated as the BN-2A Islander. The prototype, registration G-ATCT, was powered by two 210-hp Continental IO-360-B engines and first flew on 13 June 1965 at Bembridge. With an increased wingspan by 1.22 metres (4 feet) and re-engined with Textron Lycoming O-540 engines, it flew on 17 December 1965. A pre-production model, registration G-ATWU, flew on 20 August 1966.

Later variants using two Allison 250-B17C turboprops were designated as the BN-2T Turbine Islander. The AL Mk 1 was purchased by the British Army for use mainly on forward air control duties and clandestine operations during the troubles in Northern Ireland.

Of other types produced by Britten-Norman, the BN-3 Nymph never entered series production. Eighty-one seventeen-passenger BN-2A Trislanders were built, seventy-three in the UK and the balance was assembled by a US-based customer as the Tri-Commutair. However, in the late 1990s, three brand new Trislanders that had yet to be assembled in the US were returned to the Channel Islands for assembly by the Guernsey-based aero-engineering company Anglo Normandy. A distinctive aircraft, the Trislander has a third piston engine mounted high up in a much modified tail unit. First flown on 11 September 1970, a total of eighty-five Trislanders were delivered. In spite of the success of its BN-2 range of aircraft with in excess of 1,250 sold worldwide and production having once peaked at twelve a month, the company went into receivership in August 1972 to be acquired by the Fairey Group and renamed Fairey Britten-Norman. Fairey set up a new production line at their Gosselies factory in Belgium with the 500th Islander being delivered in 1973. Subsequently, the Fairey Company went into liquidation with Britten-Norman then being purchased by Pilatus Aircraft of Switzerland.

On 24 January 1979, it was renamed Pilatus Britten-Norman and production continued at Bembridge and at the Romaero works in Bucharest, Romania. New variants were introduced such as the BN2T-4S Defender 4000. The prototype, registration G-SURV, flew on 17 August 1994. The company offered a low-cost off-the-shelf Multi-Sensor Surveillance Aircraft (MSSA), the BN2T-4R, that was fitted with Westinghouse AN/APG-66 radar. Two aircraft

PBN 2T
Islander
company
demonstrator.
(*SBAC
Farnborough
brochure*)

RAF Northolt-based PBN 2T was used in Northern Ireland on FAC and intelligence gathering duties. (*Author*)

PBN 2T4R development airplane with bulbous Westinghouse ASV radar. None were sold or series produced. (*Author*)

were delivered to Westinghouse in the US for conversion in January 1995. The demonstrator (G-MSSA), a conversion from AEW Defender G-TEMI, was rolled out at Baltimore on 10 September 1995. In August 1997, Pilatus Britten-Norman delivered its first series 'Special' PBN 4000 to the Irish Garda, the type chosen in preference to rotary-winged aircraft. On 21 July 1998, Pilatus Aircraft announced it had sold Pilatus Britten-Norman to a UK-based private investment company, Litchfield Continental. The company reverted to its previous trading name Britten-Norman Ltd and remains in business in support of the delivered Pilatus Britten-Norman airplanes.

De Havilland – HSA

Sir Geoffrey de Havilland (1882–1965), an early designer and self-taught pilot, founded the de Havilland Aircraft Co. on 25 September 1920 at Stag Lane Aerodrome, Edgeware, Middlesex, having obtained financial assistance from his old Airco boss George Holt Thomas and money left to him by his grandfather. Initially, the company provided sales and support for surplus First World War aircraft while at the same time undertaking a number of its own designs. Up until the Second World War, the company concentrated mostly on civil types. In addition to aircraft, the company also became proficient aero-engine manufacturers with the opening of its engine division in 1926 when Maj. Frank Halford (1894–1955) joined to design the first of a long series of 'Gipsy' engines.

An early airliner, the eight-seat DH 34 had its maiden flight on 26 March 1922. Of the eleven built, ten were used commercially by Instone Air Line Service. Unfortunately on 7 April 1922, a de Havilland DH 18 operated by Daimler Hire was involved in the first mid-air passenger-carrying airliner collision over Thieuloy-Saint-Antoine, France, when it collided with a Farman Goliath operated by Grands Express Aériens. Seven passengers and crew were killed.

The company's first military design was the DH 27 Derby day-bomber followed by the DH 42 Dormouse high-performance, two-seat reconnaissance fighter of which only three prototypes were built. With no production orders for the reconnaissance fighter, the company once again turned to the commercial market with a four-passenger cabin biplane, the DH 50. Designed as a replacement for the DH 9C, the DH 50 was operated by DH Hire Service. Sixteen were built at Stag Lane and eleven were built in Australia, three in Belgium and seven in Yugoslavia under licence. It was a DH 50 flown by Sir Alan Cobham that completed the first England to Australia and return flight from 30 June 1926 to 1 October 1926, finally landing on the River Thames near the Houses of Parliament.

The DH 51, DH 52 glider and DH 53 Hummingbird preceded a long line of de Havilland Moths which undoubtedly became the foundation of the British light aircraft industry and with a total of 8,800 built, with most for the RAF, there can be no doubt of the type's importance to the military. The first Moth was the wooden civil DH 60 and first flown by Geoffrey de Havilland on 22 February 1922. This very aircraft epitomised private flying with 500 produced in Britain alone. Initial production was centred at Stag Lane until 1934 when the design and manufacturing activities followed the de Havilland Flying School to Hatfield. Occupying a new factory established at Hatfield, the site soon became the company's headquarters. Other DH 60 family members were the DH 60G Gipsy Moth (fitted with a de Havilland Gipsy engine); the DH 60M two-seat military elementary trainer and communications aircraft with a welded-steel fuselage; the DH 60GIII Moth Major; and the DH 60T military trainer. Moths were even developed briefly as airliners.

The DH 66 Hercules was a large seven-passenger commercial biplane constructed for Imperial Airways for use on their desert air mail service between Cairo and Karachi. This was followed by the DH 61 Giant Moth, a six to eight-seat airliner designed in 1927 to an Australia Government requirement for a replacement for the DH 50J model followed by the four-seat DH 75 Hawk Moth. Further Moth improvements resulted in the DH 80A Puss Moth of 1930. The Puss Moth is generally recognised as the first true executive business aircraft to be produced by de Havilland. The most famous of the Moth lineage was undoubtedly the DH 82A Tiger Moth IIA derived from the DH 60G. The Tiger Moth was sold worldwide to at least twenty-five countries. By the beginning of the Second World War, 1,150 Tiger Moths had been built at Hatfield and 227 in Canada. In fact, by the end of the war in 1945, some 2,751 had been built in Canada, Australia and New Zealand by de Havilland's associated companies (most for the Commonwealth Air Training Plan). The Tiger Moth differed from the Gipsy Moth by way of its staggered sweptback wings, inverted engine to improve the forward view and provide greater ground clearance for the propeller, and other detailed improvements. The prototype Tiger Moth flew on 26 October 1931 and was destined to become a 'classic' aircraft of all time with large numbers used by the military and civil operators as basic trainers. Total UK production of the Tiger Moth was in excess of 4,200 aircraft. From 1937 until 1939, Tiger Moths equipped forty-four Elementary and Reserve Flying Training Schools during the war. There were twenty-eight schools in the UK; twenty-five in Canada; twelve in Australia; four in New Zealand; seven in South Africa; two in India; and five in the Rhodesian Air Training Group as well as twenty-five Reserve Flying Schools and eighteen University Air Squadrons.

In Canada, to enable flying training to continue in the extremes of the winter weather, the DH 82C was fitted with a heated cockpit and canopy, and with an undercarriage choice of wheels, floats or skis. An all-wooden,

First flown in its DH 60T form, the revised DH 82 Tiger Moth trainer first flew in October 1931 and over 8,000 Tiger Moths were built in the UK, Canada, Australia and New Zealand. (*Flight Colour*)

ply-covered, radio-controlled version of the Tiger Moth was built for the RAF as target drones. Three hundred and eighty aircraft were supplied to the RAF and were known as the DH 82B Queen Bee. Three hundred and twenty were built at Hatfield and the remainder were constructed by Scottish Aviation Ltd. Most were completed as twin-float seaplanes.

In 1934, de Havilland introduced the manufacture and general use of variable-pitch propellers to the UK. Originally based on the American Hamilton Standard design, most new bombers, fighters and other types were fitted with de Havilland constant-speed propellers. Further airscrew development followed with the introduction of six-bladed, contra-rotating, constant-speed propellers and a Hydromatic airscrew both featuring feathering and reverse-pitch for braking, and hollow steel blades, all innovations from the Hamilton Standard Division of United Aircraft. Final Moths produced were the DH 83 Fox Moth, DH 85 Leopard Moth, DH 87 Hornet Moth and the DH 94 Moth Minor. De Havilland then concentrated on passenger airliner types starting with the DH 84 Dragon, a twin-engine development of the Fox Moth capable of accommodating six passengers. One hundred and fifteen Dragons were produced in the UK with most entering airline service.

The de Havilland Tiger Moth was used by the newly formed RAF Coastal Command for coastal patrol duties. (*Flight Colour*)

Mention should be made at this point of the DH 88 Comet long-range racing monoplane. Three aircraft were built specifically for entry in the Victorian Centenary Air Race between Melbourne, Australia, and RAF Mildenhall, Suffolk, England. The race was held on 20 October and was won by Grosvenor House in 70 hours and 54 minutes. This unique aircraft is now preserved at the Shuttleworth Trust Museum. Two other Comets were later built, one as a mail plane for the French Government and one for what proved to be unsuccessful attempts on the London to Cape Town record. The Comet Racers established the de Havilland Company as leading designers of high-speed aircraft.

The four-engine DH 86 Dragon civil airliner was an enlarged version of the DH 89 Dragon Rapide and both types were widely used by British internal airlines in the 1930s. Many remained in service for many years after the war being virtually irreplaceable for certain duties and resulted in many service DH 89A Rapides being converted back from Domonies as they were known in service use. A total of 521 DH 89As were built for the RAF. De Havilland built 186 at Hatfield with Brush Coachworks of Loughborough building the remainder. The Rapide was followed by the smaller four-seat DH 90 Dragonfly.

A civilian-operated DH 89A Dragon Rapide, the company's first executive transport. (*Author*)

RAF DH 89A Dragon Rapide light-transport and training aircraft with two 200-hp DH Queen 3 inline piston engines. Wartime code Z-CA indicates No. 189 Squadron. (*Warplane Collection*)

Built in 1939 of all wood construction, the extremely elegant DH 91 Albatross low-wing, twenty-two seat intercontinental transport entered service with Imperial Airways who purchased the five series aircraft and two prototypes along with the smaller eighteen-passenger, high-wing DH 95 Flamingo that first flew in December 1938. Three Flamingos were built for the RAF for the King's Flight (VIP standard) then based at RAF Benson in Oxfordshire. A contract for thirty fully militarised Hertfordshires (Flamingos) was reduced to one, serial R2510, delivered to No. 24 (Communications) Squadron in

RAF No. 24 (Communications) Squadron DH 85 Flamingo transport. (*Wings*)

June 1940.

An order by the RAF for 250 DH 93 Don advanced trainers was initially cut to fifty and only thirty were delivered, its demise brought about in the main by the Air Ministry who demanded too much (by way of specification) of the small training airplane.

Experience gained in the construction of the DH 91 twenty-two seat civil transport proved invaluable in the design and manufacture of the 'Wooden Wonder', the DH 98 Mosquito. Considered to be one of the most successful aircraft of the Second World War, the beloved 'Mossie' is arguably one of aviation's most outstanding aeroplanes of all time. Mosquito design began as a private venture in October 1938 as a light unarmed bomber under the watchful eye of chief designer R. E. Bishop at the remote Salisbury Hall near London Colney, Hertfordshire, and now the site of the Mosquito Aircraft (de Havilland Aircraft Trust) Museum. The first prototype Mosquito, serial W4050, flew at Hatfield on 25 November 1940 piloted by Geoffrey de Havilland Jr attaining a level flight speed of nearly 400 mph. Much to the amazement of official guests, the new light-bomber displayed near fighter-like agility. Photographic-reconnaissance, fighter, trainer and bomber variants followed.

When production ceased in 1950, 7,781 de Havilland DH 98 Mosquitoes had been built in forty variants. The type had been operated by eighty-six RAF squadrons and twelve air forces. The fact that the aircraft was constructed almost entirely of wood was a bonus for the UK. A country at war and dependant on the import of metals and iron ores from overseas, wooden construction also facilitated dispersed manufacture to subcontractors usually involved in the carpentry and joinery fields, and furniture manufacture. The aircraft was powered by two 1,460-hp Rolls-Royce Merlin 21 or 23 V12-cylinder, liquid-cooled, supercharged inline engines driving three-bladed de Havilland variable-pitch propellers. The Mosquito was produced as a bomber, fighter, night-fighter, photographic-reconnaissance aircraft and trainer. Also, from November 1944, the Royal Navy deployed the Sea Mosquito variant for some six years in the trials and training roles with its No. 700 series squadrons.

In 1943, Mosquitoes with civil markings were put on special airline duties with British Airways. They were tasked with maintaining a service to Stockholm over enemy territory, often in the face of determined efforts by German fighters to intercept them. A number of prototype 'Mossies' were built including serial W4050 (initially serialled E0234) that is now preserved for posterity at Salisbury Hall, Mosquito Museum, London Colney, near St Albans in Hertfordshire. Prototype NF II, serial W4052, and FR photo-reconnaissance variant, serial W4051, were followed by the first bomber versions, the B.IV, serial W4072, and subsequently the fighter-bombers: FB VI, serial MP469; FB XVIII, serial HJ732; and a navalised TR 33, serial LR387. Series production was carried out by de Havilland Aircraft Ltd at Hatfield and Leavesden, near Watford, Hertfordshire – nearly all Leavesden production consisted of trainer T.3 variants – and Hawarden in Cheshire. Subcontractors were Airspeed Ltd, Christchurch, Hampshire; Standard Motor Co. Ltd; de Havilland Aircraft Pty Ltd, Bankstown, Sydney, New South Wales, Australia; and de Havilland Aircraft of Canada Ltd, Downsview, Toronto.

The Mosquito returned such astonishing performance and manoeuvrability that only ten of the initial batch became bombers. Mk I, II and III designations were preserved for photo-reconnaissance fighter and training variants. The Mk IV became the standard bomber version and over 250 were built. Four 500-lb bombs could be carried and a modification to lengthen the bomb bay later permitted carriage of a single HC 'Cookie' 4,000-lb bomb. The original B.IV with its Merlin XX series engines gave way to the B.IX with more powerful Merlin 72 engines and an additional payload of two 500-lb bombs carried under the wings. A development of the B.IX, the B.XVI with a lengthened bomb bay and pressurised cabin, gave rise to more than 1,000 aircraft built by de Havilland and its subcontractors. These were later supplemented by Canadian production Mosquitoes fitted with Packard-built Merlin engines. The first, serial KB300, first flew at Toronto on 24 September 1942.

The final Mosquito variant built was the B.35 with Merlin 113/114 engines and was produced as a night-strike fighter, but emerged too late to see action in the closing stages of the war. The B.IV, B.IX and Canadian-built models were withdrawn from use in 1946 and these were followed by the B.XVI. However, the B.35s were retained and modified to continue in the target-towing role before being struck off charge at the end of 1962. Two further de Havilland designs flown before the end of the Second World War were the DH 100 Vampire – a twin-boom, Goblin-engine turbojet – and the piston-engine

The infamous de Havilland 'Wooden Wonder' Mosquito is renowned for its Bomber Command deployments in the Second World War, especially in the Pathfinder role. However, its deployment to the Far East during the Pacific campaign was marred by problems associated with its wooden construction in the hot and humid jungle environment. (*Warplane Collection*)

DH 103 Hornet and its navalised equivalent, the Sea Hornet. The latter was effectively a scaled down version of the Mosquito with a wooden fuselage and a light alloy wing. Two hundred and eighty Hornets were delivered to the RAF with a further order for 534 cancelled.

In 1948, production of the Hornet was switched from Hatfield to Chester. Navalisation of the Hornet was entrusted to Heston Aircraft Co. Ltd, the main changes being the incorporation of Lockheed hydraulics for the power-folding wings and a steel V-frame arrester hook with local strengthening of the airframe. The hydraulic main undercarriage oleos to cater for the higher rate of descent during carrier-deck landings were supplied by de Havilland. Production of seventy-eight Sea Hornet NF Mk 21s was centred at Chester where forty-three examples of the final variant, the Mk 22 photo-reconnaissance aircraft, were built.

On 13 May 1944, a production order for 120 Vampire jets was placed with the aircraft to be built at the Preston factory of English Electric Co. Ltd who were to build over 1,000 Vampires of various marks. Seventy Vampire Is were ordered by the Royal Swedish Air Force under the designation J28. Forty RAF squadrons received the Vampire and many of the 4,206 built were exported. Two Vampire Is were modified for high-speed trials. Designated as the DH 108, they were both fitted with swept wings as precursor designs for the Comet jetliner and the DH 110 naval fighter. On 27 September 1946,

The first and the last (until the Lockheed-Martin F.35 enters FAA service) fixed-wing types operated by the Royal Navy: the Sea Harrier F/A-2 and Vampire. The latter was the first jet fighter in the world to land on an aircraft carrier. (*Aviation News*)

DH 108, serial TG283, broke up over the Thames Estuary killing Geoffrey de Havilland Jr. The second DH 108, serial TG306, flown by John Derry – later killed at the Farnborough air show while display flying a DH 110 – on 9 September 1948 was the first British aeroplane to exceed the speed of sound. The third DH 108, serial VW120, had a different nose section.

All three DH 108s and their pilots were tragically lost in flying accidents. A total of 1,158 Vampires were produced in the UK for the RAF and 291 Sea Vampires Mk I and 3 for the FAA.

The DH 110 Sea Vixen was a twin-engine development of the Vampire's twin-boom configuration designed to protect the airframe tail assembly from the jet efflux. The Sea Vixen was primarily designed as a platform for the British AI Mk 17 radar. The first prototype DH 110, serial WG 236, was flown by Gp Capt. John 'Cats Eyes' Cunningham CBE DSO DFC at Hatfield on 26 September 1951. As previously mentioned, tragedy was to strike serial WG236 flown by John Derry on 6 September 1952 at Farnborough. In the subsequent crash, Derry and his flight observer, Tony Richards, and twenty-eight members of the public were killed when debris decimated the packed crowds. Subsequently, the remaining prototype DH 110 was grounded pending investigation and modifications and other design work to enhance the aircraft's flight characteristics, handling and naval specification requirements. The work was carried out under the auspices of W. A. Tamblin when production was switched from Hatfield to de Havilland's Christchurch plant in the south of England. A third prototype DH 110 was named as the

DH Vampire single-seat F.6 fighters were operated by the Swiss Air Force as jet fighter trainers with nineteen remaining operational in the early 1990s. (*Warplane Collection*)

Sea Vixen. One hundred and nineteen Sea Vixen Mk 1s were built followed by twenty-nine of the much enhanced Mk 2 variant. Production was centred at the de Havilland plants at Hatfield, Hawarden and Christchurch.

The prototype dual-seat DH 115 Vampire T.11 trainer, serial WW456, was produced by the Airspeed Works at Christchurch (a de Havilland subsidiary) having its first flight on 15 November 1950. The aircraft featured a widened cockpit to seat student and pupil side-by-side. The aircraft was similar to the DH 113 night fighter although it did not carry radar and was fitted with dual controls. Total production of the DH 115 was 804 aircraft. Four hundred and twenty-seven were built at Chester from October 1952 onwards with over 530 examples delivered to the RAF. Many T.11 and T.55s were exported to more than twenty countries with licensed production in Australia, India and Italy with six supplied to the Iraqi Air Force. Some 3,000 RAF pilots qualified for their wings on the Vampire T.11 jet trainer. In 1949, the Vampire was developed into the DH 112 Venom and Sea Venom of which production totalled 887 aircraft built at Hatfield, Chester, Christchurch, and subcontractor Fairey Aviation Co. Ltd at Ringway, Manchester.

The DH 104 Dove was de Havilland's first post-war civil aircraft entering airline service in May 1946. The Dove was a ten-passenger, low-wing monoplane and large numbers were built at Hatfield and Hawarden Aerodrome, Chester. The aircraft appeared in numerous civil variants and for the RAF as the Devon C.1 and the Royal Navy as the Sea Devon Mk.20.

The Dove was followed by the fourteen to seventeen-seat DH 114 Heron

Royal Navy DH Sea Vixen FAW.1 carrier-borne all-weather interceptor or strike fighter with two Rolls-Royce Avon 208 turbojets of 11,230-lb static thrust each. (*Author*)

airliner. The Heron, which first flew on 10 May 1950, used many Dove component parts. Four Herons entered service with the Queen's Flight in the mid-1950s. One example was the C.3 variant and the remaining three the C.4.

The DH Chipmunk DHC.1 was designed by de Havilland Canada, Toronto, where the prototype first flew on 22 May 1946. A monoplane descendant of the Tiger Moth, 158 were built in Canada and a number went to the RCAF. When the type arrived in the UK, the Air Ministry adopted it as an ab initio trainer and 735 Chipmunks were built at Hatfield and Chester for the RAF. It was only in March 1997 that the final Chipmunks still in use as basic flying trainers with the Army Air Corps at Middle Wallop were finally withdrawn from use.

The DH 106 Comet was the world's first turbojet-powered airliner. Designs were started in 1944 in response to the Brabazon Committee's deliberations into the UK's post-war air transport requirements. The prototype Comet 1, which was designed to accommodate thirty-six to forty-four passengers, first flew on 27 July 1949. Nine production aircraft delivered to BOAC were initially used a freighters and only later as passenger carriers. The Comet 1 was followed by ten Comet 1As with increased fuel capacity and range. After three disastrous structural failures, one in 1953 and two in 1954, the Comet airliner was withdrawn from use. After extensive investigations into the accidents and a series of tests carried out at Farnborough simulating pressurisation and de-

RAF Flying Training Command DH T.11 Vampires were the first jet trainers that RAF pilots qualified for their 'wings'. The type entered service in 1952 and the last operational sortie was flown in 1967. (*Postcard*)

Royal Navy DH Sea Venom FAW.22 two-seat, carrier-borne, AI radar-equipped, all-weather strike fighter with a 5,500-lb thrust de Havilland Ghost 105 turbojet engine. (*Author*)

Royal Navy DH Sea Devon light-transport, communications and liaison aircraft. (*Author*)

pressurisation in a giant water tank, it was proved that the failures were caused by the square windows (a design used in early piston-engine airliners). The corners of the square windows formed cracks resulting in the airframe being ripped open as if a tin can. Rounded windows were immediately introduced to forty-four passenger Comet IIs – of which twelve were built for BOAC – and subsequently used in pressurised airliner designs ever since. In addition, the Accident Investigation Board (AIB) found that in an effort to save weight, the aluminium fuselage skinning was too thin. Subsequently, the ten Comet IIs after modification were diverted to the RAF Transport Command at RAF Lyneham as seventy-seat passenger aircraft designated as the Comet C.2. Pioneering the use of pure jets as military transports, the Comet 4/4B/4C powered by four Rolls-Royce 10,500-lb static thrust Avon 350 turbojets operated successfully worldwide for many years. Total Comet production amounted to 112 aircraft which included seventy-four Series 4 aircraft.

Two new civil designs to emerge from de Havilland in the late 1950s were the DH 121 Trident, which had its first flight at Hatfield on 9 January 1962, and the DH 125 executive jet. Both aircraft were to be developed and constructed by Hawker Siddeley after the takeover of de Havilland in 1960 by the giant Hawker Siddeley Engineering Group. The DH 121 Trident was the first three-engine jet airliner as well as the first to land in fog. Fitted with 'auto-land', it had a fully automatic blind-landing facility. The Trident evolved from a requirement by BEA for a regional feeder airliner. The Trident 1 was followed by the Trident

DH company civil-registered DHC.1 Chipmunk with DH badge/emblem on the tail. (*Author*)

RCAF DHC.1 Chipmuck. (*Author*)

Army Air Corps (AAC) DH Chipmunk T.10 used at Middle Wallop for ab initio training of student AAC rotary-winged aircraft pilots. (*Author*)

RAF Elementary Flying Training DHC.1 T.10 Chipmunk. (*Aviation News*)

1E with a 60 per cent increase in fuel tankage and greater wingspan. After a long and protracted sales effort, the Trident 1E was sold to China who were at the time operating indigenous built designs or aircraft of Soviet origin.

The small DH 125 business jet was a small executive airliner built to the same standard as its 'big brothers'. It was originally intended to be called the 125 Jet Dragon although this name was never adopted. Indeed, it was more than thirty years after its first flight that the 125 series of executive jets had been officially named by Raytheon as the Hawker. Prior to Raytheon's acquisition, except for military types such as the RAF Dominee navigation trainer and the South African Air Force Mercurius, all 125s were designated by their respective design authority such as DH 125, HS 125 and BAe 125. All DH 125s were designated by their respective design development custodian such as DH 125, HS 125 and BAe 125. Since acquiring the 125 design on 6 August 1993, Raytheon unveiled a new variant in November 1996 to be known as the Raytheon Hawker Horizon eight/twelve seater. The Horizon is the largest of the Raythron Company's executive jets to date and is in essence a completely new and redesigned BAe 125-800 aircraft. One (Reserve) squadron of upgraded DH 125-400 Dominee T.2 navigation trainers remain in use with the RAF.

The last de Havilland design to be assembled at Hatfield was the BAe 146 regional jetliner that on its transfer to the company's Woodford plant, assumed the Avro mantle by virtue of the plant's long lineage to the A. V. Roe era.

In 1992, it was announced that due mainly to the deep economic world

Original DH Comet with high-set undercarriage, broad tyres and square windows. This was of a piston-engine transport design that the AAIB at Farnborough found to be one of the main causes of early Comet crashes. (*Wings*)

DH Comet C.2 of RAF Transport Command (later Support Command) served with No. 216 Squadron at RAF Lyneham, Wiltshire. RAF Comet 4C would later fly regular diplomatic missions to Washington DC for many years with senior technicians and avionics ground-crew engineers in case of problems that might arise en route. (*Warplane Collection*)

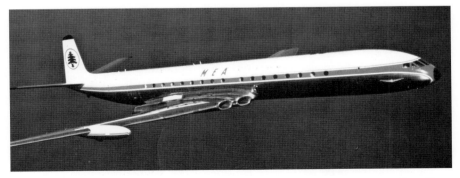

Middle East Airlines (MEA) DH Comet 4 with distinctive Christmas tree tail emblem. (*Wings*)

recession and the sharp downturn in demand for regional jets that the Hatfield plant would close and production of the 146 Avro RJ Series aircraft would take place at Woodford. Finally in 1994, the Hatfield plant closed its doors to aircraft production. The missile and space division 'Dynamics' at Manor Road had closed many years earlier with what had remained of the division moving to nearby Stevenage. De Havilland's missile department designed and developed Firestreak, the first British air-to-air missile. Other highly successful missile designs were Martel, Skyflash, Sea Eagle and the ALARM anti-radiation missile, now carried by BAe Systems' upgraded Panavia Tornado GR.4 IDS aircraft.

English Electric

The English Electric Company was founded in 1918 by an amalgamation of Phoenix Dynamo (Bradford), Dick, Kerr & Co. Works (Preston), the Coventry Ordnance Works and a number of smaller firms. All of these companies had built aircraft as subcontractors during the First World War. A series of flying boats were produced – the Cork, Ayr and six Kingstons from 1924 to 1926 – followed by two Wrens. The latter was a single-seat ultralight powered by a 398-cc ABC motorcycle engine designed by W. O. Manning and cost £350 each. The ultralights were built for the *Daily Mail* Light Aeroplane Competition at Lympne, Kent. One of the aircraft shared the first prize with an ANEC monoplane, a Wren, which is maintained at the Shuttleworth Trust's museum in Bedfordshire. A depressed business environment in 1926 forced the closure of the English Electric Company's aviation department. However, with the advent of the Second World War, the company won a substantial subcontract order and built 7,000 aircraft from 1938 and throughout the ensuing war years such as 770 Handley Page Hampden and Halifax bombers. From 1945 until 1950, de Havilland Vampires were built at the former Dick, Kerr & Co. Works, at Strand Road, Preston, and Lancashire.

After the Second World War, the company remained in aircraft construction and submitted the designs of W. E. W. 'Teddy' Petter to meet Air Ministry Specification B.3/45. The aircraft was destined to become Britain's first turbojet bomber, the Canberra, and often considered as the Mosquito of the jet age. The prototype, serial VN799, flew for the first time on 13 May 1949. At this stage, it was envisaged the aircraft would be a two-seat bomber; however, the fifth prototype was produced as a three-seater and this was the layout of the standard B.2 bomber that entered RAF service in 1951. The B.2 was superseded by the B.6 in 1954 with fuel tanks in the wings and more powerful Rolls-Royce Avon 109 turbojets. The Canberra served as a light-bomber, long-range photo-reconnaissance, two-seat light intruder, a special ECM trainer T.17, the B(I).8 with a gun pack in the bomb bay and numerous

Rollout at Hatfield of the original two BAe 146-200 airplanes delivered to No. 10 Squadron (RAF) at RAF Brize Norton for evaluation prior to the delivery of the three Queen's Flight aircraft on completion of the successful trials. (*Aviation News*)

The Royal compartment of the Queen's VIP BAe 146. The four-seat settee can be converted into a single bed. (*Wings*)

Earlier in its career, Queen's Flight BAe 146 CC.2, serial ZE700. (*Wings*)

Resplendent RAF No. 32 (Royal) Squadron VVIP BAe (HS) 146 based at RAF Northolt. In the millennium, only two of the original three aircraft delivered remain in use with one having been sold on the civil market. In 2013 No. 32 (Royal) Squadron added two BAe 146QT aircraft to its equipment inventory. (*Aviation News*)

other variants. Many served with various air forces around the world. Six hundred and thirty-one were built by English Electric with another 194 by Avro, Handley Page and Short Bros in Northern Ireland. Forty-eight were built in Australia and 403 in the US by the Martin Company as the B-57 after an extensive evaluation programme. The B-57 was a completely different aircraft than its British counterpart bar its same basic shape and straight Meteor-style fighter wings. The American aircraft was powered by Pratt & Whitney turbofans in place of the Rolls-Royce Avon engines. BAC (EE) Canberra T.17 EW/ECM trainers were used by the joint Royal Navy and RAF No. 360 Squadron based at RAF Wyton from December 1966 until its disbandment on 31 October 1994.

Several Canberra variants were used by research establishments for trials and experimental duties. A B.2 trials aircraft based at RAE Bedford in the late 1970s and early 1980s flew with the prototype A-Model AI 24 Foxhunter radar destined for the Panavia F.3 Tornado ADV. The radar was fitted into the Canberra's bomb bay. 'Wart nosed' ECM Canberra T.17s from No. 360 Squadron at RAF Wyton were also used for ECM/ECCM proving trials and carried out at the RN/RAF Bedford Thurleigh airfield. These trials were used in conjunction with an 'A' Model Foxhunter radar installed in the airfield's control tower as an experiment to combat intruding Soviet long-range Tupolev Tu-142 Bear reconnaissance-bombers and Mikoyan 'Foxbat' MiG-25Rs based in East Germany and Bulgaria during the Cold War. (The latter was the only Eastern Bloc country to operate the Mach 3.0 MiG-25R under Soviet supervision and VVS headquarters in Moscow.) A distinctive all over, orange-painted Canberra B.2, serial 99+34, was used by the German Air Force at one time for survey duties. Forty-eight Canberras designated B.20s were equipped with Australian-built Rolls-Royce Avon 109 engines while UK imports were fitted with the Avon 101 powerplant. These were built in Australia by the Government Aircraft Factory (GAF), the aircraft equipping three RAAF squadrons.

With the Canberra designs off the drawing board, Petter set about meeting the requirements set out in Specification ER.103 that called for an investigation into the production of a high-speed interceptor capable of attaining Mach 1.5 at 36,000 feet. Within two years, Petter had produced a promising design for a twin-engine supersonic aircraft with the engines located one above the other in the centre fuselage and the nose intake and ducts passing below the cockpit. In order to maintain the correct centre of gravity, the lower engine was to be located well forward of the upper powerplant. The result was the single-seat supersonic research aircraft, the P.1, serial WG760. The P.1 took to the air on 4 August 1954 from Boscombe Down with English Electric's chief test pilot, Wg Cdr Roland 'Bea' Beaumont DSO DFC, at the controls. The aircraft performed beautifully with only minor changes being required as some minor buffeting was experienced as the airbrakes were extended. The

P.1 featured an unusual ovoid intake with no centre body and this was later used on production variants to house the Ferranti A.I 23B Airpass fire control radar. The Lightning was probably the first aircraft where major airframe design parameters and calculations were processed on an early computer at the National Physics Laboratory. Designed for a top speed above Mach 2.0, the aircraft came close to Mach 0.98 on only its second flight. On 5 August and its third flight on 11 August, WG760 accelerated to Mach 1.01 and became the first British aircraft to exceed the speed of sound in level flight. The only real shortcoming of the aircraft, now designated as the Lightning, was its lack of fuel and flight endurance. Often after a 35 minute flight, there remained only sufficient fuel to sustain each engine for a further 50 miles of flight. However, the fuel load issue was not rectified until the third and definitive Mk 6 variant was produced with a ventral fuel tank.

The Lightning entered RAF service in 1960, retiring almost thirty years later in 1988. Three hundred and eighty-eight examples were built including

BAC (EE) TSR.2, probably 'the best bomber that never was', is displayed at the Imperial War Museum in Duxford. (*Author*)

thirty-four Mk 53s (similar to the Mk 6 with ground-attack capability) and six Mk 55 two-seat trainers for Saudi Arabia. With regards to the latter, some twenty-five Mk 55s were known to have returned to Warton Aerodrome in the UK as 'buy backs', part of the Saudis' deal to purchase the Panavia Tornado aircraft. Efforts by BAe to sell the repossessed Lightnings to the Austrian Air Force were thwarted when Austria purchased retired Saab 35 Drakens from Sweden. Kuwait also procured a small quantity of Lightnings: twelve F.53s and two T 55s trainers. The Lightning was one of the few RAF aircraft that was never used in anger. A number of Saudi F.53s were used with some success against ground targets in the Yemen in 1969. The Lightning was a pilot's aeroplane, the 'formula one' of the skies. However, to ground crews, the aircraft was unpopular to work on with engine changes a nightmare.

In 1959, English Electric and Vickers won a joint development contract for a Tactical Strike Reconnaissance aircraft: the TSR.2. On 9 January 1959, the English Electric Company was reorganised as English Electric Aviation Ltd that later became part of BAC on 1 January 1960. Series production of the Lightning continued at BAC's Preston Division when the English Electric name finally disappeared on 1 January 1964. A date that also saw the untimely demise of the English Electric TSR.2, a project its design office was working in at the time under the auspices of BAC.

Fairey Aviation

Formed on 15 July 1915, Fairey Aviation Co. Ltd was renowned for their long line of naval aircraft. Founded by electrical engineer C. R. Fairey, later Sir Richard 1887–1956), the company initially assembled the Short 827 seaplane and Sopwith 1½ Strutter at its factory at Clayton Road, Hayes, and Middlesex. However, Fairey soon embarked on designs of their own. Amongst early designs were the F2 three-seat bomber and the two-seat Campania seaplane, forty of which were inherited by the RAF from the RNAS in April 1918 out of the total of sixty-two built. The company's first Fairey designed aircraft was the Fairey F.2, a twin-engine biplane, long-range fighter with a 77-foot wingspan and was intended for the RNAS. Four aircraft were ordered but only one, serial 3704, was completed in April 1916. None entered production. The next Fairey type to enter series production was the Hamble Baby with fifty built and a further 130 subcontracted to Parnall. The aircraft was a redesigned Sopwith Baby fighter seaplane modified to carry a small bomb load. It featured revolutionary variable camber flaps pioneered by A. W. Judge and A. A. Holle at the Varioplane Co., but perfected by Fairey who patented the idea as The Fairey Patent Camber Gear (flaps-cum-ailerons). It was the first of its kind in the world, the principle of which still remains in use today on numerous modern aircraft designs.

The Fairey III series of biplanes, which started with the N.10 or Fairey III experimental seaplane in 1917, were produced from 1917 to 1930 in several different variants. The IIIA prototype flew on 6 June 1918. The IIIA and IIIB seaplanes were followed by the IIIC that saw service with the RAF in Russia in 1919 operating against the Bolsheviks with the North Russian Relief Force. In 1918, a new factory was built at North Hyde Road, Hayes, Middlesex, and designer Maj. Barlow was joined by Marcel Lobelle from Belgium and E. O. Tips. The Fairey IIIC was followed by the IIID three-seat general purpose aircraft. In its landplane version, the IIID was one of the first aircraft to be fitted with an oleo-pneumatic undercarriage. The IIID was destined for a place in the annals of RAF history for its first official long-distance formation and England to South Africa flights. A total of 207 Fairey IIIDs were delivered to the RAF out of 227 D models produced. The definitive version of the III series was the IIIF built as a two-seat general-purpose aircraft for the RAF or its three-seat FAA reconnaissance version. Production of the IIIF reached 662 aircraft including prototypes and export variants out of a total build of almost 1,000 III series aircraft. A number of Fairey IIIs were re-engined with 525-hp Armstrong Whitworth Panther IIA radial engines in place of the Napier Lion water-cooled engine. The converted aircraft were redesignated as the Fairey Gordon 1 of which 246 were built including sixty-eight retrospective conversions of the Fairey III already in service. Two Fairey IIIF communications aircraft, serials K1115 and J9061, were produced for use by No. 24 (Communication) Squadron (RAF) as VIP aircraft.

The next Fairey type was the Fairey Flycatcher single-seat training float-plane used exclusively by the FAA except one RAF aircraft, serial S1288, for their High Speed Flight. The Fairey Pintail was designed to meet RAF Type 19 Specification for a single-engine, two-seat, twin-float, naval fighter-reconnaissance amphibian biplane. Six Pintails were produced with three prototypes and three series production aircraft for the Japanese Imperial Navy (none were produced for British forces). The Fairey Fawn II two-seat, day-bomber derived from the Pintail was the RAF's first new light day-bomber to enter service in the 1920s replacing a number of veteran DH 9As in early 1924. The Napier Lion-powered Fairey Fawn was heavier and carried a crew of two or three. Some later models were of a metal construction adding to its weight and ultimately reduced its performance, therefore being of little improvement when compared to the DH 9A. Its lacklustre performance was not the fault of Fairey, but with the Air Ministry Specification that had stipulated a top speed of six mph less than the DH 9A! Seventy Fawn IIs were built and they equipped three RAF squadrons. However, the aircraft's ungainly appearance and poor performance meant it soon gave way to the Fairey Fox that was designed as a private venture by the company. The Fox dramatically changed views on how the light day-bomber was a slow and cumbersome aircraft. The Fox was to change all this: its sleek design and marriage to the American 480-hp Curtiss D-12 engine resulted in an aircraft that was some 50 mph faster than the Fawn and could outstrip any contemporary fighter of its day. ACM Sir Hugh Trenchard was so impressed with the aircraft on attending a demonstration in August 1925 that he ordered a squadron on the spot. The aircraft were delivered to No. 12 Squadron at Andover to replace their Fawns and from that day onwards the squadron has been known as The Flying Foxes (a fox's head adorns the official squadron badge/emblem). Despite the Foxes outstanding performance, financial constraints meant that only twenty-eight aircraft were built for the RAF and the redesigned all-metal Fox II was built in Belgium for the Armée de l' Air Belge with a small number supplied to Switzerland and Peru. A few later variants were fitted with 480-hp Rolls-Royce F.XIIA Kestrel engines that returned an even more outstanding performance. A slight disadvantage with the Fox was that the long take-off and landing runs required by the Curtiss-powered aircraft made operation from some airfields undesirable.

A failed attempt by Britain on the world long-distance record using a Hawker Horsley prompted the Air Ministry to purchase a special aircraft designed for the purpose. The Fairey Monoplane was an elegant, streamlined, long span, cantilevered wing, two seater with a fuel capacity of over 1,000 gallons giving the aircraft a range of 5,000 miles. Two aircraft were built. The first, serial J9479, was lost when the second attempt on the record ended in disaster when it crashed in Tunisia killing its occupants. Success was eventually achieved when the second aircraft, a Mk II, serial K1991, flew from RAF Cranwell to Walvis Bay in South-West Africa for a total distance of 8,544.37 km (5,309.24 miles) in 57 hours and 25 minutes. The record stood until August 1933 when it was beaten by the French. The Fairey Monoplane was also involved in a number of other long-distance flights organised by the RAF such as on 27-28 October 1931 when Sqdn Ldr O. R. Gayford and Flt Lt D. L. G. Bett flew from Cranfield Aerodrome, Bedfordshire, to Abu Sueir, Egypt.

The Fairey Gordon day-bomber was an adaption of the Napier Lion-powered Fairey IIIF series re-engined with a 609-hp Armstrong Siddeley Panther IIA double-row, air-cooled, fourteen-cylinder radial for the RAF or as the Fairey Seal for the FAA. When compared with the smaller, lighter and faster Fox, the Gordon appeared to be a retrograde step, but it had an improved range, and as with the IIIFs, could operate on floats. The Gordon equipped three home-based bomber squadrons and was used extensively overseas. A number were sold to Brazil.

In the 1930s, Fairey built twenty-five Firefly IIs at Hayes for Belgium as well as undertaking other licensed subcontract production. Twelve Fairey Fox IIs were built at Hayes and 185 were produced in Belgium by Fairey.

The Fairey Hendon heavy night-bomber, an all-metal, low-wing cantilever monoplane, was the first of its type to go into squadron service with the RAF. Only fourteen aircraft were built at the company's new and larger premises at Hyde Road, Hayes, and Middlesex. The Hendon appears to be have been an enigma for Fairey and the RAF. It was the only heavy bomber to be produced by Fairey, and although the Hendon was the most modern monoplane heavy bomber available at the time, it only served with one operational RAF squadron, No. 38. When it first appeared in 1931, the Hendon was known quite simply as the Fairey Night Bomber. With the declaration of war in September 1939, ten Hendons were replaced by Vickers Wellingtons and renumbered as ground instructional airframes at the Electrical and Wireless School, RAF Cranwell, Lincolnshire.

Of all the Fairey Second World War designs, the biplane torpedo-bomber and reconnaissance aircraft, the Fairey Swordfish, must be the most famous. Of 2,391 aircraft built, Fairey Aviation Co. Ltd built 691, the remainder were produced by Blackburn at Brough (the Blackburn aircraft were known as Blackfish). Many of the Swordfish's flying achievements and combat missions are legendary. One of the lesser known exploits is of a Swordfish that was so badly damaged by anti-aircraft fire that it has become a monoplane and was able to be flown back to the UK from the Western Desert for repair.

In 1940, series production of the Swordfish passed to Blackburn Aircraft Ltd where it was manufactured under a group scheme comprising of four major production units and hundreds of major and minor subcontractors. The Swordfish was the last of the operational biplanes and production of the type ceased in mid-1944. On 21-22 December 1941, an ASV radar-equipped Swordfish of the FAA's No. 812 Squadron sank the first German U-boat to be destroyed by an aircraft at night. In a demonstration to show the type's versatility, on 23 May 1943, a Swordfish operating from the escort carrier HMS *Archer* sank a German submarine, U-572, in a rocket attack. Swordfish operating from escort carriers were much feared by U-boat crews due to their slow speed and loiter ability. Radar-equipped Swordfish Mk IIIs were operated by No. 119 Squadron (RAF), the fitment of the under-fuselage, nose-mounted radome negating carriage of a torpedo.

When it entered service in the late 1930s, the Fairey Battle I all-metal, stressed-skin, three-seat monoplane light-bomber represented quite an advance over the Hawker biplanes it had replaced. The prototype, serial K4303, first flew on 10 March 1936; however, by 1939 and the outbreak of the Second World War, the Battle was seriously obsolete. Ten squadrons went to France with the Advanced Air Striking Force and doubts with regards to the aircraft's suitability for combat were affirmed when Battles were decimated as the Germans invaded the Low Countries and France. Remnants of the Battle squadrons slogged on with appalling losses until mid-June 1940 when they were withdrawn from frontline operational use and turned over to training duties.

Seven hundred and thirty-nine Battles were shipped to Canada for use with the Commonwealth Air Training Plan and 400 were shipped to Australia. Two hundred and two examples which served with Air Gunnery Schools were fitted with dorsal turrets. A total of 2,419 Battles were built, 1,029 by the Austin Motor Co. Ltd in Longbridge, Birmingham. Of the 200 dual-control trainers fitted with two separate cockpits in place of the long canopy, fifty were sent to Canada. Eighteen aircraft were built at Avions Fairey in Gosselles, a Belgian-based subsidiary of Fairey, and were delivered to the Belgium Air Force in 1938. The Belgian-built aircraft gave slightly better performance than its UK counterpart by virtue of its longer radiator cowling, different engine exhaust stubs and a shallow rear canopy.

An unusual seaplane spotter, the Fairey Seafox was designed for catapult operations from Royal Navy cruisers. An unusual feature was the enclosed observer's cockpit. Total production was sixty-four examples. The Fairey Albacore torpedo-bomber was intended to replace the Swordfish, but the iconic Swordfish outlasted the newly designed aircraft. Nonetheless, the Fairey Albacore proved to be a very useful aircraft in 1942 at the peak of its career. The design included a number of improvements over the Swordfish such as a more powerful engine, enclosed cockpit and hydraulic flaps. When production ceased in 1943, 803 Albacores had been built. The Fairey Barracuda was the Royal Navy's first monoplane torpedo bomber. Although designs on the aircraft commenced in 1937, it did not enter FAA service until 1943 due to the company's efforts in other areas and the requirement to accommodate the Merlin engine in place of the discontinued Rolls-Royce Vulture. After initial deliveries of twenty-five Mk 1s, 2,577 were built incorporating a Merlin engine by a number of other companies under a Group Production Scheme including Fairey, Boulton Paul, Blackburn and Westland. While in service, the aircraft carried the widest variety of stores including mines, depth charges, torpedoes, lifeboats and even containers to carry passengers under the wings. Some aircraft were RATO (Rocket Assisted Take-Off) equipped to assist in its operation from small cruisers.

Designed to follow the Fulmar into naval service, the Fairey Firefly two-seat reconnaissance fighter was one of the few Second World War aircraft to use an elliptical wing as seen with the Supermarine Spitfire. Four prototypes were built and the first, serial Z1826, flew for the first time on 22 December 1941. Fairey built 297 Firefly 1s with a further 132 completed by General Aircraft Ltd. These aircraft were followed by the production of 376 fighter-reconnaissance versions, the FR Mk 1, and thirty-seven night-fighters, the NF Mk II. Total Firefly production amounted to 1,570 aircraft including fifty-four for the Royal Netherlands Naval Air Service. The aircraft attracted a number of overseas customers including Canada, Australia, Denmark, Ethiopia,

Fairey Swordfish torpedo-spotter-reconnaissance aircraft flew with distinction with the Royal Navy and RAF (No. 119 Squadron, January-May 1945) throughout the Second World War. The aircraft shown belongs to the RN Vintage Aircraft Flight based at RNAS Yeovilton, Somerset. (*Aviation News*)

Sweden, India and Thailand.

1939-1945 were troublesome years for Fairey mainly due to its failure to meet production schedules. Many of its difficulties stemmed from overloading the main plants at Hayes and Stockport. Also, it placed too great a reliance on subcontractors as well as the slow takeover of Swordfish production by Blackburn and the troublesome progress with the Albacore due to issues with its Bristol Taurus engine. Also, Firefly production was delayed by a year and there were problems with Barracuda production. Therefore in December 1942, the Fairey Company became the first major company to be investigated by Sir Stafford Cripps, the newly appointed Minister of Aircraft Production (MAP). Only fifty Fireflies were made in 1943, but in 1944, production reached 307 plus thirty by the General Aircraft Co.

After the war, Fairey experimented with a number of helicopter designs utilising a number of new principles. The Fairey Rotodyne was an impressive forty-passenger, vertical take-off and landing airliner. It was powered by two Napier-Eland turboprops for forward flight and a pressure jet unit at the rotor-tip blades. However, although the aircraft was extensively tested and created much attention in the press, none entered series production.

Fairey also built two delta-winged jet research aircraft, the FD.1 and FD.2. The FD.2 was Fairey's last fixed-wing aircraft to be produced and with it Britain

Advanced Air Strike Force (AASF) Fairey Battle Mk III three-seat, light day-bombers. Although modern for the day, they were easy prey for the Luftwaffe during their blitz through the Low Countries during May 1940. (*Warplane Collection*)

regained the world's air speed record from the US beating the previous record set by a North American F.100 Super Sabre by 310 mph. The FD.2 was also the first British aircraft to exceed 1,000 mph and in its BAC 221 configuration carried out aerodynamic research for the Anglo-French *Concorde* project. The only other post-war design from Fairey to enter series production was the Fairey Gannet that made the first deck landing by a prop-turbine aircraft aboard HMS *Illustrious* on 19 June 1950. The aircraft was fitted with an Armstrong Siddeley Double-Mamba that consisted of two engines coupled to two contra-rotating propellers. Three hundred and forty-nine Fairey Gannets were built in five versions under the 'Super Priority' scheme. Initial series production aircraft were built at the Hayes plant, assembled at Northolt Aerodrome, and then flown to White Waltham, Berkshire, for collection by FAA pilots. Later, Stockport-produced aircraft were test flown at Ringway Manchester before delivery and others were built by Westland Aircraft Ltd at Yeovil who took over Fairey in May 1960. A number of export orders were received for the type from Indonesia, Australia and West Germany. It served for a number of years with the Royal Navy carrier fleet as an Airborne Early Warning (AEW) aircraft and on its withdrawal from use, its American-built APS radar was fitted to Avro AEW 2 Avro Shackletons of No. 8 Squadron RAF for the air defence of the UK prior to receiving the Boeing E-3 Sentry (AWACS).

Royal Navy Fairey Firefly T.1 carrier-borne and land-based deck landing trainer powered by a 1,734-hp Rolls-Royce Griffon II engine. (*Warplane Collection*)

Luftwaffe Fairey Gannet ASW aircraft fitted with a 3,035-hp Armstrong Siddeley double Mamba 101 engine. (*Author*)

British Marine Aircraft – Folland Aircraft Ltd

Folland Aircraft Ltd was originally formed from British Marine Aircraft Ltd at Hamble near Southampton. The company has been set up in February 1936 primarily to build civil flying boats. However, in May 1937, the company was reorganised when Harry P. Folland (1889–1954), the former chief designer of Gloster Aircraft Ltd, arrived to form his own company at BMA's premises at Hamble. Folland was appointed managing director and chief engineer, and the name of the company was changed to Folland Aircraft Ltd. The company had an extensive works at Hamble on Southampton Water. In the Second World War following the development of a number of engine test-beds such as the Folland 43/37 Monoplane, the company turned to subcontract manufacture of aircraft components such as the wings for de Havilland's early jets, the Vampire and Venom.

In 1950, W. E. W. 'Teddy' Petter, who had established the basic design of the English Electric P.1, joined Folland as managing director and chief engineer, and within a year had started design work on a lightweight fighter: the Fo 139 Midge. The single Folland Midge, registration G-39-1, was first flown at RAE Boscombe Down on 11 August 1954. In spite of its low-powered engine, the aircraft displayed remarkable agility and performance, and created considerable interest from a number of foreign air forces including the USAF, the Royal Canadian Navy, RNZAF, IAF and the Royal Jordanian Air Force. Unfortunately, the Midge was destroyed in a fatal accident at Chilbolton on 26 September while being flown by a Swiss pilot.

As the Air Ministry had shown scant interest in the Midge, Petter turned his attention to a scaled-up version of the aircraft: the single-seat Fo 141 Gnat G-39-2. The Bristol Siddeley Orpheus turbojet-powered Gnat – effectively a scaled-up Midge by some 10 per cent – flew on 18 July 1955. However, despite strong lobbying from the company for introduction of the type into the RAF as a ground-support fighter, it was later accepted as an advanced jet trainer. Following a series of 'hot-and-high' evaluations against the Hawker Hunter in Aden, the Gnat was discounted on its inferior performance and weapons carrying ability. However, from 1958 to 1959, the Finnish Air Force took delivery of thirteen aircraft which remained in service until 1972. The largest customer for the Gnat was India, who after the initial delivery of twenty-five examples and fifteen kits, licensed-produced a further 175 from 1958 onwards, equipping eight Indian Air Force squadrons. In Indian use, the Gnat was known as the Ajeet and operated as a single-seat fighter seeing frontline air-to-air combat in the 1970s war with Pakistan.

Eventually, interest in Britain centred on using the Gnat as a trainer for

A 'Yellowjacks' Folland Gnat trainer parked alongside two Panavia Tornado F.3 ADVs with a C-130 Hercules tail just visible in the background at the Essex International Air Tattoo. Originally held at North Weald, the show relocated to RAF Fairford, Gloucestershire. (*Author*)

The diminutive Folland Gnat was the first mount of the world famous Red Arrows. However, the original RAF aerobatic team was named as The Yellowjacks and their Gnat trainers painted yellow. (*Aviation News*)

the RAF. The enlarged two-seat Gnat trainer Fo 144, serial XM691, first flew on 31 August 1959 just before Folland, who had fought vehemently to remain independent, opted to join the Hawker Siddeley Group to safeguard the award of a production contract for the aircraft. Hawker Siddeley's acquisition of Folland was completed in 1960 and the RAF eventually received a total of 105 Gnats which included fourteen pre-production aircraft and Gnat T.1 trainers. The aircraft was the chosen mount for the RAF Red Arrows aerobatic team from 1965 until replaced by the BAe Hawk T.1 in 1979.

General Aircraft Ltd

With the closure of Beardmore, a Swiss-born engineer, H. J. Stieger, set up the Monospar Wing Co. Ltd at Croydon to develop the monospar system of construction that offered a better strength to weight ratio by adopting the Warren girder type assembly. After demonstrating his Monospar ST-1 that was built by Gloster Aircraft Co Ltd, Stieger formed a new company, General Aircraft Ltd, at Hanworth, Feltham, and Middlesex. General's first aircraft was the four-seat Monospar ST-4 cantilevered monoplane of which thirty-six were built followed by the ST-6 with its manually-operated undercarriage in 1933. In the same year, the company moved into new premises at The London Air Park, Feltham, and Middlesex. This was a fortuitous move as in 1935, General were awarded a production subcontract to produce eighty-nine Hawker Fury IIs as Hawker factories were stretched to the limit. Another contract from Hawker, received in 1938, was to convert 124 Hawker Hind two-seat, light-bombers to trainers. Late production Hawker Hinds from serial L7202 onwards left the factory as trainers. A succession of Monospar designs – the ST-10, ST-11 and ST-12 – culminated with the four-seat ST-25 Jubilee, so named to acknowledge the Silver Jubilee of King George V. There were three variants of the ST-25: the other two were the twin-fin ST-25 Universal and the De Luxe. Fifty-seven ST-25s were built before production ceased in 1939.

In the Second World War, the company built a number of smaller aircraft types and gliders in addition to undertaking work on a number of important experimental contracts and subcontract work for the Ministry of Aircraft Production (MAP). Amongst the first aircraft of the Second World War era was the GAL38 Fleet Shadower, a four-engine, carrier-based aircraft suitable for the purpose of shadowing or maintaining contact with enemy fleets at night. The role called for exceptionally low speeds and long endurance. Overall dimensions were restricted for shipboard stowage and the wings were designed to fold, but only one was built to Air Ministry Specification

S.23/37. The GAL38 was followed by the GAL42 Cygnet/GAL.45 Owlet, a two-seat trainer, and the design was acquired by General from the bankrupt Graham White Aircraft Ltd. The GAL47 was an ultralight private venture design for AOP (air observation post) duties and no aircraft entered series production. General's most prolific Second World War design was a glider, the GAL48 Hotspur. The Hotspur I glider was intended for use as a small troop transport with a wingspan of 61 feet 6 inches (18.75 metres). This version did not enter production. The Hotspur II and III – with their wingspan reduced to 45 feet 10.5 inches with modified flaps and ailerons, and dual controls for two pilots in tandem and revised entrance door and cockpit canopy – became the standard trainers for the Army Glider Pilot Regiment. The main difference between the types was that the Mk III aircraft had complete duplication of flying controls and instruments for each pilot. The initial production order for the Hotspur was 400 aircraft, but eventually 1,000 were built, most by Harris Lebus of Tottenham. The usual tugs for the Hotspur were Hawker Hectors or Audaxes. One experimental GAL48B Twin Hotspur was completed and consisted of two standard fuselages and outer wing sections joined by a new centre section and a common tailplane.

The GAL49 Hamilcar was the Allies' largest and heaviest glider of the Second World War. After a half-scale trial model had been built, the full-size prototype flew on 27 March 1942. The aircraft was capable of lifting a seven-ton tank and had a special side-hinged nose to enable vehicles to be driven straight out on landing. Of the 390 built, all but the first twenty-two aircraft were built by various woodworks subcontractors throughout the UK. The Hamilcar is renowned for its part in the D-Day landings in Normandy. The Hamilcar was towed by the Handley Page Halifax, Avro Lancaster and Short Stirling four-engine bombers. In 1944, a powered version of the Hamilcar was produced, the GAL.58 Hamilcar X. Powered by two 965-hp Bristol 31 Mercury radial engines, the aircraft was intended for use in the Pacific theatre of war against the Japanese. Although 100 Hamilcar X were ordered, only twenty-two were completed by VJ Day and the type never saw service. Two other glider types produced by General were the GAL55, a small, two-seat training glider of which only two prototypes were built, and the GAL56. The latter was a small research glider for 'flying wing' trials that began in late 1944 of which only three or four were built.

The single-engine, twin-finned light plane of General Aircraft, the Cygnet, has the distinction of being the first all-metal, stressed-skin civil aircraft to be produced in the UK. The type was used in small numbers by the military in the Second World War for communications. The final design from General in 1946 was the GAL60 Universal Freighter, a medium-range transport that became the Blackburn Beverley medium-range, high-capacity transport for the RAF. It was produced by Blackburn and General Aircraft Ltd, Brough, East

Yorkshire, after General Aircraft and Blackburn Aircraft merged in January 1949.

The Gloucestershire Aircraft Co. – Gloster Aircraft

The Gloucestershire Aircraft Co. was formed at Sunningend Works, Cheltenham, on 5 June 1917 by Airco and H. H. Martyn. By the end of 1918, the new company had built large numbers of RAF Fe.2bs, Bristol Fighters and Nieuport Nighthawks. Harry Folland, disenchanted with the Royal Aircraft Factory at Farnborough, had left during the war joining The Nieuport and General Aircraft Co. Ltd, Cricklewood, London, where he set about designing the Nieuport BN.1 and the Nieuport Nighthawk. After Holt Thomas sold Airco in 1920, the Gloucestershire Aircraft Co. took over large quantities of Nighthawk parts and Folland set about utilising the parts to produce a series of Nighthawk derivatives named Sparrowhawk of which fifty were built for the Imperial Japanese Navy. In addition, the Bamel racer, registration G-EAXZ, was later converted to the Gloster I racing seaplane to train RAF pilots for the Schneider Trophy contests in 1925 and 1927. This was followed by the Sparrowhawk I, II, III or Mars II, III, IV fleet fighters which were also sold to the Imperial Japanese Navy. The fifth derivative was the Gloucestershire Mars VI Nighthawk that differed little from the original Nieuport aircraft. It is known that thirty-one Mars VIs were flown and it is believed that a further ninety were built and stored. The final Mars conversion was the Mk X Nightjar of which nineteen were produced for the RAF.

Following on from the Gloster I, Gloucestershire Aircraft Co. produced a number of racing seaplanes to help Britain with its attempts in winning the Schneider Trophy. These were two Gloster IIIs, three Gloster IVs and Gloster V Arrows. Folland then went on to design some of the best known types developed and built by the company during the inter-war years such as the high speed and highly manoeuvrable two-seat Gloster Grebe that was derived from the Grouse I experimental trainer (a modified Sparrowhawk) and the Grouse II. One hundred and thirty-three Gloster Grebes were built and the majority were single-seat fighters with twenty-one dual-control, two-seat trainers. Grebe Mk IIIDCs were also produced. The aircraft were produced by Gloucestershire Aircraft Co. with subassemblies manufactured by Avro, de Havilland and Hawker. Three aircraft were delivered to the RNZAF in 1928, one as a two-seat trainer.

The Gloster Gamecock single-seat fighter followed the Grebe into RAF service. The initial aircraft, serial J7497, retained the Grebe tail that was similar to Folland's famous Se.5 tail pattern. Powered by a 398-hp Bristol Jupiter IV radial engine, the aircraft was also known as the Grebe Mk II.

The production Grebe II or Gamecock was fitted with the Bristol Jupiter VI engine. Ninety-one Gamecock Is were built for the RAF. The Gamecock was the last biplane fighter of wooden construction for the RAF, although as the type entered production in 1925, the Air Ministry decided to investigate the possibility of producing an all-metal variant. However, as Gloucestershire Aircraft Co. were not equipped to produce such an aircraft, the contract was awarded to Boulton Paul to produce the prototype, serial J7959. Nevertheless, when the all-metal types displayed a number of familiar spinning and flutter characteristics, the metal variant was abandoned. Meanwhile, a company-sponsored Gamecock II was being developed and although the RAF displayed little interest in the aircraft, it did form the basis for the Gamecocks ('Kukkos') for the Finnish Air Force. For the contract, Gloster completed two 'pattern' aircraft with fifteen completed under licence by the National Aircraft Factory in Helsinki. Following on from the Air Ministry's determination to fully investigate all-metal designs in May 1924, Gloucestershire Aircraft Co. was awarded a £24,000 contract to build three prototypes of an experimental single-seat interceptor. The first two aircraft were to have steel fuselages and wooden wings, and the third example would be of all-metal construction. The aircraft were known as Gloucestershire Gorcocks. There were no series production aircraft, but an ongoing programme of investigation into inline engine development with the Napier Lion in conjunction with Napier, led to Gloucestershire Aircraft Co. being awarded a further contract for three Guan prototypes. However, with numerous problems with the engines on flight trials, the third aircraft was cancelled. Although in spite of the Guan engine issues, Folland persisted with the Napier Lion engine in his excellent racing seaplanes such as the Gloster III, IV and VI when the Rolls-Royce Kestrel V12 was produced.

In 1926, Gloster Aircraft Co. was awarded a contract to build an all-metal, high-altitude version of the Gamecock. The resulting aircraft was the Goldfinch and was similar to the Gamecock Mk III, serial J8047. The idea was that the first prototype should be of conventional design with a metal wing and tail, and a mixed wood/metal fuselage. This prototype, serial J7940, was first flown in May 1927 and returned to Hucclecote to be almost entirely rebuilt in its all-metal form with a new engine, wings, fuselage and tail. In almost every respect, the new aircraft excelled in the air, but failed to attain range requirements. Also, the Goldfinch did not carry the number of rounds required for its two Vickers machine guns: only 500 for each gun instead of 600. However, although the aircraft failed to win a production contract, the experience gained was of huge value to the future development of all-metal aircraft. Indeed, the last wooden fighter to be produced by the now more commercially acceptable renamed Gloster Company was the Gloster Gambit fighter. One hundred and fifty Gambits were built in Japan by Nakajima

Hikoki for the Imperial Japanese Navy to replace their ageing Sparrowhawks. The first fifty aircraft were designated AINI and were powered by Nakajima-built Jupiter VI engines, the remaining AIN2 powered by the Nakajima Kotobuki 2 powerplant.

In May 1927, Specification N.21/26 called for a new naval fighter. The aircraft was to be an all-metal, single-seat, carrier biplane interceptor to be powered by the 450-hp Bristol Mercury IIA radial engine. It was also to possess a maximum speed of 160 mph at 10,000 feet. A most important new parameter was to provide for good all-round vision for the pilot. While a number of companies set about making alterations to existing designs to meet the requirements, Folland produced a brand new aircraft: the Gloster Gnatsnapper. Unfortunately, Gloster was letdown by the Bristol Mercury engine that proved totally unreliable and failed to produce the promised power. Delays caused by engine problems and a landing accident while the aircraft was under evaluation led to the type losing any chance of selection for series production, although this proved to be purely academic as by this time the Rolls-Royce Kestrel-powered Hawker Nimrod aircraft was available. Although two prototype Gnatsnappers were built, there were no series production aircraft.

The last open cockpit type to see service with the RAF was the Gloster Gauntlet. Powered by a Bristol Mercury engine, it could reach 230 mph, making it the fastest RAF fighter in service between 1935 and 1937. The Gauntlet SS.19B prototype, serial J9125, was first shown at the 1933 Hendon SBAC Pageant. The SS.19B was a day/night fighter development of the SS.18B and SS.19 that had utilised the same airframe with a different engine. The Gauntlet was born at the time that Hawker Aircraft had finalised their takeover of the Gloster Company in May 1934. Gloster's demise had been brought about by the effects of the depression and lack of worthwhile production contracts for four years. In 1935, Henry Folland left Gloster to set up his own company. In total, 228 Gauntlets were built with twenty-four Mk Is and 204 Mk IIs. The Gauntlet was the first RAF aircraft to make an airborne interception while directed by ground radar when a No. 32 Squadron aircraft was vectored on to a civil airliner over the River Thames in November 1937. These initial proving trials confirmed the viability of the proposed chain of coastal radar warning stations.

Delays in the delivery of the new monoplane Hawker Hurricane and Supermarine Spitfire fighters were only partially offset by the entry into service of the Gloster Gladiator biplane fighter. The Gauntlet with its truly outstanding performance remained in service far longer than intended and were transferred to lead-in training duties for the new monoplane fighters.

In 1940, Gauntlets were exported to Finland and seventeen Mk IIs were built under licence by the Flyvertroppernes Vaerksteder. With the Hawker takeover, Gloster went on to produce 7,000 Hawker types and some 600 Armstrong Whitworth AW.41 Albemarles. The Gladiator was a development of the Gauntlet which it closely resembled apart from its enclosed cockpit and more powerful engine. The Gladiator marked the end of an era for biplane fighters, an age that had spanned a quarter of a century from the earliest years of military aviation. The prototype Gladiator, serial K5200, first flew in September 1934 and was designated SS.37 with a modified Gauntlet fuselage. Production of the Gladiator was speeded up by using as many Gauntlet components as possible. Total Gladiator production amounted to 747 aircraft of which thirty-eight were converted to Sea Gladiators along with sixty new builds for the Fleet Air Arm. Over 300 Gloster Gladiators were in use in thirteen countries before the war including Latvia (twenty-six); Lithuania (fourteen); China (thirty-six); Norway (twelve); Belgium (twenty-two); Eire (four); Sweden (seventy-three); Greece (two); Portugal (fifteen); and Egypt (eighteen). During the Second World War, ex-RAF Gladiators were supplied to Finland (thirty-nine); Greece (seventeen); Egypt (twenty-seven); Iraq (nine); and South Africa (eleven). Also, it is worth mentioning the epic defence of Malta as three Sea Gladiators – Faith, Hope and Charity – fought against all odds and overwhelming numbers of a superior Luftwaffe.

The Gloster Company has the distinction of being the first aircraft manufacturer in the UK and the US to design, build and fly an aircraft fitted with a jet engine. Following Frank Whittle's successful development of his jet engine, the Air Ministry placed an order with Gloster in 1939 to design and construct an aircraft fitted with Whittle's engine. On Folland's departure, his place at Gloster Aircraft was taken by Wilfred George Carter who worked closely with Whittle to produce the airframes for his new engines. Built to Specification E.28/39, the single-engine experimental Gloster G.40, serial W4041, took to the skies on 15 May 1941. The monoplane was piloted by Flt Lt P. 'Gerry' Sayer (1905–1942), the company's chief test pilot, at RAF Cranwell and was the first ever flight of a British jet-propelled aircraft. The first of Gloster's F9/40 series production was fitted with Power Jets-built improved W.2B/23 turbojets. But Metro-Vickers and Rolls-Royce engines as fitted to early 'DG' serialled aircraft had a smaller frontal area and air intakes as did the Rolls-Royce Welland (fitted to the first fifteen F.3s) and Derwent powerplants fitted to Gloster's series production F.1, F.3 and F.4 fighters.

The first series production Meteor F.I, serial EE210, was supplied to the US for study purposes in exchange for one of America's first jet-propelled aircraft: the Bell P-59 Airacomet. Gloster Meteor fighter export sales totalled 1,183. In December 1948, Gloster produced the first jet trainer destined to go into service with the RAF – the G.43 Meteor T.7. The prototype with civil registration G-AKPK was produced as a company private venture and first flew on 19 March 1948. A total of 640 T.7s were produced of which around

500 went to the RAF with the balance exported or delivered to the Royal Navy.

From 1942 to 1955, Gloster built around 2,500 Meteors of various marks with Armstrong Whitworth producing another 1,067. A further 300 were built by Fokker in the Netherlands and thirty by Fairey in Belgium. Meteor F.4s were exported to Argentina, Belgium, Denmark, Egypt and the Netherlands. One thousand and ninety-five F.8s were produced from September 1949 to April 1954. Five hundred and ninety-five were built by Gloster and 500 by Armstrong Whitworth.

In 1951, the F.8 – known as the 'meat box' to service pilots – took part in many air-to-air refuelling experiments. Meteor F.8s were also exported to Australia, Belgium, Brazil, Denmark, Egypt, Israel (seven ex-RAF aircraft), the Netherlands and Syria with substantial licensed-production undertaken in Belgium and the Netherlands. Although RAF fighters were not used in the Korean War, the RAAF, by way of No. 77 Squadron, deployed eighty-nine ex-RAF aircraft which fought for some thirty months from February 1951 to July 1953 suffering a horrendous attrition rate of forty-eight losses to three kills. On leaving frontline duties, many Meteor F.8s assumed target-towing duties with a banner towing hook installed in the ventral tank. These aircraft were redesignated as the TT.8. Until the introduction of the special Meteor variants, the RAF relied heavily on wartime Spitfire aircraft for its photo-reconnaissance duties.

On 15 June 1949, prototype Meteor FR.5, serial VT347, which featured forward-facing and oblique cameras in the nose and a vertical camera in the rear fuselage, was brought to an abrupt end when the aircraft broke up on its first flight. Its pilot, Rodney Dryland, was tragically killed.

It was not until 22 March 1950 that the prototype G.41L, Meteor FR.9, took to the air and within two years 126 examples had been delivered to the RAF for use mainly in Germany and the Middle East. The FR.9 was followed by the G.41M, PR.10, of which the RAF received fifty-eight examples. The final Meteor variants were the Armstrong Whitworth NF.11 and NF.14 radar-equipped night fighters. Gloster were asked to investigate the possibility of producing an interim night-fighter derivative of the T.7 trainer. However, considering that the company was overstretched on other tasks, it was agreed that development of a night-fighter variant should be undertaken by Sir W. G. Armstrong Whitworth Ltd at Coventry. The new aircraft, designated AW Meteor NF.11, were fitted with an AI Mk X radar. To accommodate the radar, the aircraft's nose section was extended by 5 feet. Although the aircraft were subsonic, they did represent a substantial improvement over the ubiquitous DH Mosquito NF.36 that had entered service in January 1946. Total AW Meteor NF production amounted to 576 aircraft comprising of 335 NF.11s, 100 NF.12s, forty NF.13s and 100 NF.14s

Gloster Meteor development aircraft fitted with Rolls-Royce Welland W.2B engines as supplied to the US at the request of USAF Gen 'Hap' Arnold. (*Author*)

Post-Second World War Gloster Meteor F.3 with two 2,000-lb thrust Rolls-Royce Derwent 1 turbojets as issued to the RAuxAF. (*Warplane Collection*)

Post-Second World War RAF Gloster Meteor F.4s took part in FRL's in-flight refuelling experiments. (*Aviation News*)

Gloster Meteor F.4s of No. 43(F) Squadron. Four Gloster Meteors of No. 54 Squadron were the first RAF combat jets to fly across the North Atlantic to the US. (*Wings*)

The Gloster GA.5 prototype was fitted with two 8,000-lb thrust Armstrong Siddeley Sapphire SA 6 axial flow turbojets. Series FAW aircraft featured a large 42-inch radome to house the various AI radar equipment and scanner that comprised either a British AI 17 or American AI 21/AI 22. (*Wings*)

No. 5 'Maple Leaf' Squadron Gloster Javelin FAW.7 all-weather night fighters on a conventional RAF Fighter Command line. (*Warplane Collection*)

In addition, 330 Meteor F.8s were built by Fokker in Holland c/n 6315-6644. Also, Belgium (Fairey) built sixty-seven Meteors, thirty with component parts and assemblies supplied by Fokker and thirty-seven from Gloster-made components. In total, 933 aircraft were exported. Eight hundred new builds and 133 refurbished aircraft were delivered from the UK. However, Fokker also produced a number for export of which at least two were supplied to Israel.

The last Gloster aircraft was the Javelin two-seat, all-weather fighter specifically designed to replace the AW Meteor NF.14. The Gloster Javelin was the first twin-jet, delta fighter in the world to operate in all weathers thanks to its sophisticated AI radar. Total production for the RAF of all Javelin marks amounted to 428 aircraft and included twenty-two T.3 trainers. The T.3 prototype, serial WT841, was assembled by Air Service Training at Hamble, Hampshire, having its first flight on 26 August 1956.

In 1960, Gloster were awarded a major programme of modification work in converting 116 FAW.7s – of which seventy-six had not left the factory – to FAW.8 standard, but retaining their British AI 17 radars and as such were redesignated as the F (AW) Mark 9. Forty examples were designated FAW 9R having been fitted with in-flight refuelling probes. The very last aircraft to be manufactured by Gloster was a Javelin F (AW).8, serial XJ165, in August 1960. In October 1961, Whitworth and Gloster became the Whitworth Gloster Division of Hawker Siddeley with both firms eventually losing their corporate identities on 1 April 1965.

Grahame-White Aviation Co. Ltd

The Claude Grahame-White Aviation Co. Ltd produced a number of aeroplanes in 1910 at Hendon Aerodrome, Middlesex, after Grahame-White had learnt to fly in 1909. The aircraft were familiar sights at Hendon and various flying meetings in the hands of their private owners. In August 1911 at the coronation of King George V, the Grahame-White Aviation Company firmly established themselves in the annals of British aviation by carrying more than 130,000 cards and letters between London and Windsor Castle inaugurating (along with other countries such as France, Germany and the US) the first airmail services. The Grahame-White Type 6 single pusher-engine, two-seat fighting biplane – which was similar to the Royal Aircraft Factory Fe.3 – was designed by nineteen-year-old John North who had joined Grahame-White in 1912. It followed the familiar pusher configuration and featured a Colt machine gun in the nose nacelle. Only one aircraft was built and there was no series production or military serials.

From 1911 to 1919, Grahame-White built a succession of aircraft, mostly biplanes, as subcontractors for the Burgess Aircraft and Morane-Saulnier. Grahame-White redeveloped the Burgess Baby Biplane into the New Baby and produced Morane-Saulnier monoplanes for the War Office. The company's own designs included the five-seat pusher Type 10 Aerobus followed by the Type 11 Warplane two-seat military biplane flown by Louis Noel at Hendon in May 1914. Noel reported that the aircraft had very poor longitudinal stability and control. His report convinced John North that there was no point in developing the aircraft further and so only one prototype was built. The two-seat Scout Type 13 was developed as a seaplane intended for the 1914 Round Britain Race (which was cancelled). However, prior to the aircraft's first flight, the pilot on opening the throttle caused the aircraft to nose over into the water. The aircraft was repaired and rebuilt with a wheeled undercarriage. However, the War Office were not impressed, possibly due to the extended distance between pilot and observer that made crew communication difficult (this was before the introduction of the wireless). The single prototype flown on 7 October 1914 was used at Hendon by the RNAS. A number of GW Type 15 two-seat biplane trainers were also used extensively by the RFC and RNAS during the early stages of the First World War. The Grahame-White Type 20 was a small biplane and believed to have flown in 1916. Its top speed was only 80-90 mph and it is unlikely that the War Office or Admiralty displayed interest in this type either. A refined variant of the Type 20, the Type 21, appeared in 1917. Although the aircraft appeared to be of excellent design for a scout aircraft, its only drawback was that it appeared a year after its contemporaries from other manufacturers and consequently no orders were received.

Grahame-White then entered into the design of a number of civil types and the GWE 4 Ganymede bomber of 1918 was converted for civil use as the GWE 9 Ganymede. Other civil types followed such as the GWE 6 Bantam single-seat sporting biplane designed by Frenchman M. Baudot who had joined Grahame-White from the small F. C. Nestler Ltd of Westminster, London. As a result, three GWE 6 Bantams were built at Hendon in 1919. One flew in the Aerial Derby at Hendon that year. The Bantam was followed by the GWE 7, a four-seat, luxury passenger-transport with folding wings. From 1920 onwards, the Grahame-White Aviation Company Ltd undertook subcontract work for Avro building the Avro 504K night fighter.

Handley Page Ltd

Having first established himself at Cricklewood Works, North London – and later moving to Radlett Aerodrome at Park Street, near St Albans, Hertfordshire – Frederick Handley Page (later Sir Frederick) built a number of biplanes and monoplanes at premises in Woolwich, Fambridge, and Barking Creek. Founded on 17 June 1909, Handley Page Ltd became the first limited company to build aeroplanes in the UK. In 1911, Handley Page started work on the then largest aircraft made in Britain, the O/100 heavy night bomber.

The O/100 had its origins in a naval specification for a twin-engine, sea-patrol plane dated December 1914. The specification was exceeded on the advice of Cdr Murray Sueter in order to develop a super bomber aka the mighty 'Bloody Paralyser'. It was powered by two 250-hp Rolls-Royce engines and sixteen 112-lb bombs could be carried. Also, there were Lewis machine gun positions in the nose and above and below the fuselage. The aircraft featured folding wings, an enclosed cabin with bullet-proof glass and armoured protection, and armoured nacelles for the engines. On 9 December 1915, the prototype was moved by road from Cricklewood Works to Hendon where it made its first short flight on 17 December 1915. The first O/100 delivered to the RNAS was flown over to the Independent Force 5th Wing at Dunkirk in November 1916. The third aircraft to be ferried over unfortunately landed by mistake at Laon behind the enemy lines, thus making a present of Britain's latest war machine to the Germans. A number of improvements to the O/100 gave rise to the O/400 with its twin 360-hp Rolls-Royce Eagle VIII engines. One aircraft went to No. 1 Squadron, Royal Australian Flying Corps, in Palestine and fifteen were ordered by the Standard Aircraft Corporation in the US, but none of these saw action. Four hundred and forty-six were built from 1918-1919: forty-six O/100s and 400 O/400s. At the end of the war, a number of O/400s were pressed into civil use as O/7s carrying passengers between Croydon and the continent. Initially, three aircraft were pressed in to use as freighters followed by nine aircraft, each converted to carry up to twelve passengers. There were two variants of the O/7 – the O/10, a twelve-passenger version, and the O/11, a passenger/freighter aircraft. Seven O/7s were supplied to China.

The success of the converted O/400s led the company to produce its first civil transports, the W.8, W.9 and W.10, which helped pioneer the early British commercial airlines. Featuring an enclosed cabin for the passengers, the pilots of these aircraft were exposed to the bitter elements in an open cockpit. The W.8 first flew on 4 December 1919 followed by the W.9 of which only one was built, followed by the sixteen-passenger, twin-engine W.10. In reality, Handley Page civil airliner ventures were not particularly successful returning a loss of £606,000 in 1920.

It was about this time in 1923 that Frederick Page and other aeronautical engineers independent of each other discovered that the addition of a miniature 'winglet or slat' had the effect of delaying the breakdown of airflow before the aerofoil gave rise to the stall effect. By the war's end in 1918, Page had developed a workable system and Handley Page Ltd applied for world patents. Almost immediately, a number of air arms became interested in this new development, among them the US Navy who in 1921, approached Handley Page with an order for three naval fighters to be equipped with the new device. The order gave rise to the HP.21, a cantilevered low-wing monoplane experimental aircraft although it is not certain whether all three airframes were built; however, it is known that performance and handling trials were conducted at Martlesham Heath, near Ipswich, Suffolk. At least one aircraft was delivered to the US where it received the designation HPS-1 – Handley Page Scout-1.

Another of Handley Page's early heavy bombers designed in 1917 was the V/1500. The largest British bomber of the First World War, the 'Super Handley' was intended to bomb Berlin. It was of a conventional design similar to the O/400 except for its size and was the first bomber with four engines in two pairs of 375-hp Rolls-Royce Eagle VIII pusher and tractor powerplants mounted in tandem. It was designed to carry 7,500 lbs of bombs, although for the Berlin trip this would have been reduced to around 1,000 lbs. However, as the war ended – almost coincidently with the type's entry into service – it remained in use for only a short period. Of the planned order for 255 to be built, only three were delivered by the war's end and only about twenty in total were delivered to the RAF. Handley Page at Cricklewood produced twenty V/1500s with about twelve more from appointed subcontractors Beardmore Ltd and Harland and Wolff Ltd in Belfast. Most V/1500s were cancelled as it was too expensive to operate in peacetime either as a bomber or a commercial aircraft.

A military development of the W.8 gave rise to the HP.24 or W.8D Hyderabad heavy night bomber. Designed to a 1922 specification, it had a deeper fuselage and a 'stepped' nose that enabled the pilot to see over the front gunner's position. The Hyderabad was the first aircraft to be fitted with the patented Handley Page upper wing, leading edge automatic slots, although the feature was not included in production aircraft of which a total of thirty-eight were built. The HP.36 Hinaidi II was a development of the Hyderabad differing mainly in its all-metal, fabric-covered construction and fitment of 480-hp Bristol Jupiter VIII radial engines enabling it to carry a slightly increased bomb load. Total production of Hinaidis amounted to forty-five aircraft.

In 1928, a troop-carrier version of the Hinaidi was produced to Air Ministry Specification C.20/27 and originally named Chitral. Later renamed as the Clive, Clive I, serial J9126, first flew in February 1928 and was followed by an all-metal version, the Clive II. Only two Clive IIs were built serving with the RAF's Heavy Transport Flight at Lahore, India, from 1931 to 1934.

The HP.50 Heyford was the last of the RAF's biplane heavy bombers. The aircraft's most notable feature was that its fuselage was attached to the upper and not the lower wing. This brought the added advantage that rapid rearming could be achieved as the bomb load was stored in the thickened centre section. Initial production Mk 1 and IA Heyfords were powered by two 575-hp Rolls-Royce Kestrel IIIS engines and featured open cockpits. The Mk II and III variants were powered by Kestrel VI engines and the Mk III had an enclosed pilot's cockpit and protected positions for the top gunners. A total of 124 Heyfords were produced for the RAF before production ceased in July 1936.

Eight HP.42 airliners were produced for Imperial Airways for use on their European and Eastern routes between 1918 and 1939. With the passenger cabin laid out like a Pullman railway carriage, the aircraft proved outstandingly reliable, flying in total in excess of 2.3 million miles up to the outbreak of war without incident or accident. In April 1937, the HP.54 Harrow transport was conceived although it was built as a high-wing monoplane bomber developed from the earlier HP.51 troop carrier that first flew on 8 May 1935. However, the Air Ministry had decided upon the Bristol Bombay as a standard troop carrier and the Harrow was seen as an interim bomber that could be quickly put into production under their existing Scheme C Expansion Programme. Harrows were produced in two versions – the first twenty-six as Mk Is with Bristol Pegasus X engines and 100 Mk II examples with Pegasus XX engines. In service use, most early Mk Is were brought up to Mk II standard, but a limited number of turrets were available and many aircraft entered service in the spring of 1937 with faired-in turret positions. The prototype, serial J9833, was used at the Ford in-flight refuelling experiments and two years later the first production Harrow, serial K6933, and two other civil-registered aircraft were loaned to Sir Alan Cobham's Flight Refuelling Limited (FRL) for similar experiments. By 1939, the Harrow had assumed its bomber trainer role having been superseded in frontline service by the Vickers Wellington as it was considered too vulnerable for operational bomber use. A few aircraft did see operational service with No. 93 Squadron in the winter of 1940-1941 when they were used as aerial minelayers. One hundred Harrows were ordered by the Air Ministry in August 1935 and were frequently known as Sparrows in service use. On withdrawal from bomber duties, a number of Harrows were converted as transports with their turrets removed and a redesigned streamlined nose similar to the HP.51. A number of Sparrows were allocated to No. 271 Squadron and a few participated in the infamous Arnhem operations by flying out casualties. They were also used extensively as transports for the frequent squadron moves around the UK and of the few Harrows/Sparrows which survived the war, most that not been destroyed on the ground by enemy action were scrapped in July 1945.

The HP.52 Hampden I (only two Mk IIs were built) prototype first flew on 21 June 1936 and entered service in December 1940. The bomber did not meet its promising expectations and its highly unorthodox fuselage shape and slender tail-boom earned it the 'Flying Panhandle' nickname. Also, the Hampden was often confused by British air defences with the Luftwaffe Dornier Do 17 'Flying Pencil' and three were hit by anti-aircraft fire in the first week of the war.

In 1940, pilot Flt Lt R. A. B. Learoyd and wireless operator/air gunner Sgt John Hannah were awarded Bomber Command's first Victoria Crosses by landing a seriously damaged and burning Hampden. Although the Hampden possessed exceptional speed and agility for a bomber, its lack of adequate offensive/defensive armament and serious problems of crew fatigue on long flights was soon reflected in the heavy losses experienced by the type on its initial deployment on day bombing offensives against Germany. On switching the type to less hazardous night bombing operations and with provision of improved defensive armament, the Hampden performed excellent work for Bomber Command and from September 1942, was employed as a minelayer and interim torpedo-bomber by RAF Coastal Command as the Hampden TB. A number of TBs, which operated against German shipping along the Norwegian coast from Russian bases, were handed over to the Soviet Air Force. Five hundred Hampdens were built by Handley Page with 770 produced by English Electric at its Preston factory and 160 in Canada by Canadian Associated Aircraft Ltd. Most Hampdens ended their lives in Canada in early 1944 with operational training units. Almost identical to the Hampden, 100 Handley Page Herefords were fitted with two 955-hp Napier Dagger VIII engines instead of the Bristol Pegasus built by Short Bros & Harland at Belfast. However, teething issues and unreliability of the Dagger engines relegated the Hereford to non-operational duties and those that were not converted to Hampdens were used as bomber crew trainers from 1940 onwards.

The HP.57 Mk I and HP.61 Mk VI Halifax were the second of the four-engine 'heavies' to enter RAF service and was conceived from the same Heavy Bomber Specification P.13/36 that produced the ill-fated Avro Manchester. However, the Halifax proved to be an excellent aircraft and unlike its more famous counterpart the Avro Lancaster, was also employed as a glider tug and coastal reconnaissance aircraft. Manufacture of the Halifax was undertaken by a 'Production Group' led by the parent company who acted as technical advisers and consultants to the group as a whole and included The English Electric Co. of Preston, the London Passenger Transport Board, Rootes Securities Ltd, Speke, and the Fairey Aviation Co. Ltd in Stockport. At the peak of production, the group operated forty-one factories and dispersal units, 660 subcontractors and a total of 51,000 employees completing one new aircraft every working hour. Of the 6,177 Halifax bombers built, English Electric produced 2,145, Rootes 1,070, Fairey 662 and the London Aircraft Production Group 710. By any standard, the Handley Page Halifax was a very effective heavy bomber. During the Second World War, it made 75,532

The twin-engined Hampden powered by Bristol Pegasus Mk XVII piston engines was nicknamed as the 'Flying Panhandle' and mistaken by the Royal Observer Corps as Luftwaffe Dornier Do 17 bombers during the Battle of Britain.

sorties and carried a total of 227,610 tons of bombs to the enemy. Both the B.II and B.V models were adopted for Coastal Command and thereby became the GR.II or V. The Mk III variant with four 1,675-hp Bristol Hercules VI or XVI engines – which had a ventral gun position and H2S navigation/bombing equipment as standard – became the backbone of RAF Bomber Command. Further improvements saw the introduction of the Mk V1 with its Bristol Hercules 100 engines. Although these engines were in short supply, a Mk VII variant using Bristol Hercules XVI engines and a revised fuel supply was introduced to maintain production. When adapted for Coastal Command, the Mk VI became the GR.VI. The Halifax also operated as a glider tug in the Arnhem and Rhine crossings and was the only aircraft that could efficiently tow the tank-carrying Hamilcar glider.

A range of Halifaxes powered by the Hercules XVI were adopted for transport duties as the A.VII of which an improved variant, the A. IX, was used post-war. During the post-war years, 161 Halifaxes were converted as civil airliners and designated as the C.VIII. This also included the twelve-passenger HP.70 Halton 1 for BOAC and a number of smaller operators such as the Lancashire Aircraft Corporation. In early 1946, all Rolls-Royce Merlin-engined variants were scrapped and within a year the remainder, with the exception of the Mk VI and Mk VII, were converted for weather reconnaissance. A number of Mk 7s were used as transports and some were transferred to the Armée de l' Air

Handley Page Victor B.2 bombers were converted into B (K).2 in-flight refuelling tankers by BAe at their Woodford factory near Manchester. (*Flypast Calendar*)

and Egyptian Air Force. Before the end of the Second World War, Handley Page had a number of transports on the drawing board including the HP.67 Mk 1 and 2, and the HP.64 Mk IV Hastings four-engine, long-range transport aircraft, the prototype, serial TE580, first flown at RAF Wittering on 7 May 1946. A total of 146 Hastings were built of which eight C.1s were converted by Airwork at Blackbushe to Hastings T.5s for training bomb-aimers in the use of modern V-bomber electronic NBS radar bomb-aiming equipment until they were finally retired in 1977.

Britain's first modern four-engine airliner after the war was the Handley Page Hermes that had its first flight on 3 December 1945. Twenty-five, sixty-five seat improved Mk IVs were supplied and used by BOAC from 1950 until 1954. A number were later used by charter operators Silver City and Skyways until the early 1960s. The HPR.5 Handley Page Marathon was originally designed by Miles Aircraft Ltd of Woodley, Reading. Handley Page assumed responsibility for production of the type at Woodley Aerodrome, Reading, Berkshire, when it bought Miles Aircraft Ltd in 1948 and at which time only two prototypes had been built. A new organisation, Handley Page (Reading Ltd), was formed on 5 July 1948. Orders from BEA for Marathons were subsequently cancelled, although six twenty-two seat Marathons were built for West African Airways

Corporation in 1952 and a further three were sold to the Union of Burma Airways. Twenty-eight aircraft were ultimately delivered to the RAF as T.11 trainers. The Marathon T.11 differed from the civil version mainly in its interior arrangement being equipped to carry a pilot, air signaller, navigation instructor and two student navigators. The cabin was fitted with three navigation plotting tables and rear facing seats. In subsequent years, as with a number of other manufacturers, Handley Page built a number of research aircraft to investigate supersonic flight, new wing shapes and tailless configurations of which some were incorporated in the design of the Handley Page HP 80 Victor B.1 V-bomber. The last of the trio of V-bombers to enter service was prototype, serial WB771, that made its first flight on Christmas Eve 1952 with a second, serial WB775, flying in September 1954 two months after WB771 had crashed.

The first production Victor B.1 was rolled out early in 1956 and powered by four Bristol Siddeley Sapphire 200 turbojets. A developed variant, the B.2 carried the Avro Blue Steel standoff bomb. The revised aircraft was powered by Rolls-Royce Conway 11 turbojets in place of the Bristol Siddeley Sapphires and incorporated an enlarged tail radome plus a wing with a 10-foot increase in span. The air intakes had been considerably deepened to cater for the more powerful engines and there were retractable dorsal air scoops in the fuselage close to the fin root to assist high-altitude operation. Although another fatality occurred with the first B.2, sufficient data was obtained from the second production aircraft to enable the type to enter RAF service with Bomber Command in 1959 as its high-speed, high-altitude bomber and reconnaissance aircraft. A total of eighty-three series Victors were built of which twenty-four were the B Mk 1, twenty-five B Mk 1A and thirty-four B Mk 2 B/SR.2 Bomber Strategic-Reconnaissance. In 1965, Victor B.1s were modified to replace the ailing Vickers Valiant tankers which were hastily withdrawn from use with metal fatigue. Avro at Woodford converted six Victor B.2 aircraft to the B(K).1A, ten to K.1 and fourteen to K.1A standard and in 1975, a similar action took place when a further twenty-four B.2s and SR.2s were converted to K.2 in-flight refuelling tankers to replace the ageing K.1. In the twilight of its career, sixteen Victor tankers of No. 55 Squadron from RAF Marham, Norfolk, played a prominent role in the Falklands conflict. When operating out of Ascension Island, they made some 600 refuelling sorties flying over 3,000 hours and supported Avro Vulcan B.2BB 'Black Buck' bombers, Hawker Siddeley MR.2 Nimrods, Lockheed C-130 Hercules transports and BAe GR.3 Harriers en route to the South Atlantic.

The high-winged, short-haul HPR.7 Dart Herald airliner appeared in 1958 and forty-eight were built between 1959 and 1968 along with the smaller eighteen-seat HP 137 Jetstream that entered large scale production at Radlett. However, the company's refusal to take part in the government-sponsored mergers of the early 1960s and high cost of developing the Jetstream forced

Handley Page into voluntary liquidation on 8 August 1969. On 1 June 1970, the company ceased to exist and another famous name in British aviation had died. The Jetstream was later redeveloped by British Aerospace as a successful regional turboprop airliner with substantial sales in the USA.

H. G. Hawker – Hawker – HSA

It is ironic that the accomplished Australian test pilot Harry G. Hawker OBE (1889–1921), who in 1920 stepped in to help his friend and colleague Thomas Sopwith save his company when it was faced with crippling tax demands, died in a flying accident the same year. It is also ironic that the newly formed H. G. Hawker Engineering Co. Ltd should then receive a contract to repair and rebuild Sopwith Snipes and Camels for the RAF. On Hawker's death, Thomas Sopwith was appointed chairman of the newly formed Hawker company and although the new company was kept busy with reconditioning work, it was not long before its design office under Capt. B. Thomson embarked on its own designs.

The first was the parasol-wing Duiker reconnaissance monoplane while the first fighter was the Hawker Woodcock I. The Woodcock was flown in late March 1923 and displayed some very unpleasant aerodynamic characteristics and as Thomson had left Hawker by the time the aircraft had its first flight, W. G. Carter was appointed chief designer in his place. Carter immediately set about a redesign of the Woodcock producing the Mk II interceptor and night fighter. The prototype Mk II, serial J6988, was evaluated at RAE Martlesham Heath in August 1923 and was found to be a considerable improvement over its predecessor. It was synonymous with a long line of superb Hawker fighters and sixty-two Woodcocks were delivered to the RAF and a three-seat naval reconnaissance variant named Hedgehog was delivered to the FAA. Meanwhile, Sidney Camm had also designed an ultralight, the Cygnet, of which some 1,924 were built.

Before George Carter left Hawker in 1925 to join the Gloucestershire Aircraft Company, he started work on the Hawker Hornbill, a single-engine, single-seat biplane interceptor. On evaluating the aircraft's performance, Hawker's chief test pilot, Flt Lt Paul Ward Spencer Bulman MC AFC, immediately expressed his disappointment at its poor performance that he believed to be caused by the fine-pitch Watts propeller. The aircraft was returned to Kingston and extensively modified to designs prepared by Carter's deputy, Sidney Camm, who had joined the company two years previously from G. H. Handasyde. Camm, on becoming chief designer carried out further innovations to both the Hornbill and Woodcock designs. Only one Hornbill prototype, serial J7782, was built, but after further modifications it was officially reclassified as an experimental aircraft and amassed 1,080 flying hours by the time of its last flight on 18 May 1933.

When Bulman was asked for his assessment of the aircraft, it led him to say 'The Hornbill was too clever by half. The designer seems to have almost forgotten that the pilot is an important part of the design.' Sidney Camm was never to forget these remarks. At first sight, the Heron single-seat fighter appeared as just another biplane fighter; however, it was a very significant aeroplane for Hawker as it was the first predominantly metal aircraft to emerge from the Kingston factory. At the beginning of the 1920s, Hawker realised that the Air Ministry were looking to the industry to introduce all-metal fighter designs and to this end in 1923 they began to introduce limited metal construction into designs at the Canbury Park Road plant. The Heron was undertaken as a private venture, the design of which was delegated by Carter to Sidney Camm in 1924. The Heron, serial J6989, was flown by company pilot Raynham in May 1925 after a prolonged evaluation at Martlesham Heath where it was nicknamed the Tincock by service pilots. The aircraft was returned to Kingston and transferred to the civil register as G-EBYC. It was entered in the 1928 King's Cup Air Race but as it was being taxied to the start line, Bulman struck a parked car and the starboard wing was severely damaged. Although the aircraft was repaired, it was decided not to seek renewal of its airworthiness certificate and was struck off charge in January 1930.

The Hawker Horsley two-seat day and torpedo bomber was named after Harry Hawker's residence at Horsley Towers. There were three marks of the 112 aircraft built. The Mk I was of all-wood construction and the Mk II was of composite part wood and metal construction. Of all metal, thirty-five Mk IIIs were produced in 1929 and incorporated Hawker's system of steel or duralumin tubes, rectangular sectioned at the ends and joined by various patterns of flat steel plate. This made the fuselage easier to assemble and repair and was arguably more cost effective to manufacture than the welded structure as pioneered by the Germans during the First World War.

In 1925, a Hawker Woodcock II was demonstrated to the Danish Government who placed an order for three pattern aircraft and negotiated terms for the licensed production of further aircraft. The Danecock as it was named was powered by a 385-hp Armstrong Siddeley Jaguar IV fourteen-cylinder radial engine. Various modifications were designed by Sidney Camm before initial deliveries commenced in February 1926. A further twelve aircraft were built at the Royal Danish Navy Dockyard from 1927 to 1928 and the aircraft served with the Danish Army Air Service as well as No. 2 Naval Squadron. One of the aircraft established a Scandinavian altitude record of 28,028 feet in January 1927 and the record stood for eight years.

First flown in 1927, the prototype Hawker Hawfinch, serial J8776, was Hawker's first all-metal structured fighter. The wing spars consisted of a pair of light gauge steel strips and were rolled to an octagonal section and connected by a corrugated steel plate web. Patented in 1927 by Roy Chaplin, Camm's assistant designer, the Hawfinch was built specifically to Air Ministry

Specification F.9/26 that was ultimately fulfilled by the Bristol Bulldog fighter. The Hawfinch was the second Hawker aircraft of the era to officially be designated as an experimental aircraft until it was finally struck off charge at Martlesham Heath in 1934. By 1928, it was clear to Camm and a number of other designers that the days of the large air-cooled radial engine were numbered. Camm therefore decided to build Hawker F.20/27, serial J9123, which although powered by a Bristol Mercury radial engine could with relative ease be modified to accept the new Rolls-Royce F.XI inline engine. After its evaluation at Martlesham Heath, the unnamed F-20/27 interceptor was not proceeded with and only one example was built. In the same year, the all-metal fabric-covered Hawker Tomtit was chosen for evaluation and had extended trials by the RAF's flying training organisation. Although the Tomtit proved to be an excellent training aircraft, only twenty-five were built for the RAF and a few were used at RAF Northolt as a communications aircraft.

Designed to replace the Fairey Flycatcher (Naval Specification N.21/26), the Hawker Hoopoe, which had flown at a similar time as the F.20/27, was a private venture instigated by Camm to demonstrate that there should be no reason why a naval fighter derived from a landplane should have an inferior performance. After evaluation, this was another aircraft to be placed on experimental charge, being flown by Armstrong Siddeley and the RAE until 1932 when it was scrapped. The Hawker Hart light biplane bomber, which had its first flight in June 1928, was a superb aircraft with an excellent turn of speed. When it first entered service, it could easily outdistance the Armstrong Whitworth Siskin fighter. Four hundred and thirty Harts were delivered to the RAF and included fifteen pre-production development aircraft delivered in January 1930. Series aircraft were built by the parent with subcontract production by Armstrong Whitworth, Vickers and Gloster. Sixty-four aircraft were delivered to the RAAF in March 1934 and forty-two were built under licence in Sweden. Including Hawker Hart fighter derivatives such as the two-seat Demon, Hector, Audax, Hardy and Osprey, 2,700 examples were produced and the type was manufactured by more companies than any other British aircraft between the wars. A civil variant known as the Hawker Hart II fitted with a 525-hp Rolls-Royce Kestrel IB engine was flown on 15 September 1932.

The Hawker Fury was the first RAF aircraft to exceed 200 mph and at 245 mph was the fastest biplane in RAF service. The aircraft was aptly named as Sidney Camm, Hawker's chief designer, had a furious disagreement with the Air Ministry over its title although he eventually won the day. The Fury was a development from two of Camm's early fighter designs, the Mercury-engined

Hawker Horsley Mk II torpedo-bombers with a 665-hp Rolls-Royce Condor IIIA engine carried an 18-inch torpedo. (*Warplane Collection*)

F.20/27 and Hornet. Some 264 Furies were built and included 112 of the more powerful Fury II and licensed production in Yugoslavia. A naval counterpart of the Fury was the Hawker Nimrod and fifty-six Nimrod Mk 1s and thirty Nimrod IIs were built. A fast two-seat fighter reconnaissance aircraft, 129 Hawker Ospreys were built for the Fleet Air Arm. Specially constructed from stainless steel for research purposes, three examples of the Osprey III were built.

The two-seat Hawker Hart bomber returned such an outstanding performance that it spawned a whole series of fighters, trainers and army co-operation aircraft such as the two-seat Audax. Six hundred and fifty aircraft were produced by the RAF, 114 by Hawkers, fifty by Gloster, 141 by Bristol and 287 by Avro which included forty-three transferred from a Westland contract. A number of Audax aircraft ended their days fitted with de-rated Rolls-Royce Kestrel X engines and served as advanced trainers or target tugs. A direct derivative of the Audax was the Hardy that was designed as a general-purpose aircraft and not purely as an army co-operation aircraft. The Hardy was characterised by its 'doughnut' heavy-duty tyres suitable for rough desert landing grounds. Production of the Hardy was subcontracted to Gloster at Brockworth who built forty-seven examples. The first high performance, two-seat interceptor fighter derived from the Hart bomber was the Demon. The Demon was fitted with a fully supercharged Rolls-Royce Kestrel engine, twin

This Hawker Tomtit was from a batch of eight serials, K1781-1786, six of which would later receive civil UK registrations. Airworthy 1928 Tomtit K1786 belongs to the Shuttleworth Trust Museum in Bedfordshire. (*Flight Library*)

Hawker Fury Mk 1s with Rolls-Royce Kestrel engines equipped three RAF fighter squadrons. (*Warplane Collection*)

front guns and a cutaway rear cockpit with a tilted gun ring to improve the arc of fire. The type reintroduced a two-seat fighter to the RAF for the first time since the First World War.

In 1934, it was announced that Royal Aux Air Force Squadrons were to become fighter units equipped with the new Hawker 'Turret' Demon fitted with its Fraser Nash turret. Deliveries commenced in 1936. By the time of the Munich Crisis of September 1938, RAF Fighter Command fielded eight Demon squadrons. A navalised variant of the Hart was the Osprey, a two-seat biplane carrier-borne or seaplane fighter-reconnaissance aircraft that appeared in four different variants. Hawker Fury aircraft were sold to Yugoslavia, Iran, Spain and South Africa. Further development of the Fury was investigated by way of producing a monoplane variant, but this idea was soon to manifest itself as an entirely new design, the eight-gun Hawker Hurricane monoplane fighter.

In response to a requirement for a Hawker Horsley bomber replacement, Sidney Camm produced his first Hawker Harrier, which although performed reasonably well at official trials at Martlesham in November 1927, it could not really be considered as a Horsley bomber replacement and was abandoned. The Hawker Hind light day-bomber has the distinction of being the most prevalent type in the RAF's peacetime history. From 1935 onwards, over twenty regular RAF squadrons and eleven Auxiliary Air Force units were equipped with Hinds. It remained in production for almost two years of the RAF's pre-war expansion programme utilising the same facilities as the Hart light bomber and maximised resources with production staff needing only minimal retraining. With Thomas Sopwith having arranged for a number of other manufactures who were having a lean time to complete outstanding orders for Hart, Audax, Hardy and Fury fighters, Hawker produced all 527 Hinds that were delivered to the RAF in just two years. However, the Hind was hardly an advanced design and few doubted that it was purely an interim measure prior to the introduction of a new breed of bomber. It was therefore of little surprise that as the new monoplane bombers started to enter service, the Hind underwent the swift transition to a dual-control trainer to which ab initio pilots transferred from their de Havilland Moths. It is important to note that this little and light Hawker bomber was conceived and built by a company better known for its fighter aircraft along with Sidney Camm and Thomas Sopwith's tenacity and foresight formulated the concept of work distribution to meet peaks of demand. It laid the seeds of survival for the British aviation industry almost a decade after the Second World War had ended, paving the way for the rationalisation and consolidation of the modern aircraft manufacturing industry as we now know it.

In 1936, Hawker Hinds were foremost in the inventory of the RAF's new Bomber Command and later as a trainer that equipped most of the flying training schools and the Royal Air Force College at Cranwell who at one time had fifty-eight on charge. Many Hinds were also later used as glider tugs. Hawker's success with its outstanding run of amazing little biplanes led to the formation of Hawker Aircraft Ltd on 18 May 1933 and with the purchase of Gloster in June 1934, the establishment of Hawker Siddeley Aircraft Co. Ltd. Embracing Hawker and Gloster were Sir W. G. Armstrong Whitworth Aircraft, Armstrong Siddeley Motors, Air Service Training and A. V. Roe.

Luckily for Britain, Thomas Sopwith realised that the Second World War was inevitable and entirely at Hawker's own risk laid down series production for no less than 400 Hawker Hurricanes, the first RAF monoplane fighter capable of more than 300 mph. Throughout the Second World War, Camm and Hawker produced a distinguished line of single-seat fighters as had their Sopwith ancestors during the 1914-1918 conflict. A steady process of evolution produced the Hurricane, Typhoon and Tempest. The origins of the Hurricane can be traced back to October 1933 with the design of the Fury Monoplane powered by the new Rolls-Royce PV-12 engine. It is difficult to quantify what impact these three Hawker designs had on the outcome of the war. First, the Hurricane played a far greater part in winning the Battle of Britain in 1940 than the Spitfire. Then, while production of this versatile fighter continued for service in many parts of the world on many different battlefronts, the Typhoon was put into production. Some Hurricane production was delegated to the Gloster Aircraft Co. (1,750), the Austin Motor Co. (300) and the Canadian Car and Foundry Co. (1,451). Canadian-produced variants were fitted with Packard-built Merlin engines and designated as the Mk X, XI, XII and XIIA respectively.

The announcement by the South African Government in 1934 that it was to expand its air force to 250 aircraft within four years led to an agreement between Oswald Pirow, the South African Defence Minister, and the British Government to develop a version of the Hawker Audax for light support and bombing duties. This gave rise to the Hawker Hartbees, sometimes referred to in South Africa as the Hartbeest, sixty-five of which were licensed-built in South Africa.

Expansion of the RAF, which began in 1934, created many new squadrons, except with no new aircraft types to equip them. As an interim measure, orders were placed for a Hart variant: the Hind. With many minor improvements and a more powerful Rolls-Royce Kestrel V engine, the Hind possessed a far better performance at altitude. In the Second World War, Sea Hurricane conversions (there were no new builds) were undertaken by General Aircraft Ltd and Austin Motors Ltd. From 1941 to 1944, Sea Hurricanes served aboard CAM ships (catapult-armed merchantmen) in protection of Allied shipping crossing the North Atlantic from the US as well as Royal Navy carriers. Out of a grand production total of 14,533 Hurricanes built, Hawkers produced 10,030 examples. The first 500 delivered to the RAF were with a fabric-covered wing with the metal-winged version appearing in March 1939. The Hurricane was exported to many countries including Finland, Canada, South Africa, Belgium and Portugal. A major user was the Soviet Union that received some 3,000 under the American Lend-Lease Act.

The Typhoon was the first of the RAF's 400 mph fighters that carried on the Hawker tradition – just as the Hurricane was the first fighter to exceed 300 mph and the Fury the first to exceed 200 mph. Although its early career was plagued with design issues including a series of unexplained crashes where the tail unit failed under stress, the Typhoon became a highly successful ground-attack fighter with the RAF's 2nd TAF in Germany. A total of 3,330 were built. The Typhoon was followed by the Tempest air superiority fighter which was a natural progressive development as the initial design of the type was undertaken as part of the Typhoon programme. After seeing action in 1944 against V1 flying-bombs, the Tempest moved to the continent and by the end of the war eight squadrons were equipped with the type. Tempest V Mk IIs were produced too late to see service during the war, but it did serve with the RAF until 1951 and was supplied to the Indian and Pakistani air forces. The Tempest gave rise to the second Hawker Fury that was first flown in 1944 although was eventually produced for export only. A naval counterpart, the Hawker Sea Fury was the last naval piston-engine fighter to enter service after the end of the war seeing operational service with the Fleet Air Arm during the Korean War in 1950-1953.

Companies forming the Hawker Siddeley Group were responsible for providing approximately 30 per cent of all equipment supplied by the British aircraft industry to the RAF throughout the Second World War. Factory space increased from a floor area of 2,000,000 square feet in 1938 to 15,000,000 square feet in 1944 and the rate of new aircraft production rose from sixty to 600 per month. Total Hawker Group deliveries consisted of approximately 40,089 aircraft and 38,564 aero-engines. In addition, it repaired 11,010 aircraft and 9,777 aero-engines. Aircraft production rose from 1,753 in 1938-1939 to a peak of 8,795 in 1943-1944, which did not include a further 2,190 aircraft repaired or reconditioned from 1943-1944. Engine production rose from 2,175 in 1938-1939 to 8,008 in 1942-1943.

After the war, Hawker produced the Sea Hawk, a single-seat, carrier-borne, ground-attack fighter of all-metal stressed-skin construction. The basic design stemmed from the company's first jet, the P.1040, which had its first flight on 2 September 1947. Sea Hawks entered service with the FAA in 1953 and took part in the Suez operation of 1956 before finally retiring in 1960. Export versions were supplied to West Germany and the Netherlands, and the type also saw action with the Indian Navy against Pakistan in 1971.

This was followed by the P.1067 prototype, serial WB188, subsonic jet

Hawker Hurricane F.1s equipped RCAF 'Ram' Squadron at RAF Odiham in March 1940 before moving to RAF Northolt in October where it remained until converting to Supermarine Spitfire F.2as in 1942. (*Aviation News*)

Opposite top: Hawker Hurricane F.1 of No. 1 (F) Squadron in its Battle of Britain livery. (*Wings*)

Opposite middle: Hawker Hurricane F.1 with wartime code GN F indicates it was a No. 249 Squadron airplane. (*Wings*)

Opposite bottom: The Shuttleworth Trust Hawker Hurricane with wartime code 7 L indicates it was a No. 59 Operational Training Unit (OTU) airplane. (*Author*)

fighter that first flew on 20 July 1951. The prototype of the Hawker Hunter was universally acknowledged as a thoroughbred with virtually vice-less handling characteristics and was epitomised by the fact that the Empire Test Pilots' School at Boscombe Down used a pair of dual-seat Hunter T.7s, serials XL564 and XL612, for many years to introduce and instruct student test pilots on the vagrancies of inverted spin and spin recovery. The 'Raspberry Ripple' Hawker Hunter T.7 aircraft of the ETPS, Boscombe Down, used for spin recovery training was finally replaced by a leased Saab JAS-39 Gripen (Griffen) in the new millennium.

Arising out of a 1948 Ministry of Supply requirement for a single-seat, day interceptor fighter (F.3/48), the Hunter F.1 with a 7,500-lb thrust Rolls-Royce Avon RA.7 engine entered service with the RAF in July 1954. By the time production of the Hunter had ended in 1960, some 2,350 Hunters were constructed. Built in parallel with the Mk 1 was the Mk 2 variant with an 8,000-lb thrust Armstrong Siddeley Sa.6 Sapphire engine. Along with the Mk 5 version, the Mk 2 was to suffer less from engine issues which occurred

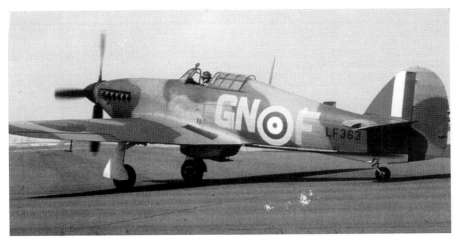

Hawker Hart biplane fighters were used by the SAAF with special broad tyre undercarriages for 'rough field' use in the bush and the type was known as Hartbees. (*Author*)

when the aircraft's 30-mm Aden cannon was fired on earlier marks.

A number of aircraft were involved in trials work associated with the introduction of the ground-attack variant, the FGA 9. FGA 9s were converted F.6s fitted with a 10,000-lb thrust Avon RA.28 engine, although the lesser-powered interim Mk 4 equipped no less than twenty-two RAF squadrons for some three years until replaced by the higher-powered F.6. By now, the RAF had the day fighter they wanted. Forty surplus F.4s at a unit price of around £33,000 each were transferred to the Royal Navy for tactical training purposes and subsequently redesignated as the GA.11. The GA.11 went on to serve with the Fleet Requirements and Air Directions Unit (FRADU) which among other tasks helped to train Fleet Air Arm fighter controllers at the Yeovilton base.

Rolls-Royce Ltd used the Mk 6 prototype, serial XF833, for experiments with a thrust reversal system for reducing landing runs although a simple parachute braking system was fitted to the FGA 9. Three aircraft, serials WW594, WW598, and XF378, were involved in a trials programme to equip Hunters with Firestreak air-to-air missiles and AI Mk 20 radar in place of the limited capability Plessey Ranging Radar. These aircraft were designated P.1109B. However, as a result of the 1957 Labour Government's Defence White Paper, all work on the Hunter Interceptor Programme was stopped. One aircraft, serial WW598, was flown to the Middle East to undertake trials work for the RAE with low-level, high-speed flights in high ambient temperatures to investigate the effects of severe gust loading on the

The Tempest was significantly faster at low level over other Allied and Axis fighters except jets such as the Me 262. This statement was made by Wg Cdr Roland 'Bea' Beaumont who commanded the RAF's first Tempest Wing at Newchurch, Kent, in April 1944. (*Flight Colour*)

aircraft. Much of the data collected was used in relation to the Blackburn Buccaneer low-level, maritime strike-bomber development and the cancelled BAC TSR.2. Another project that was proposed was a two-seat, all-weather fighter, one fitted with an Avon engine designated P.1114 and one with a Sapphire P.1115. Neither was built, but a Hunter F.6, serial XG131, was flown with slim wing-tip fuel tanks as it had been proposed that on the all-weather fighter, the under-wing tank pylons should carry air-to-air missiles instead.

The P.1114/1115 concept also gave rise to investigations into rear side fuselage 'clam style' air brakes as it was envisaged the all-weather Hunter would demand increased deceleration under certain operational conditions. During Sea Harrier development, two Hunter T.8Ms, serial XL602 and XL603, were fitted with Ferranti Blue Fox radar to develop the nav-attack systems for the Sea Harrier. The aircraft later joined No. 899 NAS and were used for training Sea Harrier pilots.

Following the cancellation of 150 Hunter F.6s as a result of the Wilson Labour Government 1957 Defence White Paper, India placed an order for 160 Mk 56/Mk 6s to be followed with a further order for fifty-three Mk 56As in 1965 while placing an order to upgrade all aircraft to FGA 9 standard. A further seventeen aircraft of various marks including two-seat trainers were also ordered. Switzerland placed an order for 100 Mk 58/F.6s followed by an order for fifty-two Mk 58As modified Mk 4s to F.6 standard.

Royal Navy No. 806 NAS at Yeovilton, Somerset, was the first to equip with the straight-winged Hawker Sea Hawk F.1 jet. (*Author*)

The Swiss Flugwaffe finally retired their Hawker Hunter aircraft in 1994.

On completion of the last 'new build' F.6 variant on 5 October 1960, a programme of refurbishment and modification that was to span some fourteen years was embarked on. Surplus RAF aircraft and those of other air arms were repurchased and reworked by Hawker and resold to at least eleven air arms around the world. This included twelve FGA 9s for Zimbabwe (then Rhodesia); four Mk 57s for Kuwait; eighteen Mk 59As and four Mk 59Bs for Iraq; four Mk 60s to Saudi Arabia; three Mk 70s to Lebanon (who in 1997 were seeking to refurbish between three to six Mk 70s as a basis on which to rebuild an air force); twenty-eight Mk 71s and FR 71s to Chile; two Mk 73s, thirteen Mk 73As and three Mk 73Bs to Jordan; twelve FGA Mk 74s, four FR Mk 74s and twenty-two FR Mk 74Bs to Singapore; seven FGA Mk 76s and three FR Mk 76As to Abu Dhabi; three FGA Mk 78s to Qatar; and four Mk 80s to Kenya.

The Hurricane and Hunter must rate among Sidney Camm's most famous designs. Total Hunter production amounted to 2,372 aircraft which included licensed production in the Netherlands (189 aircraft) and Belgium (256 aircraft). Well over 1,000 single-seat fighters were built for the RAF and over 400 new and refurbished aircraft were sold worldwide. Although the Hunter cannot be regarded as a superior interceptor due to the British Government's unwillingness to invest in its further development of the FGA 9 variant, it was an extremely robust and versatile fighter. Relatively inexpensive to operate

Painted bright red, the Hawker Hunter prototype as P.1067, serial WB188, established a new FIA world speed record of 727.6 mph and was flown by Sqdn Ldr Neville Duke in September 1953. (*Wings*)

This Hawker Hunter 'Raspberry Ripple' F.6 was used by the Empire Test Pilots School (ETPS) at Boscombe Down. (*Author*)

and easy to maintain, the Hunter served many nations throughout the world to counter threats to their sovereignty. The aircraft was also invaluable to Hawker and the British aviation industry as a whole, playing a major part in ensuring its very survival at a time when it was faced with extinction. A small number of Hunters remain in use today. In 2001, Brazilian aircraft manufacturer Embraer acquired a Hunter T.7 trainer variant for use as a company chase plane.

Following the Hunter, Hawker produced a number of experimental designs such as the P.1052 single-seat, research fighter and P.1072 twin-engine, jet/rocket research aircraft. Hawker developed the P.1052 into the P.1081, a single-seat, swept-wing fighter, with a view to meeting a requirement from Australia. However, interest in the aircraft cooled and serial XV279 crashed

Of the many Hunter F.6 airframes reworked by Hawkers were the F.74 single-seaters supplied to the Singapore Air Force for air defence duties. (*Aviation News*)

Land-based Hawker Hunter G.A.11s were used by the Royal Navy at RNAS Yeovilton as advanced fighter trainers. (*Author*)

A sole dual-seat 'Raspberry Ripple' Hawker Hunter T.7 was used for many years by the ETPS at Boscombe Down to teach students the vagaries of 'spin recovery'. (*Author*)

on 3 April 1951 at Farnborough killing Hawker's chief test pilot, Sqdn Ldr T. S. 'Wimpy' Wade DFC AFC. Subsequent 'Hawker' designs carried the Hawker Siddeley HS nomenclature when in 1963, original group members were joined by other famous industry names giving rise to the Hawker Siddeley Aviation HSA Group.

Hawker Siddeley Aviation

On 1 July 1963, Hawker Siddeley Aviation came into being and assimilated a number of new members into the reorganised Hawker Siddeley Group giving rise to Hawker Siddeley Aviation HSA and Hawker Siddeley Dynamics HSD for the company's missile designs. New members brought the group up to eight: Hawker, de Havilland, Gloster, Armstrong Whitworth, Armstrong Siddeley, Avro, Folland and Blackburn. All aircraft originating from the group carried the HS Hawker Siddeley nomenclature as did existing inherited designs. The HS.681, which started life as the Armstrong Whitworth 681 jet V/STOL freighter, was cancelled; however, most of the other company's designs survived. Among the products that were assimilated was the DH Sea Vixen naval all-weather fighter that began life as the DH.110. A total of 146 were built and the type was withdrawn from frontline Fleet Air Arm service in 1972.

The Trident, a medium-range airliner, was also an original de Havilland design and was the first airliner in the world to be specifically designed for operation in all weathers including fog with its revolutionary fully-automatic landing system. However, as has often been the case with British civil types, the Trident was the right aircraft at the wrong time as Boeing were obtaining a fierce stranglehold on the civil airliner market. Although the Trident was the first three-jet airliner to fly – appearing a year before the rival Boeing 727 – fifteen were ordered by the People's Republic of China and sales peaked at a meagre sixty aircraft. Nonetheless, de Havilland's six to eight-seat executive business jet, the DH.125, went from strength to strength with over 350 aircraft delivered under the HS banner and in excess of ninety aircraft retrofitted with the up-rated Garrett TFE731-3R-1H engines. As well as civil variants, the RAF used two specific types: the Dominie T Mk 1 navigation trainer (since upgraded to T.2 for use well into the 21st century) and the HS 125 CC1, CC2, CC3 communications and VIP variants of which six remained in use in 2009 with No. 32 (Royal) Squadron RAF at Northolt, North London. A total of sixty-nine HS.650s, formerly AW.650 Argosy Freighters, which included fifty-six of its military counterparts, the AW.660 Argosy C.1, were built.

The Hawker Siddeley 748 started life as the Avro 748 powered by two Rolls-Royce Dart engines and over 350 civil and military versions named Andover were sold worldwide. The type was also licensed-produced by HAL Hindustan

Aeronautics Ltd in India. HAL developed and trialled an AEW 748 variant that subsequently crashed after years of trials and was written off in 1999.

The de Havilland Comet airliner was developed by Hawker Siddeley into the Nimrod MR.1 maritime reconnaissance aircraft that was destined to serve the RAF for at least another thirty years until 2030 with a major upgrade programme. The Nimrod MRA.4 upgrade was virtually a complete rebuild with in excess of 70 per cent of the airframe including wings, engines and avionics being replaced. But in 2010, the Nimrod MRA.4 was cancelled in the UK coalition defence review and all twelve airframes were cut up at BAe Systems' Woodford plant near Manchester. In the military field, Hawker Siddeley continued development of the Folland Gnat advanced trainer, licensed-produced by HAL as a single-seat fighter as the Ajeet single-seat fighter, and the Hawker Siddeley Blackburn Buccaneer two-seat, low-level strike and reconnaissance aircraft. A total of 189 Buccaneers were produced for the Royal Navy, RAF and the SAAF. Some fifty-four of the original sixty delivered to the Royal Navy transferred to the RAF when Britain decided to phase out its fixed-wing aircraft carriers.

Another famous Hawker/Hawker Siddeley design was the Harrier Jump Jet born out of an idea conceived in 1957 when Sir Stanley Hooker, the Sidney Camm and Ralph Hooper senior project engineer at Hawker's Kingston facility, produced a V/STOL design. The P.1127 was powered by a Bristol Siddeley BS.53 turbojet and four exhaust nozzles could be directed downwards for vertical take-off and rearwards for normal forward flight. The P.1127 was eventually to spawn the Hawker Siddeley Kestrel that ultimately led to the AV-8A and subsequent AV-8B MDC/BAe Harrier II. The iconic Harrier was the world's only operational fixed-wing V/STOL strike aircraft and under another defence review, the RAF's entire Harrier fleet was withdrawn from use and many airframes were sold to the USMC at a knockdown price as a spares source.

On 29 April 1977, Hawker Siddeley Aviation and Hawker Siddeley Dynamics were forced into an amalgam with BAC and Scottish Aviation to form British Aerospace, later renamed BAe Systems when it merged with GEC/Marconi Avionics in the late 1990s.

Hunting Percival Aircraft Ltd – Hunting

In 1954, Hunting Percival Aircraft Ltd was formed when Hunting Engineering at Ampthill, near Bedford, acquired Percival Aircraft Ltd. A number of designs were in production at Percival's Luton Airport facility including the P.50 Prince, a civil feeder-liner and executive transport that had first flown in August 1948. The P.50 gave rise to two military variants, one for the Royal Navy (P.66 Sea

The RAF Hunting Jet Provost T.1, which first flew in June 1954, was derived from the earlier piston-engined P.56 Provost trainer as is clearly shown by this photograph. (*Warplane Collection*)

A few Jet Provost T.4s based at RAF Finningley with No. 6 FTS were used by No. 100 (TT) Squadron as Forward Air Controllers. (*Author*)

RAF Percival (Hunting) Pembroke C.1 two-crew utility transport of No. 60 Squadron based at RAF Wildenrath in West Germany. (*Warplane Collection*)

Prince) and the P.66 Pembroke for the RAF. The main difference between the P.50 and P.66 was that the military variants had a greatly increased wingspan of 64 feet 6 inches as opposed to 56 feet. In addition, one of the RAF's famous post-war training aircraft was in production – the P.56 Provost, a successor to the less powerful P.40 Prentice. The P.56 was followed by the P.84 Jet Provost incorporating major design features from the piston-engined aircraft. The Jet Provost was to become the RAF's standard basic trainer for many years with over 450 built.

In 1957, Hunting dropped the Percival name from its title becoming Hunting Aircraft Ltd and was to become controlled by the newly formed British Aircraft Corporation in September 1960. Under BAC's auspices, Hunting continued with work on two new projects: the H.126 Jet-flap research aircraft and the H.107 forty-four to fifty-five seat airliner that was to be redesignated as the B.107. The B.107 entered production as the BAC1-11.

In 1965, Hunting's aircraft design office was closed although the company continued to be a leading player in the munitions field. Its most famous product must undoubtedly be the JP 233 dispenser and associated air-launched munitions pod as carried by the IDS Tornado. Used to such devastating effect in the first Gulf War in 1991, the weapon was subsequently withdrawn from use following strong protestations from the anti-mines lobby led by H. R. H. Lady Diana Princess of Wales.

Marshall Aerospace

No review of British aviation history can be undertaken without recall to the contribution made by Marshall Aerospace of Cambridge. Almost from its inception, Marshall has been involved in some way with practically every significant British aircraft programme. Between the 1950s and 1960s, many of the great names of British aviation industry were merged into what is now British Aerospace. Each company blended into one corporation as costs of development and production of aircraft spiralled beyond the capabilities of individual independent companies. Marshall, however, would appear to have avoided the melting pot and continue today as a significant independent player in Britain's aviation industry.

In 1909, David Gregory Marshall, steward and manager of the University Pitt Club in Cambridge, started a car vehicle business in Brunswick Gardens providing chauffeured transport for wealthy dons and undergraduates. The business soon moved to larger premises in King Street and then to new premises in Jesus Lane leased from Jesus College in 1912 (the site remains to this day as the company's main city centre garage). The company's first encounter with aviation took place in 1912 when *Beta II*, a Royal Flying Corp airship, made a forced landing at Jesus Grove behind Jesus College close to the Marshall garage when mechanics helped with engine repairs. In 1926, David Marshall was joined by his son, Arthur, who had just completed an engineering degree at Jesus College.

In 1928, Arthur Marshall learned to fly at Norwich and in the following year, the first Cambridge aerodrome was opened on a farm behind the family home at Whitehall on the outskirts of Cambridge. A spectacular flying display marked the opening which included an air race by three RAF pilots – one of whom, F/O Waghorn, went on to win the Schneider Trophy later in the year – and F/O Boyle who eventually became AM and CAS. With the opening of the airfield, flying training commenced in October 1929 and in 1930, the Marshall Flying School Ltd was formed.

In 1935, the company purchased new farmland slightly out of Cambridge where in October 1937, the company established Cambridge Airport. Pilot training continued with courses run by Arthur Marshall with such famous names as Norman de Bruyne (who invented the glues used in the production of the all-wooden de Havilland Mosquito), Hawker test pilot Bill Humble, and de Havilland test pilot H. G. Barrington, all gaining their wings with

The Marshall Flying School Ltd used DH Tiger Moths to train hundreds of new recruits to fly for the RAF before and during the Second World War. (*Wings*)

Marshall. The formal opening of the airfield by Sir Kingsley Wood, Secretary of State for Air, took place on 8 October 1938. The opening coincided with the 'Munich Crisis' and the flying display included the first public showing of the Supermarine Spitfire fighter, the type having recently entered service with No. 19 Squadron at the nearby RAF Duxford aerodrome.

In 1938, a RAFVR Flying School operated by Marshall was opened at the new Cambridge Airport. The company pioneered efficient flying training programmes and by the outbreak of the Second World War in September 1939, over 600 pilots had been trained with a grand total of 20,000 pilots, flying instructors and observers being trained at the Marshall Flying Schools from 1939 to 1945. In addition, the post-war future of the company had been secured as over 5,000 aircraft had been repaired or converted by Marshall for the war effort. A further development of the company's activities was the repair of RAF training aircraft such as Hawker Hart, Audax, Hind and Fairey Battle prior to war breaking out with repair and modification work continuing throughout the conflict. The workshops now handled a huge range of aircraft including Armstrong Whitworth Whitneys, Airspeed Oxfords, Gloster Gladiators, Avro Ansons, Supermarine Spitfires, Hawker Hurricanes, Vickers Wellingtons, Bristol Blenheims, Ablemarles, Boeing B-17 Flying Fortresses, Mosquitoes, Hawker Typhoons and Douglas C-47 Dakota transports.

The company even undertook conversion of Hamilcar gliders into powered transports by adding two Bristol Mercury engines. Repair and structural work continued post-war, the company being awarded a major maintenance contract for the RAF's fleet of Douglas Dakota transports. This was followed by repair, modification and rebuild contracts for over 1,600 aircraft including de Havilland Vampires and Venoms, English Electric Canberras, Vickers Viscount turboprop airliners and Vickers Valiant bombers. The company has had some involvement in every UK military and civil design since the war. It designed and built the 'droop-snoot' nose assemblies for the Aerospatiale/BAC *Concorde* and was the only company outside of British Aerospace with fully delegated design authority for the SST. In 1953, the company funded a fully engineered concrete runway and in 1955, the first of the large post-war runways were built to accommodate aircraft such as the BAC VC 10, Vickers Valiant and Bristol Britannia. In 1965, the establishment of this facility enabled Marshall to bid for the contract to receive, paint and carry out pre-delivery checks on the RAF's new Lockheed C-130K Hercules transports arriving from the US. Since the 1960s, Marshall has built up successful relationships with a number of major US manufacturers such as Gulfstream, Cessna Citation and Lockheed with the RAF's fleet of Lockheed C-130J Hercules II and Lockheed L-1011 tanker transports.

In 1960, the company was appointed the sole Gulfstream service centre outside the US and in 1974 became the approved UK Cessna Citation service centre. Major overhauls and engine changes can be undertaken on both types and the company specialises in complete interior refits for corporate and personal jets.

In 1962, the company changed its trading name to Marshall of Cambridge (Engineering) Ltd and 1966 saw the company appointed as the UK technical centre in support of the sixty-six Lockheed C-130K Hercules transports purchased for the RAF. From this modest beginning in its association with the Hercules, the company became established as the first Lockheed appointed service centre and has carried out modification and repairs on the Hercules from up to seventy different operators involving over 1,250 different requirements for servicing and modification work. Subsequently, the company was awarded the support contract for twenty-four of the new RAF C-130J Hercules II variant of Lockheed's venerable workhorse. The company was involved in the proving trials of the Allison AE2100 turboprop engines and Dowty six-blade propellers for the new C-130J fitted to an RAF C-130K, serial XV181. Lockheed have estimated that £2.2 billion pounds of work would accrue to UK aerospace companies should the new aircraft attain its estimated worldwide sales of 700 aircraft. Among other notable technical achievements by Marshall Aerospace was the design and build of a space-sled for medical research that flew 121 orbits in the Space Shuttle *Challenger* in 1985.

Lockheed C-130K Hercules were delivered 'green' to Marshalls where they were prepared to meet RAF requirements and painted before delivery (note the white cockpit area cabin roof). (*Wings*)

RNetAF Lockheed C-130 Hercules I in fifty-fifth anniversary livery dispensing chaff for self-defence. Marshalls Aerospace is the official Lockheed-appointed European design authority for the Hercules I and undertake any specialised work on the type as well as routine servicing. (*Air Power International*)

In 1982, Marshall applied itself to the needs of the nation by executing the rapid conversion of a number of RAF Hercules aircraft to receive air-to-air refuelling by the addition of in-flight refuelling probes within twenty-one days of receiving the request in support of the Falklands conflict. In 1983, Marshall received a contract to convert six RAF Lockheed Tristar aircraft to the tanker/freighter/passenger role to a Marshall design. As a result, the company was appointed as the UK technical centre for Lockheed Tristar aircraft. An unusual project spawned from Marshall Tristar associations was the conversion of a L.1011 for the Orbital Sciences Corporation of California for the carriage of Pegasus, an airborne satellite launcher. The work entailed strengthening the airframe to carry the launcher and undertaking a number of

One RAF Lockheed TriStar was flown for several months with a fourth Rolls-Royce RB.211 engine fitted inboard under the starboard wing as a possible method of transporting spare engines to overseas locations. However, this experiment was not continued. (*Air Power International*)

Marshalls Aerospace as the European design authority for the Lockheed Tristar converted a number of RAF L1011 aircraft as tanker transports. (*Air Power International*)

structural and flight tests using a dummy.

As a result of the economic recession in the early 1990s, Marshall declined along with many other aerospace companies such as Lucas and Dowty, etc. However, The Marshall Group including Marshall Garages, Marshall Special Purpose Vehicles and Marshall Aerospace remains as Cambridge's largest single employer with some 2,500 employees. Marshall Aerospace employs between 1,100 and 1,200 people and is organised into three profit centres: the design centre, the maintenance and manufacturing division, and the hangars and airport. In the new millennium, Marshall are the credited Lockheed Hercules service agent for Europe and have maintained all of the RAF's

C-130Ks since the 1960s and the latest C-130J Hercules II now in service. The weather reconnaissance C-130 'Snoopy' has been reconverted to a standard C-130 to serve as an Airbus Military A400M transport engine development test bed and the original BAe-146-300 prototype regional jet was converted to assume Snoopy's role for the UK's Meteorological Office.

Martin-Baker

In 1929, Capt. James Martin (1893–1981), later Sir James Martin CBE, set about building his first aeroplane, the M.1, a side-by-side two-seater. Unfortunately, the onset of the Great Depression forced him to abandon his venture. However, in 1934, he joined forces with Capt. Valentine Baker by setting up Martin-Baker Aircraft Co. Ltd to produce the MB.1, an all-metal experimental two-seater based on the M.1. The MB.1 used a unique system of steel tube lattice girder construction evolved by James Martin and only one aircraft was built. The MB.1 was followed by the MB.2 fighter, serial P9594, fitted with a 1,000-hp Napier engine. The aircraft was built at Heston, Middlesex, to where the company had relocated in 1937 and it had its first flight on 3 August 1938. The company built a number of aircraft from 1934 to 1936 but none were selected for production. In 1939, the company built a single-seat, multi-gun monoplane fighter to an Air Ministry order. The machine made use of the Martin system of steel tube construction, yet nothing was to come of the venture. Two further prototype fighters were produced, the MB.3 and MB.5, before accepting an invitation by the Ministry of Aircraft Production to investigate the possibility of providing a practical means of escape for pilots from fighter planes. Turning its back on aircraft construction, Martin-Baker Aircraft Co. Ltd concentrated its resources on the development and production of ejection seats. The MB.3, fitted with a 2,000-hp Napier Sabre engine, was followed in 1946 by the MB.5 fitted with a 2,340-hp Rolls-Royce Griffon engine driving contra-rotating propellers. It was capable of attaining a top speed of 465 mph. After undertaking a number of successful test and trials flights, the MB.5 – which resembled the North American P-51 Mustang – was abandoned. The advent of the jet-propelled fighter negated any chance the MB.5 may have had of success.

The company now concentrated on the development of aircraft escape systems, namely the ejector seat. On 20 January 1945, company employee Benny Lynch volunteered to take part in experiments being shot 4 feet 8 inches high into a 16-foot static test rig. Subsequently as testing became increasingly vigorous and with one volunteer, a technical journalist, hospitalised with a crushed spinal vertebrae, the first dummy ejection in flight was made in a piston-engine Boulton Paul Defiant on loan from MAP and piloted by Brian Greenstead on 11 May 1945. A further six successful dummy ejections were made from the Defiant at varying speeds up to 300 mph. For tests at higher speeds, a Gloster Meteor F.3 jet fighter was greatly modified to fit ejection apparatus in the ammunition bay behind the pilot's cockpit. On 24 July 1946, Benny Lynch took part in the first live test firing of a Martin-Baker ejection seat at a speed of 320 mph at 8,000 feet.

Meanwhile, the US Navy was showing great interest in the work going on in the UK. Following a demonstration at the company's Denham Works, the US Navy placed an order for a 110-foot test rig to be erected at the NAF Yard in Philadelphia. It also asked for an ejection seat to be fitted to a Douglas A-26 Invader, which following a number of dummy ejections, the first successful live ejection was made at Lake Hurst on 1 November 1946 by Lt Furtek USN.

In the UK, and in a completely redesigned seat Mk.1 suitable for mass production, Lynch made a final ejection on 19 August 1947 at 420 mph at 12,000 feet with no ill effects. By June 1947, the authorities had decided that Martin-Baker ejection seats should be fitted to all new British service jet aircraft. Arrangements were immediately put in hand for fitment of the seat to the Meteor, Attacker, Wyvern and Canberra light bomber followed by the Sea Hawk and Venom. Later with higher speeds demanding further development and low-altitude ejections, the company used a modified dual-seat Gloster Meteor T.7, serial WL419, which has been used by Martin-Baker for the last fifty years in developing its successful range of ejection seats. Martin-Baker has delivered in excess of 70,000 ejection seats to eighty-eight air forces. Company records reveal that some 7,061 aircrew lives have been saved by Martin-Baker ejection seats on an average of two to three a week (until June 2004). Martin-Baker has a 75 per cent share of the Western market and 80 per cent of its sales are exported.

Miles Aircraft Ltd

Miles Aircraft Ltd was established by the brothers Frederick George Miles and George Herbert Miles in October 1943. They took over Phillip & Powis Aircraft Ltd, a public company established in March 1935 to manage the manufacturing operation of Phillip & Powis (Reading) Ltd that was established in 1931 at Woodley Aerodrome, Reading. Frederick George Miles (1903–1976) had become interested in aircraft after having been taught to fly by the pioneer Cecil Paisely in an Avro 504. He set about his first design, the Gnat, which he did not complete although it did lend its name to a flying school, Gnat Auto, with which Frederick George Miles was associated. Following on from Frederick George Miles' second design was the M.1 Satyr aerobatic biplane. A highly modified Avro Baby, the M.1 Satyr was built by Parnall at

Yate in Gloucestershire. Frederick George Miles became the chief designer at Phillips & Powis producing a number of designs for them before assuming control with his brother in 1943.

Their first design was the Miles M.2 Hawk that had its first flight on 29 March 1933. Miles designs fell into four categories: the Hawk, Magister, Messenger and Gemini. The Hawk was followed by the M.3 Falcon and the five-seat M.4 Merlin; all were powered by de Havilland Gipsy engine. Another racing monoplane was the M.5 Sparrowhawk. 1939 saw the enlargement of the Woodley factory to handle the large series order for the M.9 Master two-seat, high-speed advanced trainer monoplane powered by a 720-hp Rolls-Royce Kestrel XXX engine. The Kestrel/Master was Miles' first twin design. A total of 3,450 Miles Masters had been built when production ceased in 1942 to free the factory production lines for the high speed Miles Martinent TT target tug.

The design of the famous M.14 'Maggie' Magister owed much to the civil Cirrus Hawk series. A Hawk Major was supplied to the RAF in 1936 who were suitably impressed and went on to order a total of 1,293 examples for its Elementary and Reserve Flying Training Schools. Total Magister production was 1,303 including 100 built in Turkey. The Magister was at the time the only monoplane in the UK to be approved by the Air Ministry for ab initio instruction of RAF pilots and was used in RAF training establishments both at home and overseas. The success of the Master and the Magister meant Miles Aircraft Ltd had joined the 'big league' and became a limited company in 1936. Forty-five M.16 Mentors were supplied from 1938 to 1939 for use on radio instruction and communication duties. Miles Magister M.14A trainer, serial P6382, can be seen at The Shuttleworth Collection, Old Warden Aerodrome, near Biggleswade, Bedfordshire.

At the start of the Second World War, Miles were well placed in terms of production contracts with full order books for the Magister and Master designs. Frederick George Miles had become managing director as well as chief designer. However, as the business continued to expand and Frederick George was forced to spend more time on administrative duties, his brother was to take on the mantle of chief designer.

Frederick George, always keen to exploit a possibility, convinced MAP that it would be expedient to have a stop-gap fighter in case there were insufficient Spitfire and Hurricanes available to fully equip planned RAF fighter squadrons. But his initial design, the Miles M.20, was rejected as Frederick George proposed to use the Rolls-Royce Peregrine engine that had been reserved for the twin-engine Westland Whirlwind fighter. Also, production of the Peregrine had been cut to enable production of the Rolls-Royce Merlin to be stepped up. Undaunted, Frederick George persisted with his idea and having won approval from MAP, entrusted redesign of the aircraft, the Miles M.20/2, to Walter G. Capley.

In just nine weeks and two days, the prototype made its first flight at Woodley on 15 September 1940. The original M.20 owed much of its design to the Master 1 advanced trainer, but Capley eliminated the Master's cranked wing and added a Rolls-Royce Merlin XX engine giving the aircraft a top speed of 333 mph at 20,400 feet and was faster than the Hawker Hurricane I. However, after evaluation of the M.20/2 and its successor, a proposed naval fighter, the M.20/4, at A&AEE at Boscombe Down in April 1941, it was not seen as a success and as the Spitfire and Hurricanes were readily available, further development of the Miles M.20 was suspended.

The M.25 Martinet was the first RAF aircraft to be specifically designed as a target tug. Its design was based on the Master trainer which it superseded on the Woodley production lines in 1942. In 1941, a replacement for the 'Whitney Straight' was proposed, a training-liaison type with a retractable undercarriage and the M.28 Mercury was its unofficial name. However, as the aircraft had been developed and produced without MAP approval, Frederick George unfortunately found little support for his new design in official circles. Frederick George won the day when his famous M.38/M.48 Messenger, which first flew on 12 September 1942, was accepted for series production. The Messenger was an excellent AOP or communications aircraft for the RAF and a number were used in the Second World War by high ranking Allied commanders as personal transports. Field Marshal Montgomery had his own personal Miles Messenger with the military serial RG333.

In the early war years, Frederick George not wishing to become stereotyped as a designer of trainers and target tugs stepped up his interest in blended wing and aerofoil fuselages. He was fascinated by the theories of the Russian Voevodskii on the subject. By 1938, he had sketched a number of designs using the blended fuselage theory, but the Air Ministry showed little interest. Nevertheless, the undaunted Frederick George decided to go it alone and produced a number of designs to exploit his theories, the aircraft aptly named the X-Series. The Air Ministry, however, were unmoved and Frederick George was forced to concentrate his efforts on wartime production. A specification calling for a high-performance, twin-engine, target tug capable of meeting the diverse requirements of the RAF and the FAA was met with the usual enthusiasm by Miles. The result was the M.33 Monitor that was to have a disastrous effect on the company's fortunes when it was forced into receivership in 1946. MAP had placed orders for 600 M.33s and Frederick George in his usual optimism had set up the infrastructure to produce three times this amount, but only twenty series aircraft were produced. The M.35 Libellula that followed was a research aircraft for a revolutionary fleet fighter with a canard layout and single pusher engine. The aircraft was designed, built and flown in six weeks.

Miles M.14A Magister trainers were used by RAF elementary flying schools during the Second World War. This example is part of The Shuttleworth Trust Collection. (*Author*)

Designed as a target tug, the two-seat, wooden-structured Miles Martinet made its first flight in April 1942. In 1943, a radio-controlled version called the Queen Martinet was produced with sixty-five built. (*Flight Colour*)

On 26 August 1944, Miles Aircraft Ltd was awarded a contract against Specification E24/43 calling for a single-seat, experimental supersonic aircraft capable of speeds in excess of 1,000 mph. The work was to be carried out in association with Frank Whittle's Power Jets Ltd and two experimental aircraft were ordered, serials RT133 and RT136. The project was to give rise to the Miles M.52. A mock-up was built and amid great secrecy Frederick George set about designing his dream and was confident that the aircraft would be ready for flight tests in 1946. However, much to his horror, all work on the project was terminated with no explanation given in February 1946. All manner of speculative reasons have been expounded. One was it was too dangerous and put test pilot lives at risk. But it would appear that a short-sighted government took the decision purely on the grounds of cost, not realising the devastating effect it would have on Britain's cutting edge technological base and in terms of revenue lost in the field of design and development of high-speed aircraft.

Meanwhile, minds were concentrating on designs to keep the company in business on the cessation of hostilities in 1945. Frederick George proposed a twin-engine freighter that would have both civil and military applications also with a view to developing the aircraft into a four-engine variant. This produced the M.57 Aerovan light freighter. Unfortunately, Miles Aircraft Ltd once again fell victim of the Ministry of Aircraft Production by evolving another design without them knowing, resulting in an order going out to the company to stop all work on the project. The delay caused incalculable damage to the company and it never recovered losing its foothold in the market place for its aircraft.

Larger developments such as the M.68 Boxcar and M.71 Merchantman did not enter series production and a four-engine Aerovan, the M.72, was started but not finished. Another aircraft that was to help drive the final nail into Miles Aircraft Ltd was the M.60 Marathon, the requirement having emanated from the Brabazon Committee. It had been hoped that the Marathon would keep the company afloat after falling behind production of the short-lived Monitor series run, but the type was beset with design and development problems. With a lack of orders, the loss of the prototype led to the project being taken over by Handley Page who were to refine a larger variant of the M.73 into the Handley Page Herald. While still having a reasonable order book, the crippling cold winter of 1946-1947 resulted in a loss of production of its all-wood goods due to the plummeting temperatures.

In the spring of 1947, it was realised the company was in a desperate 'cash flow' situation. On 19 November 1947, the official receiver was called in and Miles Aircraft Ltd went into receivership. George Herbert Miles went to work for de Havilland at their Airspeed offices at Christchurch in the south of England for a time, helping to design the Vampire T.11 trainer. Frederick George Miles set up a new company, F. G. Miles Ltd, at Redhill, Surrey, in

1951, undertaking the assembly of unfinished Gemini aircraft and developing the M.75 Aries.

In 1953, F. G. Miles Ltd moved to Shoreham, Sussex, where he was joined by his brother George. The brothers now set themselves up as consultants and undertook 'special' development projects. They developed a neat jet trainer, the M.100 Student, which made its first flight on 15 May 1957. However, it failed to attract orders from the market it was aimed at, losing out to the Hunting Jet Provost.

In 1961, most of the Miles designs were absorbed into Beagle including the M.114 that became the Beagle Pup. The last Miles type was the M.218 four-seat, light twin that flew at Shoreham, Sussex, on 19 August 1962. The M.218 was a new Gemini for the 1960s employing much fibreglass in its construction. However, Beagle chose not to develop it and opted for the Bristol Type 220 which became the Type 206 Beagle Basset.

National Aircraft Factories

In October 1917 after much deliberation, it was announced that in order to meet increased demands for military aircraft, three new aircraft works to be known as National Aircraft Factories were to be built at Waddon near Croydon. However, only the National Aircraft Factory was built. NAF No. 2 was eventually set up at Heaton Chapel, Stockport, in a requisitioned factory taken over while under construction and NAF No. 3 was never started. The site chosen for NAF No. 1 was 240 acres of farmland that lay to the east of Beddington Aerodrome, later to become Croydon Aerodrome, near the village of Purley. It was proposed that land to the west of the new factory site known as New Barn Farm should be levelled to provide a flying field for test flying and proving of new aircraft. The airfield was soon known as Waddon Aerodrome. The new factory was to be constructed by one of the country's leading building contractors at the time, W. Cubitt & Co. It was estimated that the three new factories would cost in the region of £1.5 million, a tremendous sum at the time. Official approval for the project was given on 16 September 1917 and work commenced on 20 September. The complex was to consist of a total of fifty-eight single-storey buildings covering a total area of 645,483 square feet of floor space. A quarter of a million square feet of glass was used in the construction of the roof so as to provide the plant with plenty of natural light. As it happened, it was impossible to provide the plant with any 'black out protection'.

The complex was also to be served by its own rail track, about half a mile in length, complete with two sidings giving direct access for delivery of materials such as timber, engines and airscrews. As each building was completed and machines installed, workers were engaged and production got under way.

In this way, production commenced on 15 January 1918 and by 14 March 1918, the first series production aircraft was completed: an Airco DH.9, serial D451, day bomber. The first of an order batch of 500, it would appear that only 276 examples were built. Two hundred and forty-one were completed within a year. Serial D451 was flown to the Aircraft Acceptance Park by Capt. Frank Barnard who was to become closely associated with Croydon Airport in its pioneering days. The whole factory complex was completed in record time by July 1918.

While the plant had continued under fairly arduous conditions with completion of the complex going on around staff as they worked, DH.9s continued to be built at a rapid rate. On 5 June 1918, an order for the production of a new type was received: the Handley Page O/400. The order was for 100 bombers, serials F5349-F5448, to be powered by American Liberty engines against an anticipated shortfall of Rolls-Royce Eagle VIII engines. In the event with the signing of the armistice in November 1918 bringing the First World War to an end, the NAF failed to build one complete O/400 bomber. Serial F5349 was constructed by American personnel at Ford Airfield for use by the US Signal Corps. The aircraft was subsequently flight tested at Cricklewood.

With the official closure of the factory on 31 December 1918, some 1,000 of 1,500 staff were dismissed while wages were drastically cut. These actions were to bring about mass demonstrations at Croydon Town Hall. Nonetheless, the fact remained that the factory and its output of new aircraft were no longer needed. The original O/400 order was cut to seventy examples and the last three of the previous batch, serials F5414, F5417 and F5418, were moved to Cricklewood for final assembly and testing before assuming civil registrations. From its auspicious start in the middle of 1917 within less than two years, NAF No. 1 had become the ignominious Salvage Depot for the storage and disposal of huge stocks of used and unused materials, airframes, engines, spares, components and accessories offered for sale by the newly created Aircraft Disposal Board. Items for disposal were grouped in four main categories: A-new, B-used, C-second-hand (serviceable) and D-scrap. Complete engines were carefully overhauled, thoroughly cleaned and stored with the crankshafts turned over at regular intervals. Nearly 1,000 aircraft were stored at NAF No. 1. Having been carefully stored, any potential owner could have the airframe of their choice assembled, tested and flown away from the adjacent airfield. Another function undertaken by the Salvage Depot was the acceptance and breaking of trainloads of smashed and damaged aeroplanes from the Western Front and elsewhere in the country. Nothing was wasted. Every part of the aeroplane was stripped down to the nuts and bolts and other metal fittings.

In 1920, Sir Handley Page acting on information received from a contemporary reporter made a bid for the Salvage Depot. This bid was accepted and on 4 March 1920, the new Aircraft Disposal Company Ltd was registered with a capital of £600. Within a fortnight, Handley Page Ltd was appointed as its sole agent. Furthermore, Handley Page Ltd on registration of its new Aircraft Disposals Company Ltd issued debentures to the value of £1,080,000 charged against the company's property, the purchase price of the stock being valued at £1,000,000 plus 50 per cent of all profits on the eventual sale of more than 10,000 airframes, 30,000 aero engines and other stores including 1,000 tonnes of ball bearings, 100,000 magnetos and 350,000 spark plugs. Also, Aircraft Disposals Company Ltd immediately engaged three test pilots: H. H. Perry, Maurice Piercy and R. H. Stockton. In addition, on 14 May 1920, it presented King Albert of Belgium with two suitably modified Bristol F.2bs for his personal use. By 15 July 1925, £1.25 million had been paid to the Treasury as part of the profit sharing agreement. In spite of this, Handley Page Ltd needed to inject some £179,000 of its own cash into the company to permit its recovery after spending in the region of £800,000 in an abortive attempt to establish air transport services to India, South Africa and Brazil. The following is a representative list of complete airframes advertised for disposal by Aircraft Disposals Company Ltd, *c.* 1920:

Armstrong Whitworth FK8
C8633, C8634 and C8673: built by Armstrong Whitworth at Newcastle-on-Tyne.
F3465/F3473: built by Angus Sandeson & Co.

Avro 504K
E505: built by Harland & Wolff Ltd, Belfast.
E944: built by Grahame-White Aviation Company Ltd.
H2062: built by Sunbeam Motor Car Company Ltd.
H2517: built by parent.
H9730/H9809: built by Grahame-White Aviation Company Ltd, Hendon.

Bristol F2B
H1307, H1308, H1331, H1364, H1365, H1372, H1373, H1374, H1379 and H1380 built by parent company.

De Havilland DH.9
F1259/F1270: built by Waring and Gillow Ltd, Hammersmith.
H5575, H5576, H5834, H5839 and H5851: built by Alliance Aeroplane Co., Hammersmith.
H9174, H9195 and H9350: built by parent at Stagg Lane, Hendon.

De Havilland DH.10
E5470: built by parent at Hendon.

Sopwith 7F1 Snipe
E6535: built by Boulton Paul.
H367, H368, H369 and H372: built by Ruston Proctor.
J452, J453, J455, J456, J457, J460, J462 and J465: built by Boulton Paul.

In 1923, Aircraft Disposals Company Ltd bought the manufacturing rights, goodwill and stock of Martinsdyne Ltd, Woking, with a view to building its F-4 single-seater as a scout in competition with Armstrong Whitworth's Siskin. The aircraft was fitted with a 385-hp Armstrong Siddeley Jaguar radial engine and before its first flight from Croydon on 11 October 1924, was redesignated as the ADC.1. In spite of its superior speed of 163 mph over its competitors, it was not selected for the RAF requirement although in 1926, eight examples were sold to Latvia. In 1926, a Nimbus-powered variant appeared and two were built with the civil registrations G-EBOJ and G-EBOL. Although the former was modified in 1927 by adding a faired 'cleaned up' cylinder head and undercarriage in an attempt to make it more appealing to potential operators, none were sold.

By this time, it had become clear that the days of Aircraft Disposals Company Ltd were numbered. It had passed its peak of activities by far and in 1930, all trading had ceased and the remaining tasks was to 'break up' Aircraft Disposals Company Ltd and the two Nimbus-powered prototypes. Manufacture of the Cirrus engine continued for almost four years at Croydon until the takeover by Blackburn marked its move to Hull. The former buildings of the National Aircraft Factory, NAF No. 1, were taken over for other industrial purposes.

Percival Aircraft

Capt. Edgar W. Percival's (1897–1984) first attempt at aircraft design was the Saro-Percival Mailplane that led to sixteen Spartan Cruiser aircraft. In 1932, this resulted in the three-seat, low-wing Gull. Twenty-four Percival Gulls were built by George Parnall & Co. at Yate Aerodrome. The success of the Gull led Capt. Percival to establish the Percival Aircraft Co. Ltd in association with Lt-Cdr E. W. B. Leake by setting up their own manufacturing facility in 1934 at Gravesend, Kent. The early Cirrus Hermes IV-engined Gulls were followed by the Gull Major and Gull Six with DH Gipsy Major and Gipsy VI engines respectively. A specially-built racer, the P.6 Mew Gull, was derived from the

P.2. The first of the Vega Gulls appeared in November 1935 and fifteen were impressed into military service in the Second World War.

In 1937, Percival relocated its works to Luton Airport, Bedfordshire. Concurrent with its move to Luton, the company introduced its Q6 Petrel followed by the very successful Proctor navigation trainer and communications aircraft both based on the Vega Gull. The Proctor was so successful that 1,154 were built in total with 437 examples produced by F. Hills and Sons of Manchester. The all-metal P.48 Merganser, which led to the twelve-passenger P.50 Prince medium feeder-liner, was first flown on 13 May 1948. The basic P.50 was developed into the P.54 Survey Prince and the military P.66 Pembroke/Sea Prince for the Royal Navy and the six-seat executive President. In 1944, Percival Aircraft was acquired by the Hunting Group and W. A. 'Bill' Summers, who had resigned before the outbreak of war, returned as managing director. He replaced Capt. Peter Ackland who had run the company since the resignation of Capt. Percival. Under the new management, the letter designation of the projects was dropped in favour of the numbers prefixed by the letter 'P', thus the Prentice became the P.40 and the Proctor V, although an earlier product, but still being built when the Hunting Group assumed control, was allocated the P.44 project number. The sales manager, Y. Galitzine, allocated 'P' numbers to all previous designs from the Gull onwards as well as all paper designs that were never built, purely to record all project designations of the Hunting Group.

Edgar Percival, having left Hunting Percival, started a new company at Stapleford Tawney, Essex, where he set about building his EP9 agricultural aircraft. Twenty-one were built before he sold the business to Samlesbury Engineering who was to reform in 1960 as the Lancashire Aircraft Co. producing a further twenty-eight EP9s up until 1963. Named as the Prospector, a number were exported to Australia. In 1954, the company was renamed Hunting Percival Aircraft Ltd and in 1957, Hunting dropped the 'Percival' from its title and another famous name disappeared from British aviation industry history.

Royal Aircraft Factory

The first design from the Royal Aircraft Factory (RAF) at Farnborough, Hampshire, was the de Havilland No. 2. It was a design that the War Office had purchased from Geoffrey de Havilland for the sum of £400 when he joined the RAF as an assistant designer and test pilot in December 1910. It was redesignated as the FE.1 by way of its similarity in appearance to the Farman Experimental FE aircraft. At the time de Havilland joined the Royal Aircraft Factory, it had already embarked on the design of six basic types while under the auspices of Her Majesty's Balloon Factory who had not been authorised to build aircraft. The six design categories were as follows:

BE (Bleriot Experimental tractor type)
BS (Bleriot Scout fast single-seat tractor)
FE (Farman Experimental pusher)
RE (Reconnaissance Experimental two-seat tractor)
SE (Santos Experimental tail-first or canard)
TE (Tatin Experimental propeller behind tail)

On 1 April 1911, the Army Aircraft Factory, as a section of the Royal Engineers Balloon Group, was established becoming 'Royal' exactly one year later. Geoffrey de Havilland's FE.1 had crashed, but was rebuilt with a 50-hp Gnôme engine and redesignated as the Fe.2. In 1913, it was fitted with a 70-hp Renault engine, but crashed again in 1914. Meanwhile, de Havilland had prepared a new design based on the Fe.2 but it bore little resemblance to it. Designated as the Fe.2a, it was designed as a fighter from the outset so that 'FE' now stood for 'Fighting Experimental' although the 'FE' was of a pusher configuration. Twelve aircraft were immediately ordered for the Royal Flying Corps powered by a 100-hp Green engine. In the event, it was underpowered and modified to accept the 120-hp or 160-hp Beardmore engines giving rise to the Fe.2b that was used experimentally on night-flying duties during 1915 and 1916. This was followed by the special short-distance night-bombing unit, No. 100 Squadron RFC, which was formed and sent to France in March 1917. The bombers made effective attacks on aerodromes and railway stations, and production of the aircraft, which had been allowed to run down, was stepped up. With the fitment of the 250-hp Rolls-Royce Eagle engine, the type emerged as the Fe.2d that could carry 340 lbs of bombs and was one of the few aircraft armed with Vickers 'pom-pom' guns for use against trains. Nearly 1,500 Fe.2s were built and they remained in service until the end of the First World War. A number of Fe.2ds was built by Boulton Paul including serials A6351-6570 and B1851-1900.

The next designs of note from the Royal Aircraft Factory were the Be.2a/b reconnaissance aircraft. Designed by Maj. Frederick Green and Geoffrey de Havilland, the prototype Be.2 was flown by de Havilland at the military trials of 1912. The Be.2a/b were pure reconnaissance types, but the next design, the famous Be.2c, had been strongly influenced by Edward Teshmaker Busk who was the assistant physicist at the Royal Aircraft Factory. Busk closely studied the flying characteristics of the Be.2a and had compiled the first data on the stability and flight characteristics of an aeroplane, much of which was used in the design of the Be.2c. These Be.2 variants were without doubt the best aircraft used by the Royal Flying Corps in France during the First World War. However, with the introduction by the Germans of the forward-firing Fokker Eindecker E.III scout, the Be.2s suffered horrific losses. Converted Home

Defence single-seat fighters armed with an upward-firing Lewis machine gun proved to be highly successful, its inherent stability being a distinct advantage on night-flying operations when the aircraft were frequently used as bombers. Of the 1,300 Be.2cs and 2ds delivered to the Royal Flying Corps and Royal Navy Air Service, only three Be.2cs survived the war.

From the Be.2c, the Royal Aircraft Factory created two further successful variants: the Be.2d and the Be.2e. The former was externally similar to the Be.2c, but fitted with dual controls and featured a revised fuel system that incorporated an external gravity tank under the port upper wing linked to a tank in the fuselage top decking. By the autumn of 1915, four batches of Be.2ds were on order, two batches to be built by the British and Colonial Aeroplane Co. (later Bristol) and one each from Vulcan and Rushton, and Proctor. Many of these aircraft were modified either during or immediately after production to have the unequal-span mainplanes introduced with the Be.2e. The improved performance of the prototype Be.2es – which were flying before production Be.2ds became available – prompted large-scale orders of this variant and deliveries to the Western Front commenced in June 1916 and continued well into 1917. By this time, however, technological advances in aerial warfare and equipment meant that the Be.2e was no match for the well-armed German Halberstadt and Albatros fighters. Having seen service in the Middle East, India, Macedonia and Palestine as well as in Britain with the Home Defence squadrons where they struggled against Zeppelin airships and Gotha bombers, they remained in service until the armistice where most Be.2 aircraft were relegated to the training role. The Be.8 was a rotary-engine derivative of the Be.2, the prototype of which is thought to have flown in early 1913. To meet demands from the War Office for a single-seat fighter, the Royal Aircraft Factory adapted a Be.2c to form the Be.12 that in turn inspired the Be.12ae by adding a top wing similar to that on the Be.2e. This was found to do little to improve the type's performance and the design was soon reverted to that of the Be.12a followed by the Be.12b night-fighter version powered by a 200-hp Hispano-Suiza engine. In 1915, two newcomers to the Royal Aircraft Factory, S. J. Waters and Henry Folland, were tasked with designing a ground-attack aircraft. This gave rise to the Fe.4a, a large twin-pusher biplane of which only two examples were produced as it was declared obsolete by its first flight; however, one of the prototypes, serial 7993, did spend some time with the Central Flying School.

In spite of the War Office's continued reluctance to recognise the possibilities of using the aeroplane as a bomber and that this type of mission was not as yet regularly undertaken by the fledgling Royal Flying Corps, the Royal Aircraft Factory in its wisdom decided to develop a bomber. This ultimately resulted in the production of twenty-four Re.5 reconnaissance-bombers at Farnborough. To date, this was the largest series run for the Royal Aircraft Factory who had

The Se.5a was arguably the best Allied fighter of the First World War with a total of 5,205 built. (*Flight Colour*)

The last remaining airworthy Se.5a, serial F904/H, belongs to The Shuttleworth Trust Museum and was rebuilt in the early 1960s by RAE Farnborough apprentices. (*Aviation News*)

previously subcontracted work out. The aircraft was a tractor design fitted with a 120-hp Austro-Daimler, water-cooled, inline engine. Four aircraft – the fifth, sixth, twelfth and thirteenth examples – were single-seaters and sometimes unofficially referred to as Re.5As. By the outbreak of war, some fifteen aircraft had been built with production totalling twenty-five when the Re.5/Re.5A was superseded by a new variant, the Re.7, of which around 252 were built, once again by subcontractors.

The Re.8 reconnaissance bomber, nicknamed the Harry Tate, did not owe any allegiance in its development to the Re.5 or Re.7 and evolved from a RFC requirement to meet the ever increasing threat from German fighting scouts. It was of all-wood construction and incorporated a number of features from the earlier Be.2e and Be.12. Two prototypes were built, the first, serial 7996, was flown by the Royal Aircraft Factory's chief pilot on 17 June 1916. Of the 3,000 Re.8s built, about 67 per cent saw service on the Western Front, being the most widely used reconnaissance type flown by the RFC. While satisfactory as an artillery spotter when used on reconnaissance duties, it offered little improvement over the Be.2 it had replaced. Also, its distinct lack of manoeuvrability, which made it extremely vulnerable to enemy fighters, was marred by a number of fatal accidents with aircraft mysteriously entering into a spin at low altitude. On hitting the ground nose first, the engine would be pushed back into the fuselage, rupturing the fuel tanks and setting the aircraft on fire. However, subsequent investigations revealed that the main cause of the accidents, although probably aggravated by frequent failure of the RAF's 4a engine, was 'pilot error' brought about by inadequate training. Later with various modifications, including greatly improved armaments by 1918, the Re.8 was in service with no less than nineteen squadrons and despite its shortcomings, when flown by a well trained and experienced crew, it could hold its own and adequately defend itself in aerial combat.

The Royal Aircraft Factory's BS.1 tractor scout that crashed in March 1913 was rebuilt as the BS.2. This was redesignated as the SE.2 Scout Experimental and with further minor changes and modifications led to the SE.2a. Only one SE.2a was built although it did serve with the RFC for a while over the Western Front proving beyond any doubt the soundness of the design. The SE.2a eventually gave rise to the superb Se.5/Se.5a designed by Henry Folland, John Kenworthy, and Frank Goodden, but not before Folland had applied himself to designing the fastest aeroplane of the era, the Se.4. It attained a top speed of 135 mph and was the fastest aircraft of its time. The Se.4 was followed by the Se.4a in an attempt to develop the Se.4 for series production, but only four examples were built. In 1915, the War Office had ordered fifty 150-hp V8 liquid-cooled, inline Hispano-Suiza engines designed by Swiss engineer Marc Birkigt. The outstanding success of the Royal Aircraft Factory's excellent Se.5 fighter owes much to the War Office's undoubted foresight in acquiring manufacturing rights of this engine. A total of 5,205 Se.5as were built serving twenty-four RFC and RAF squadrons. When the First World War ended, the RAF had about 2,700 of these superb fighters in service. A much modified variant, the Se.5b, was built but not did not develop further nor did it enter series production.

In its short history, the Royal Aircraft Factory produced 533 series aircraft of twenty-eight different types. With the formation of the Royal Air Force on 1 April 1918, the factory was renamed Royal Aircraft Establishment RAE and from then on was to devote itself to purely research and test activities leaving design and development of aeroplanes to commercial companies.

S. E. Saunders – Saunders-Roe – Saro

Having established the famous Avro company in 1928 with his brother, Alliott Verdon Roe left the company and joined forces with John Lord in acquiring a controlling interest in S. E. Saunders Ltd, a small company at East Cowes on the Isle of Wight. The proximity of the company to the sea led unsurprisingly to a main interest in amphibious aircraft which was to become the speciality of Henry Knowler. At the age of twenty-three, Knowler had become S. E. Saunders' chief designer, a role he was to later to assume with the new formed Saunders-Roe Ltd and which he was to occupy for the next twenty-nine years.

The first aircraft produced by Saunders-Roe Ltd was the Saro A.17 Cutty Sark, a twin-engine, four-seat flying boat introduced in July 1929. However, prior to this, Knowler had designed a 'multi-gun' fighter prototype, the Saro A.10, which was a private venture design aimed at the plethora of fighter specifications issued by the Air Ministry during the 1926-1928 period. The A.10 had its first flight on 10 January 1929, but after experiencing a number of cooling problems with its radiator situated under the engine crankcase, the project was abandoned. Knowler's next venture into fighter design was the SR.A/1 flying-boat fighter that appeared at Cowes for its first flight in July 1947. In the meantime, the company were to produce a larger Cutty Sark variant, the A.19 Saro Cloud, of which twenty-one were built, seventeen for the RAF and four for civil use. The Saro Cloud was well liked by the RAF and was adopted as an amphibian crew trainer and had a spacious fully enclosed crew cabin with plenty of room for chart tables with an uninterrupted view of the ground afforded by its high-wing layout. The Cloud was followed in the post-war period by the A.21 Windhover, the successful Saro A.27 London reconnaissance biplane and Saro S.36 Lerwick. The latter was superseded by the only all Saro design to emerge in the Second World War, the half-scale Model A.37 Shrimp that was subsequently cancelled. The Second World War saw Saunders-Roe heavily involved in major subcontract work for Supermarine.

In all, 461 Supermarine Walrus amphibious biplanes (191 with wooden

Supermarine Walrus four-seat amphibians were used extensively during the Second World War by the RAF on ASR duties. Its single 775-hp Bristol Pegasus VI radial piston engine was set high up between the planes to protect it against sea water. (*Warplane Collection*)

The Saro SRA.1A Squirt jet flying-boat fighter was built to an Air Ministry specification for a small jet fighter to be used in a planned 'island hopping' campaign in the Far East should the war continue beyond 1945. (*Author*)

hulls) and 250 Sea Otters were built under licence. Also undertaken was the conversion of many American Lend-Lease flying boats to British standards, mostly carried out at Beaumaris, Anglesey, North Wales. (Later, a less venerable site was selected to carry out these vital tasks in the Menai Straits near the suspension bridge with deep water and a safe mooring area with a reasonable amount of shelter.) A small estate nearby called Friars about a mile from the town of Beaumaris was selected to locate the factory and a new slipway was built to give access to the water. The Beaumaris site handled over 300 Consolidated Catalina flying boats carrying out various modifications such as the installation of armament, radio equipment, ASV radar and Leigh-Lights.

The cancelled A.37 was reconfigured to meet Saro and Short Bros' solution to Specification R.14/40, the Short S.35 Shetland with Saro responsible for some design and construction of the wing. Only two Shetlands were built and as the first aircraft, serial DX166, did not appear until late 1945 by which time the type was no longer needed, the project was abandoned. After the war, wide rationalisation took place at Saro's Isle of Wight plant as demand for military aircraft plummeted, although the boat-building side grew in strength along with many other interests. However, the late 1940s and early 1950s saw a remarkable procession of aircraft designs emerge from the company. The first had originated as a result of wartime Specification E.6/44 for a single-seat, fighter flying boat: the Squirt. The Saro SRA.I had been intended for use in the Pacific theatre for use against the Japanese. It was to be capable of operating in sheltered coastal waters in a series of planned 'island hopping' operations. As it happens, only three Squirts were built, serials TG263, TG267 and TG271. The latter is displayed at Duxford, Cambridge, IWM, and the other two were lost in accidents. Although the third aircraft, TG271, was fitted with the larger thrust Metropolitan-Vickers Beryl M.VB.2 engine, armament of four 30-mm cannon and a good turn of speed at 516 mph in 1950, further development was abandoned.

Throughout the war, Saunders-Roe continued to carry out studies on ever larger flying boats, both military and civil. This and the Brabazon Committee's post-war, civil air transport suggestions gave rise to the giant SR.45 Princess flying boat accommodating some 200 passengers. The Princess was powered by ten 3,780-hp Bristol Proteus 600 propeller-turbines, eight of them coupled. It had a span of 67 metres (219 feet), and with a capacity of 14,500 gallons of fuel housed in integral tanks in the inner wings, the aircraft weighed in at 156,492 kg (345,000 lbs). The aircraft was a formidable technical achievement for what was by now a relatively small company, although by this time Knowler had been joined by Arthur Gouge from Short Bros. However, in spite of progress on both airframe and powerplant design, the programme slipped and with ever escalating costs and the project grossly overspent with no potential customers, all work was cancelled in the mid-

Saro Skeeter Mk 12s were used by the British Army for observation and communication duties *c*. 1958. (*Postcard*)

1950s. Of the three airframes completed, only one flew, civil-registration G-ALUN, and in spite of innumerable attempts to resurrect and re-engineer the aircraft, eventually all work on the project ceased.

The demise of the flying boat as a civil transport had a profound effect on Saro and January 1951 saw some rapid diversification occurring at the Cowes plant with the formation of the Helicopter Division after the takeover of the Eastleigh-based Cierva Autogiro Company.

Using the Cierva W.14 as a base and after a long period of development, the company produced the Saro Skeeter, a single-engine, light helicopter that provided the company with its biggest series production run to emanate from one of its own designs. Seventy-four examples were built, sixty-four for the British Army Air Corps, six for the German Army and four for the German Navy. The company's subsequent helicopter design, the all-metal, five-seat P.531 was taken over by Westland in 1959 and was produced in two variants for the Army Air Corp as the Scout and for the Royal Navy as the very successful Wasp. In 1952, Knowler had become technical director and Maurice Joseph Brennan had been appointed chief designer. As well as a marine aircraft expert, Brennan had acquired a great deal of knowledge of rocketry which was to be extremely useful when in February 1952, Air Ministry Specification F.124T called for a rocket-powered, target-defence interceptor. Eventually in May 1953, an order was placed for three Saro prototypes to the amended F.138D Specification. This was to influence the production of two

SR.53 aircraft and a more refined SR.177 to meet the shift in the requirement towards a more comprehensive interceptor to include AI radar and infrared homing missiles. In September 1956, an order for twenty-seven SR.177s was placed with the eventual planned procurement of at least 300 to be shared by the RAF and Royal Navy; however, the notorious 1957 Defence White Paper saw the sudden cancellation of the programme with the Ministry of Supply withdrawing all support for the project dealing a shattering blow to Saro from which it never fully recovered. As with the English Electric/BAC TSR.2, the completed airframes were cut up, an instruction believed to have been issued by Prime Minister Wilson who is quoted to have said 'There must be absolutely no chance that these projects can ever be resurrected in the future.'

Meanwhile, flight testing of the Saro SR.53 continued due to an interest shown by the West German Government until the second aircraft, serial XD151, was destroyed when it crashed in June 1958 killing its pilot John Booth. In March 1959, Brennan resigned. While the company's helicopter interests were taken over by Westland Helicopters Ltd of Yeovil, Somerset, a smaller portion of the company was acquired by de Havilland.

Scottish Aviation Ltd – Jetstream

Scottish Aviation Ltd (SAL) was formed in June 1935 at Prestwick Aerodrome, Scotland, primarily to run a new airport. A flying school was established and the company later moved into aircraft repair work. The main exponents were the Marquis of Clydesdale (who led the first flight over Everest on 3 April 1933) and David McIntyre who were both enthusiastic aviators. In 1938, the company moved into the repair, maintenance and modification field as well as subcontract work. In July 1940, SAL received instructions to assemble sixteen US-built aircraft at Abbotsinch supplied under the Lend-Lease Agreement that were followed by a number of Grumman, Northrop, Chance-Vought and Curtiss fighters. In November 1940, SAL took on responsibilities for servicing and modification of all landplanes ferried across the Atlantic from the US. At Prestwick, SAL worked on Lend-Lease Liberators, Dakotas, Mitchell B-25s, Hudsons and Boeing B-17 Flying Fortress aircraft. As many as thirty aircraft would sometimes arrive overnight. The company was also responsible for receiving aircraft ferried across from Newfoundland. Initially, aircraft were received at Greenock on the Clyde where SAL were operating a facility overhauling and preparing flying boats for the RAF. SAL had another facility at Largs in Strathclyde, which by 1943, was the reception base for all Lend-Lease flying boats arriving in the UK including Consolidated Catalinas and Martin Mariners. Also in 1943-1944, SAL produced fifty DH Queen Bee radio-controlled target drones for the RAF which were licensed-assembled from de Havilland.

After the Second World War, SAL worked on the conversion of ex-military aircraft, mainly Douglas C-47 transports, for the UK's aviation transport industry. SAL was to later maintain and overhaul Canadair F-86 Sabres used by the RAF in Germany and Lockheed F-104 Starfighters used by many European air forces at the time. The company also entered into the design and development of aircraft in response to Air Ministry Specification 4/45 for a light communications airplane capable of operating from confined airfields and landing strips. This led to the appearance of the three-seat, high-wing monoplane, serial VL515, powered by a DH Gipsy Queen 34 engine. This was the predecessor to the more famous Scottish Pioneer that started life as the four-seat civil variant, the Pioneer I. On fitment of the more powerful 520-hp Alvis Leonides engine, it became the Pioneer II, the prototype of which first flew in June 1950. The aircraft had excellent STOL characteristics, taking off in 75 yards with a landing run of only 66 yards. Forty were ordered by the RAF under the designation C.C.1. The success of the single-engine Pioneer led to the development of the distinctive larger twin-engine, triple-tailed Twin Pioneer that first flew on 25 June 1955 with the first military 'Twin Pin' flying on 29 August 1957. In total, fifty-nine Pioneers and eighty-seven Twin Pioneers were produced. Forty Twin Pioneers were delivered to the RAF and SAL also built Lockheed C-130 Hercules parts for the RAF's order of sixty-six aircraft. It is of interest that it was a Scottish Aviation 'Twin Pin' that fired the RAF's first air-to-air missile.

The closure of Handley Page in 1970 led to Scottish Aviation – after a short spell under the auspices of Jetstream Aircraft Ltd between 1970 and 1972 – taking over the development and production of the HP Jetstream light-transport aircraft along with the Beagle Bulldog primary trainer with the demise of Beagle Aircraft in December 1969. On 29 April 1977, Scottish Aviation was nationalised and became part of British Aerospace.

Short Bros – Short & Harland Ltd. – Shorts Bombardier

Short Bros was the oldest established firm of aeroplane designers and producers in the UK. It was founded in 1898 by three brothers, Albert Eustace (1875–1932), Horace Leonard (1872–1917) and Hugh Oswald (1883–1969), their interest in flight stemmed from the earliest days of ballooning. Indeed, for some years their work centred on the manufacture of spherical balloons. Short Brothers (Rochester & Bedford) Ltd was formally established in November 1908 from which time they have featured prominently in the history of British aviation. Their first aeroplane was based on the Wright Flyer but it did not

After the Second World War, the Short Sunderland flying boat was upgraded for civilian use as the Short Sandringham. (*Wings*)

fly. They had more success with the six licence-built Flyers they produced in 1910-1911. They also produced a biplane of original design for J. T. C. Moore-Brabazon that was the first all-British aeroplane to fly over a one-mile course and winning a £1,000 first prize for its owner. Initial interests centred on biplanes such as the S.27 that was based on a Henri Farman design. This was followed by the first British aircraft to carry military serials – No. 1 being the Short S.34 pusher, No. 2 the Short S.38, No. 3 the S.39 'Triple Twin', No. 4 the S.47 'Triple Tractor' and No. 5 the S.45. These aircraft were used to establish the Naval Flying School at Eastchurch, Kent, in 1911.

In 1911, Short's long association with seaplanes started, the company building a number of successful torpedo-carrying seaplanes. The first new seaplane to be produced almost immediately after the death of Horace Short on 6 April 1917 was the Short N.2B designed by Francis Webber under the supervision of Oswald Short. Although eight prototypes were ordered, only two were built, serials N66 and N67. One of Short's most successful First World War aircraft was the two-seat reconnaissance, bombing and torpedo-carrying seaplane, the Short Type 184. The Type 184 has the distinction that it was the first aircraft in the world to sink an enemy ship by means of a torpedo attack. The idea of a torpedo-carrying aircraft for the RNAS came from Cdr Murray F. Sueter, later Rear-Adr. Sir Murray Sueter, who was Director of the Air Department of the Admiralty in the formative years of the RNAS. Early versions of the Type 184 were known as the '225', the horse power of the engine. Later, up-rated versions with 260-hp Sunbeam engines were known as 'Dover Types'. Final builds introduced in 1918 were powered by 275-hp Sunbeam Maori III engines. The Type 184 was noted for its outstanding

The Short Skyvan was sold to a number of small overseas air forces for light transport and liaison duties. (*Aviation News*)

Short Sherpa C.23A two/three-crew utility transports were ordered by the USAFE for their European 10th Military Airlift Squadron based in West Germany and the type remains in service with the USAF having been returned by the US Army. (*Aviation News*)

reconnaissance flights during the Battle of Jutland in May 1916. A landplane bomber variant served with No. 3 Wing of the RNAS in 1916-1917. Total Short Type 184 production amounted to some 900 aircraft.

Between the wars, having survived the post-war slump by turning to boat building and coachwork in the 1920s, a long line of highly successful all-metal flying boats were built by Short. These designs prompted the Silver Streak landplane that first flew on 20 August 1920. One of the company's earliest flying boats was the Short S.8 Calcutta used on British commercial air services from 1928 onwards. The Calcutta was designed by Arthur Gouge based on experience gained with the Singapore 1 of 1926. A Singapore 1 was loaned by the Air Ministry to Sir Alan Cobham, founder of Cobham Plc, for his 23,000-mile flight around Africa in 1927-1928. In 1930, the Singapore II appeared although it did not enter series production. However, in March 1935, the Singapore III entered production with thirty-seven examples delivered to the RAF. The Calcutta gave rise to a military derivative: the Rangoon long-range reconnaissance flying boat for the RAF. This was closely followed by the S.17 Kent, an enlarged four-engine development of the Calcutta that first flew on 24 February 1931. The S.14 Sarafand flew on 30 June 1922 and was the second largest flying boat in the world after the Dornier Do X. At the same time, Short produced a number of landplanes such as the S.16 Scion feeder-liner and many civil variants were impressed into military use in the Second World War including the Scion Senior and Scylla, a landplane derivative of the S.17 Kent flying boat.

Having received an order from Imperial Airways for fourteen flying boats (later increased to twenty-eight), the S.23 C-Class Empire four-engine commercial flying boat appeared in July 1936. Eventually, thirty-nine Empires were delivered to Imperial Airways. Other developments of the C-Class Empire were the larger S.30 fitted with the new Bristol Perseus XIIC sleeve-valve engine and the S.26 G-Class launched in June 1939. Three S.26 G-Class aircraft were taken over by the Air Ministry at the outbreak of war and converted for military use. One, the Golden Fleece, was lost on active service.

In June 1936, Short Bros Ltd in collaboration with Harland and Wolff Ltd, the well-known Belfast shipbuilders, formed a new company known as Short & Harland Ltd. The Second World War forced the closure of the Rochester works as it was considered too small as well as being located beside the River Medway and vulnerable to German attacks, especially as a number of direct hits had occurred. As a consequence, the Rochester facilities were moved to the new Short factory established at Queen's Island in Belfast. Wartime activities involved much subcontract work as well as production of a number of its own designs such as the four-engine S.25 Sunderland maritime-patrol and reconnaissance flying boat for the RAF that was accredited with twenty-nine U-boat kills. German crews feared the Sunderland and dubbed it the

The Short Tucano T.1 replaced the BAC Jet Provost at No. 1 FTS at Linton-on-Ouse in Yorkshire and remain operational at the same base in the new millennium. (*Aviation News*)

Only ten Short Belfast long-range strategic transports were built. Having first flown in January 1964, they entered RAF Transport Command (later Support Command) service with No. 53 Squadron in January 1966 at RAF Fairford. They later moved to RAF Brize Norton in May 1967 where they remained flying worldwide until 1976 when they were withdrawn and sold on the civil register to Heavylift. A Short Skyvan is seen overhead. (*Warplane Collection*)

The turboprop Short Tucano built in Belfast and exported to Kenya were equipped with a ground-attack capability and operated in an all-over camouflage scheme with red spinner as shown by the 'Baby Tucano' displayed alongside its RAF-livered flying trainer. (*Author*)

'Fliegendes Stachelschwein' ('Flying Porcupine) as it bristled with machine guns. After the Second World War, some twenty-four Mk IIIs were handed over to British Airways in March 1943 and renamed as the civil Hythe and Sandringham.

Also at this time, Short were building one of the RAF's first four-engine heavy bombers, the S.29 Short Stirling. Initially a half-scale model, the S.31, powered by a Pobjoy Niagara engine, was built for evaluation. Unfortunately, the first full-scale prototype Stirling, serial L7600, powered by four Bristol Hercules HE.1M engines crashed at Rochester airport on 14 May 1939 when landing after its maiden flight. The second prototype, serial L7605, also flew in 1939 shortly after the outbreak of war, but production of the initial order for 100 aircraft was hampered by the lack of Bristol Hercules XI engines. The first few aircraft were delivered with Hercules II engines with the bombers designated Mk I Series I with the remainder Mk I Series II. Teething problems with the undercarriage were experienced and the Rochester works where initial production was underway was bombed and six aircraft nearing completion were destroyed. Aircraft with a dorsal turret in place of the retractable periscopic-sighted ventral turret were designated Mk I Series III and those aircraft with dual turrets the Series IV. Aircraft fitted with more powerful Hercules XVI engines and a dorsal turret produced the Mk III Stirling that became the standard Bomber Command aircraft until the type was withdrawn from bombing operations in September 1944. A number were retained on electronic countermeasures work while the majority were handed over for transport duties. A few interim Mk IIs were Mk Is fitted with Wright Cyclone engines pending availability of the Hercules. From 1943 onwards, Stirling IIIs were fitted for glider-towing duties equipping four squadrons – Nos 190, 196, 299 and 620 – all with an establishment of twenty-two Stirlings and fifty Horsa gliders. A new designation in the form of Mk IV long-range troop transports involved service conversion of Mk IIIs where the rear turret was retained as a token measure of self defence. A Mk V variant had no defensive armament and a redesigned hinged nose was fitted to permit ramp entry of small military vehicles. This variant could also be used in the CASEVAC (casualty evacuation) role fitted out with up to twelve stretchers. Production that had started at Rochester was transferred to Belfast, this being supplemented by subcontractors at the Austin Motor Co. at Birmingham, although plans to produce the aircraft in Canada did not materialise. Total Short Stirling production amounted to 2,375 aircraft even though large orders were cancelled and the bomber declared obsolete with the introduction of the Avro Lancaster bomber and transport variants as the Avro York C.1.

The Short Sunderland flying boat was developed into the Seaford and S.45 Solent. A post-war type, the Sturgeon, was a high-performance, carrier-borne target-tug and the first twin-engine aircraft specifically designed for naval use. This was followed by the SA.6 Sealand, an all-metal amphibian carrying up to seven passengers. In the 1950s, Short built a number of experimental aircraft, many related to other designs such as the SC.1, a five-engine VTO aircraft developed in parallel with the Hawker P.1127 V/STOL aircraft. The early 1960s saw the introduction of a range of 'boxlike' utility aircraft to be designated as the Skyvan. The Short Skyvan was ultimately developed into two very successful twin-turboprop regional airliners, the SD-330 and the SD-360, that were first flown on 22 August 1974 and 1 June 1981 respectively. A militarised variant, the C-23A Sherpa, was sold to the USAFE initially for use in the European theatre for the transportation of parts and engines. However, these aircraft were eventually transferred to the US Army who went on to order more.

The Short SC5/10 Belfast – a large, long-range strategic-freighter – was ordered for the RAF and was the first British aircraft designed from the outset for the long-range military transport role. It was also the first military transport to be fitted with a fully automatic landing system. In the event, initial orders were cut drastically in favour of the Lockheed C-130K Hercules. The Short SC5/10 Belfast had a vast cargo hold and could typically hold up to ten Land Rovers with trailers, three Westland Whirlwinds and two Wessex helicopters, a Chieftain tank, three Saladin armoured cars and two Polaris missiles or three Ferranti Bloodhound surface-to-air missiles with launch equipment. But following defence cuts, all Belfasts had been phased out of RAF service by September 1976, although a number were used by civilian cargo carrier Heavy Lift for a number of years. The aircraft was variously employed by a number of companies such as BAe, Fokker, Short and Learjet to transport new fuselages, wings, tail units and other subassemblies to final production sites such as the custom-built BAe 146 assembly hall at Hatfield (before 146/RJ final assembly was moved to BAe's Woodford plant in 1992-1994).

The last complete aircraft project to be undertaken at the Short Belfast plant was the licensed production of the highly modified variant of the Brazilian Embraer EMB-312G Tucano turboprop basic trainer for the RAF. In excess of 130 examples built, some for export (notably Kenya), final deliveries were completed in early 1993.

Having been acquired by the Canadian Bombardier Company on 4 October 1989, a considerable amount of new investment was made at the Belfast plant by way of new facilities and machinery with modern equipment, new systems and updated working practices. The two manufacturing centres at Newtown Abbey and Dunmurry cover some 27,871 square metres (300,000 square feet) of production floor area allocated to the manufacture of components for Boeing, Rolls-Royce, International Aero Engines, British Aerospace – and until their demise in 1996 – complete wing sets for all Fokker 70 and 100 aircraft. In addition, Short have a major undertaking with their Canadian parent for the design and manufacture of the 32-foot-long centre section of the fuselage, the forward and aft fuselage extension plugs, wing flaps, ailerons, spoilers, spoilerons, vanes and nacelles of the Canadair Express Regional Jet. In September 1992, the company announced it would build complete fuselage and tail units for the Learjet 45 mid-size business jet with the first fuselage delivered by a Heavy Lift Short-built Belfast on 18 October 1994. Also in March 1994, Short announced it would undertake at least 10 per cent of the BAe work-share in the Airbus Industrie FLA transport aircraft project, since designated as the EADS Airbus Military A400M. It was also announced that it had teamed with GKN Westland (now AgustaWestland) to produce the Apache WAH-64D attack helicopter for the British Army Air Corps. In 1993, the company took over the world famous Bournemouth-based international aviation support company, Airworks.

In the new millennium, Shorts Bombardier manufactures and supplies assemblies and components for Boeing 737, 747, 757 and 777 aircraft. In addition, its Nacelle Systems Division specialises in the design and manufacture of nacelles and turbofan components for many Rolls-Royce aero-engines.

The Sopwith Pup entered service on the Western Front in late 1916 and was much liked by its pilots with almost STOL qualities and excellent handling. (*Flight Colour*)

Sopwith Aviation – H. G. Hawker

The Sopwith Aviation Company founded at Kingston-upon-Thames by Thomas Sopwith (1888–1989) in 1912 produced more than a dozen or so mediocre designs before the outbreak of the First World War. One aircraft, however, was of note: the Sopwith Bat Boat No. 1 that appeared in 1913. It was the first flying boat to be built in Britain and at the outbreak of war flew sea patrols from Scapa Flow until November 1914. Almost coincidental with the Bat Boat, Sopwith produced the Sopwith three-seater Tractor Biplane. Another early design was the Sopwith Churchill, a two-seat, side-by-side biplane so called because the idea for the aeroplane came from Winston Churchill (another title was the Sociable). One of three Sopwith Seaplanes, ANZANI participated in the naval manoeuvres of 1913. Six seaplane trainer pusher biplanes, the Sopwith Gunbus, were built for the Greek Naval Air Service, but were taken over by the British Admiralty in 1914. The Gunbus was followed by the Sopwith Admiralty Type 807 seaplane, twelve of which entered RNAS service in 1914 – a number were carried aboard HMS *Ark Royal*. The Sopwith Two-Seat Scout known as the Spinning Jenny was a

Based on the fuselage of the Sopwith Pup, the Sopwith Triplane first flew in May 1916 and proved to possess a phenomenal rate of climb. Although built in small numbers, it helped the Royal Flying Corps regain air superiority over the Western Front. (*Warplane Collection*)

landplane variant of the Type 807. Twenty-four were delivered to the RNAS who used them on anti-Zeppelin patrols.

In 1914, a modified Sopwith Tabloid fitted with floats won the Schneider Trophy at an average speed of just over 86 mph. In November 1914, these aircraft were ordered into production and aptly named Sopwith Schneider of which 186 were built, all by Sopwith. The improved Blackburn-built Sopwith Baby was fitted with a 110-hp Clerget rotary engine in place of the 100-hp Gnôme Monosoupape. The Sopwith Baby saw service aboard carriers and cruisers in the Middle and Far East where they were modified to carry two 65-lb bombs. The Schneider and Baby were also used by the US Navy where the initial order for 100 Sopwith Babies was delivered by Sopwith from September 1915 to July 1916. The Sopwith Tabloid has the distinction of being the first British aircraft to destroy a Zeppelin, the new Z.IX, in its shed at Düsseldorf on 8 October 1914. The attack was carried out by Flt Lt R. L. G. Matrix, who from a height of some 600 feet, bombed the airship in its berth with flames rising to some 500 feet within 30 seconds of the bombs hitting their target. The two-seat, single-engine, torpedo-carrying, twin-float seaplane, the Sopwith Admiralty, failed to launch a torpedo in anger, although it is believed a small number of the eighteen built did see service with the RNAS.

In mid-1916, Sopwith built a tiny biplane for the personal use of his Australian-born test pilot Harry Hawker. It was named the Sopwith Bee. The Bee was later adapted as a test-bed for a fighting scout, but did not enter series production. The Sopwith 1½ Strutter was so called on account of the shortened inboard wing struts being attached to the upper longerons and not extending down to the lower wing spars. The 1½ Strutter was ordered by the Admiralty and War Office as a light bomber and the official Sopwith designation was LCT (Land Clerget Tractor). It was the first of a series of very successful warplanes produced by Sopwith and was the first British military fighter to enter service fitted with synchronising gear, permitting the front-fixed machine gun to fire forward through the propeller arc. In 1916, Sopwith 1½ Strutters of the 3rd Wing RNAS based at Luxeuil were the first aircraft to carry out strategic bombing raids on German industrial centres. The French, who were looking for a replacement for their pusher biplane bombers, were so impressed by the Strutters that the French Government placed orders for licensed production of the type for the French Air Service. The two-seat Type 9400 bomber variant was designated SOP.1B2 and the single-seat Type 9700 version the SOP.B1. Some had 110-hp or 130-hp Clerget rotary engines similar to the British version and others had the French 110-hp or 130-hp Le Rhone. Unfortunately, French production was extremely slow and by the time the type began to reach the frontline in the summer of 1917, they were already outdated and outclassed. Also, they were underpowered and of limited range unless carrying a small bomb load. However, the French day-bomber escadrilles had no other choice than deploy the type until their own Bréguet 14 became available in November 1917. Sopwith 1½ Strutters were also the first two-seaters to take-off from a British warship in April 1918. The RNAS were supplied with two versions of the Strutter designated as the Sopwith Type 9700 and comprised of 420 two-seaters and 130 single-seaters. British and French Sopwith Strutters were supplied to Belgium, Russia, the American Expeditionary Force (AEF), Romania and Japan. The Sopwith 1½ Strutter led to the smaller single-seat fighting scout: the Sopwith Pup. Perhaps the most outstanding fighter of the First World War, the Pup was designed and built within six weeks and saw service in nine months. Prototype, serial 3691, was delivered to the RNAS in early 1916. The official RFC title for the Pup was the Scout, but the RNAS named it the Type 9901.

The Sopwith F.1 Camel, the inspiration of Thomas Sopwith, must be regarded as the most successful British fighter of the war with a total of 5,825 built. With its legendary manoeuvrability, it destroyed some 1,294 enemy aircraft and at least three airships (purported to have been the highest number of downed machines by a single type on either side). However, the Sopwith Camel was reportedly not the easiest of aircraft to fly, but in the hands of a skilled pilot, it was a truly deadly fighting machine. Such was the versatility of the type, it appeared in a number of variants such as the TF1 trench ground-attack fighter, 2F1 naval variant with folding wings, Camel seaplanes and 386 F.1s used by the RNAS. A number of other variants designated HD 'Home Defence' were modified for night-fighting duties. The cockpit was moved aft and the two Lewis machine guns were placed above the wings to eliminate muzzle flash which tended to blind pilots. In March 1918, to counter the German offensive, Camels were used in the ground-attack role and also as ship-borne fighters by the RNAS.

An order for 266 Sopwith Triplanes for the RFC for use in France was supplemented by stored RNAS French Spad S.7s with only 145 examples arriving. The Sopwith Triplane was inspired to counter the infamous German 'Red Baron' Fokker Triplane. Although it is believed that Fokker's fighter was a direct copy of the Sopwith Triplane, it was a totally new design. Only two Sopwith triplane prototypes were built and first flew in June 1916. A total of one hundred and forty-five aircraft were built – ninety-five by Sopwith, forty-seven by Clayton and three by Oakley – with 130-hp Clerget 9B engines.

The prototype Sopwith T.1 Cuckoo had its first flight in June-July 1917. The Cuckoo biplane torpedo-carrier suffered the ignominy of having its frontend extensively modified to house the 200-hp Sunbeam Arab engine after the original Hispano-Suiza powerplant was diverted to the Royal Aircraft Factory for their Se.5A fighters. Unfortunately, the subcontractors chosen to series-produce the type had little experience of aircraft production and of the 350 Sopwith Cuckoos ordered, only 232 were built. The Cuckoo was the first land plane torpedo-carrier capable of operating from a flying deck.

Of over 1,500 Sopwith 5F1 Dolphin biplane fighters built, only four squadrons were equipped with the type on the Western Front from January 1918 onwards. Conceived in 1917, the type was distinguished by its back-staggered wings. The subsequent 7F1 Snipe did not enter RAF service on the Western Front until September 1918. However, although less than 100 were in service before the armistice was signed in November 1918, it had established itself as a superb aircraft. Also, the Snipe was destined to become the RAF's standard single-seat fighter, remaining in service in a variety of roles well into the mid-1920s, the last squadron relinquishing its aircraft in late 1926. Before the end of the First World War, several had found their way into naval service and a long-range variant, the 7F.1A, had evolved by fitting an additional 50-gallon fuel tank beneath the pilot's seat. At the end of the war, many brand new Snipes were scrapped, but by 1921 when the fledgling RAF was desperately short of aircraft due to wartime attrition, AM Sir John Salmond KCB CMG CVO DSO, ordered the wanton destruction of aircraft to cease. An urgent programme of repair and restoration was started and some 200 or Snipes destined for destruction entered squadron service. A number of Snipes even remained in RAF use long after disappearing from squadron service by way of forty-two or so two-seat, dual-controlled trainers found at flying training schools. Had the war continued into 1919, it was planned to equip thirteen RAF squadrons with the ground-attack variant, the Sopwith Salamander. It is thought some 180 Salamanders were built and although quantity orders were placed, none served operationally.

Another post-war Snipe development was the Dragon and a number of private venture types were designed and built in late 1917-1918, namely the Sopwith 2B.2 Rhino triplane bomber, the Sopwith Swallow monoplane fighter with its Camel fuselage and parasol wing fitted unusually close to the fuselage, and the Sopwith Dragon biplane fighter in 1919. After the prototype, serial E7990, some 200 airframes minus their engines were produced and stored (this production replaced the cancelled order for 300 Snipes). None of these aircraft ever entered service although a number were withdrawn from storage with a possible six to twelve fitted with engines. It is known at least two went to Farnborough for use as engine test-beds and one, serial J3628, was sent to the US for evaluation.

In 1918, Sopwith returned to a triplane design to meet RAF Specification Type 1 for a heavily-armed aircraft as the Sopwith Snark was only considered as an experimental aircraft and never considered for series production. The last in the long line of Sopwith fighters was the Sopwith Snapper, a single-seat, single-engine biplane fighter. While the type did undergo service trials at RAE Martlesham Heath in September 1919 and returned a good sense of speed, it was not accepted for series production.

Also in 1919, a number of tourers and competition aircraft were produced including the two-seat Grasshopper, Wallaby, Antelope and Dove. Also, the single-seat Schneider, Rainbow and Scooter from which the Swallow had been developed were produced. Others include the three-seat Gnu cabin aircraft and the Atlantic with which in May 1919, Harry Hawker and Lt Cdr K. Mackenzie-Grieve attempted an Atlantic crossing. However, the aircraft was forced to ditch in mid-ocean and luckily the two intrepid aviators survived having been picked up by a passing steamer.

Although the Sopwith Aviation Company, unlike many of its competitors, was well placed at the end of the First World War to continue in the field of aircraft production, a crippling tax bill against wartime profits forced the company into liquidation in September 1920. Harry Hawker, the company's chief test pilot and personal friend of Thomas Sopwith, stepped in to save the company with the formation of The H. G. Hawker Engineering Company. Unfortunately in the same year that his new company was formed, Hawker lost his life when he crashed at Hendon. Ironically, Hawker Engineering Ltd soon became profitable by repairing and rebuilding Sopwith Snipes that had originated from the Sopwith Aviation Company.

Pemberton Billing – Supermarine – Vickers Supermarine Vickers Armstrong

In September 1913, Noel Pemberton Billing, a pioneering aviator who had established a fully equipped aerodrome in Essex, started the design of a marine aircraft at a small factory he had acquired at Woolston, Southampton. Officially designated Pemberton-Billing PB.1, Billing adopted the name Supermarine. The Supermarine PB.1 was shown at Olympia in March 1914 having its first flight in June 1914, but it did not enter series production. With the advent of the First World War, Billing turned his attention to a tractor biplane scout using a Gnôme seven-cylinder rotary engine that delivered 50 hp. It was designed in a day and built in a week, hence it was often referred to as the 'Seven Day Bus'. Officially designated as the Pemberton Billing PB.9, it had its first flight in August 1914. Although believed to be difficult to fly and not selected for series production, the aircraft, serial 1267, was used for training purposes by the RNAS at Hendon. In 1915, Pemberton Billing Ltd came into being and was renamed in late 1916 as Supermarine Aviation Works Ltd when Billing was elected as a Member of Parliament and sold his interests in the company. However, Billing's influence was such that a number of his designs were produced by Supermarine such as the PB.23 and PB.25 pusher fighters, the PB.29 anti-airship aircraft and its derivative, the Supermarine P.B.31 Night Hawk, a quadruplane anti-airship patrol interceptor. None were to enter series production.

The first aircraft to enter series production with Supermarine was the AD Air Department Flying Boat designed by Harris Booth at the Air Department of the Admiralty. The AD patrol boat was followed by the single-seat flying boat pusher fighter, the Supermarine N.1B Baby. This was followed by the private venture Sea King II amphibian flying boat fighter that was modified and redesigned by R. J. Mitchell as the Sea Lion I. The Sea Lion single-seat racing seaplane had been entered in the 1919 Schneider Trophy race, but sank during the race. It was subsequently salvaged, redesigned by Mitchell and displayed as a fighter at the 1920 Olympia Aero Show. Supermarine's first flying boat after the First World War was the civil Swan from which the military Southampton was derived. The Swan also inspired the Scapa, an all-metal modernised and re-engined development of the Southampton that had its first flight on 8 July 1932. Initially, the Scapa was known as the Southampton Mk IV receiving its official Scapa name in October 1933. The Southampton was ordered 'off the drawing board' and proved to be an excellent flying boat design and served with the RAF for over a decade, a record only surpassed by the Short Sunderland more than a decade later.

In 1921, the Supermarine Seal deck-landing, amphibian fleet-spotter was produced and further developed to become the Seagull I. The Seal and Seagull were the first Supermarine amphibian flying boats to use tractor configuration as all previous Supermarine designs favoured the pusher layout. The Supermarine Seagull II was the first post-war flying boat to enter RAF service in 1923, the prototype, serial N158, having been displayed at the 1922 RAF Hendon air display. The Seagull V, serial K4797, which appeared in June 1933, was a very different airplane from its predecessors having an all-metal hull and had returned to pusher configuration. Initial designs were delivered to the Australian Government retaining the Seagull V designation. The type was later accepted by the Fleet Air Arm and in 1935 named the Walrus, although it was to become universally known as the 'Shagbat'. Not particularly pleasing to look at, the Walrus was well-liked by crews and the aircraft was employed on search and rescue, spotter and other duties around the world throughout the war until replaced by the Sea Otter that had supplemented it. The Sea Otter was the last biplane in squadron service with both the RAF and FAA. It had continued in service for a number of years after the war, but with the adoption of the helicopter, soon disappeared from service heralding the end of flying boats in use with British air forces. The last of the flying boat designs to emanate from Supermarine and Reginald Mitchell was the Stranraer general reconnaissance flying boat originally designated Southampton V. Only seventeen examples of the Stranraer were ordered for the RAF although adoption of the type for use by the RCAF led to an order for forty that were built by Canadian-Vickers, Montreal, from 1938 to 1941.

Supermarine also specialised in the design and production of high-speed seaplanes earning an enviable reputation by winning the Schneider Trophy four times using successive Mitchell-designed marks of high-speed racing seaplanes including the Supermarine S.4, S.5, S.6 and S.6B in 1922, 1927, 1929 and 1931 respectively.

In 1931 – on the same day that Britain won the trophy outright having won three competitions in a row – the S.6B, serial S1596, captured the world absolute speed record at 379 mph. As is well known, success with these racing seaplanes inspired Mitchell with his famous Spitfire fighter design.

The Spitfire is one of the most outstanding and famous aircraft of all time. Unfortunately, Mitchell did not live to witness the many successes achieved by his superb fighter having died of cancer before war was declared. Total production of the Rolls-Royce Merlin-powered Spitfire was 18,298;

Supermarine Seagull ASR Mk 1 three-crew ASR and coastal reconnaissance amphibians with an ability to fly as slow as 35 mph possessed a long range and ability to loiter and land on water. (*Warplane Collection*)

production of Griffon-engine variants was in the region of 1,836. The last Spitfire to be produced was F.24, serial VN496, that left the South Marston factory on 20 February 1948, bringing the final total Spitfire production to 20,351 examples. Three hundred Spitfire Is with Merlin III engines were ordered until Expansion Scheme F was introduced on 3 June 1936 to be completed by 31 March 1939. Supermarine had never before received such a large order and the Woolston factory was not equipped for mass production on the scale required. With a workforce of only 500, subcontracting was the obvious answer and the main companies chosen for large scale subassembly production in the early days were Aero Engines Ltd (ailerons and elevators); J. Samuel White & Co. (fuselage frames); Singer Motors Ltd (engine mountings); Folland Aircraft Ltd (tailplane and rudder); General Aircraft Ltd (wings); Pobjoy Motors Ltd (wings); General Electric Co. (wing tips); The Pressed Steel Co. (wing leading edge); G. Beaton and Son Ltd (wing ribs); Westland Aircraft Ltd (wing ribs); and Supermarine, Woolston (fuselage). At the Eastleigh Aerodrome in Southampton, final assembly of all parts took place in two assembly halls.

Series production of the Spitfire had begun in March 1936, but it almost turned into disaster due to the elliptical wing that was allegedly inspired from the German Heinkel He.70 high-speed transport plane and numerous other issues. By the end of 1936, only six fuselages had been completed along with

The Supermarine Spitfire LF XVI was based on the Mk IX variant and powered with an American-built Merlin 266 in place of the Mk 9's Rolls-Royce Merlin 66. Serial TB752 can be seen at The RAF Memorial Building in Manston, Kent. The aircraft was just one of 1,492 built by Vickers Armstrong at Castle Bromwich during the Second World War. (*Author*)

four sets of useless wings. Also, further internal design work was necessary. An Air Ministry official visited Supermarine in early 1937 and saw a number of fully-equipped fuselages awaiting the installation of their wings. The main subcontractor responsible, General Aircraft Ltd, had previously received an order for 100 wing sets, the first of which were not delivered until twelve months later. By February 1938, the Air Council realised that deliveries of the Supermarine Spitfire was going to be seriously delayed. The main bottleneck was the subcontracted wing sets and it was suggested that the Spitfire programme be abandoned, not only due to its many production woes, but also to problems with the aircraft. A second plan put to the Air Ministry was for Supermarine to only complete 310 Spitfire Mk 1s after which they would produce the Bristol Beaufighter under licence. But fortunately for Supermarine, the planned successors to the Spitfire and Hurricane – the Hawker Tornado and Typhoon and the twin-engine Westland Whirlwind – were also experiencing development problems, and for this reason it was impossible to cancel the Spitfire programme.

After the annexation of Austria by Germany, it was realised that war was inevitable and on 24 March 1938, Supermarine received a second order for 200 Spitfire Mk 1s. Certainly, Supermarine had a lot of luck with the introduction of the Spitfire into series production. The first three aircraft were delivered in July 1938 followed by two in August, two in September and thirteen in each of the following three months. The full total production of Spitfires for 1938 was only forty-six aircraft and at this rate of production it would be impossible to supply the requested 300 fighters by 31 March 1939.

By 3 September 1939 and the outbreak of hostilities between Britain and Germany, total deliveries to the RAF reached 306 aircraft and of these thirty had been lost. At this time, only 187 Spitfires equipped ten fighter squadrons and the aircraft was significant only by its absence in the RAF's battle order.

In 1939, peak monthly average production output was only forty-six aircraft, but production output slowly increased during the first months of 1940. However, in June 1940, much urgent supplies arrived from the shadow factory at MAP Castle Bromwich that had been set up by Lord Nuffield. By the war's end, 96.6 per cent of Spitfire output was from the two Vickers plants: Vickers built 11,939 Spitfires, Supermarine 7,727 with Westland Aircraft a meagre 685. Average peak monthly output increased to 232 in 1941 and then to 359 in 1942. But in 1943, production decreased to 351 and despite continuous development and the introduction of many new variants and subtypes, the increased production was absorbed by the need for replacements. Nevertheless, Britain produced Spitfires up to the very end of the Second World War for the same reason that Germany continued to build the Messerschmitt Me 109. Production lines for both aircraft were well established and it would have been difficult to introduce a new type into series

All-over sky blue and unarmed Supermarine Spitfire PR.XIXs operated on post-war 'peacetime' high-altitude reconnaissance missions from RAF Brize Norton as did their Second World War counterparts before them.

production without seriously affecting production output. It was also for this reason that the many design problems with the aircraft during the war such as undercarriage, engines, cockpit and armament were ignored. Despite this, the Spitfire was arguably the finest fighter of the war. Four thousand Supermarine Spitfire Mk VA/Bs with Rolls-Royce Merlin 45 or 46 engines were built and were the first Spitfires to be capable of carrying an under-fuselage fuel tank or bomb.

From the 20,351 Spitfires produced, the RAF only had 5,864 left on 31 May 1945: 1,335 had been exported to Russia and the US received a number. The Supermarine Seafire was the naval version of the Spitfire especially adapted for operation from aircraft carriers. Early Seafires were purely 'hooked' ex-RAF Spitfire VB conversions (except the Spitfire Mk VIII). As the war developed, specific navalised new builds had folding wings, catapult spools, deck-arrester hook and other specialised equipment. The decision to adapt the Spitfire for naval use with the Fleet Air Arm was taken in 1941. During the Second World War, series production of the Seafire included 1,811 Merlin-engined variants (428 converted ex-RAF aircraft) and 384 Griffon-engine variants. Post-war developments of the Spitfire and Seafire gave rise to the Spiteful and Seafang respectively. Handling problems which resulted in the loss of the first Spiteful prototype, serial NN660, were eventually cured after a prolonged development and modification programme found to be associated with the design of the wing. The unavoidable delays ultimately led to only seventeen aircraft built of an original order of 373 Spiteful fighters. The Spiteful, however, claimed a first when it reached a top speed of 494 mph in level flight, believed to be the fastest speed achieved by a British piston-engine aircraft. Of the 150 naval Seafangs ordered, only sixteen were produced, ten Mk 31s and six Mk 32s.

In the post-war years, Supermarine produced the world's first turbojet-powered experimental flying boat, the SRA/1, which first flew on 16 July 1947. The succeeding naval Supermarine Attacker has a special place in Fleet Air Arm history being the first jet fighter to enter frontline naval squadron service on 17 August 1951 with No. 800 NAS Fleet Air Arm. The last in the line of famous Supermarine fighters culminated in the Scimitar, a single-seat, carrier-borne interceptor and strike fighter for the Royal Navy, and the Swift, a single-seat fighter for the RAF. The Swift, originally proposed as a backup for the Hawker Hunter, was in its interceptor-fighter configuration an absolute disaster. In May 1955 and less than a year into its service with RAF Fighter Command, the Swift was withdrawn from operational use where it was redeveloped as the Swift FR.5, a fast tactical-reconnaissance fighter. In its fighter-reconnaissance role, the aircraft served the RAF well and remained in use for almost six years after entering service with No. 2 Squadron of the 2nd TAF in Germany. Except for a dozen or so Swift F.7s that were used by the No. 1 Guided Weapons Development Unit at RAF Valley, Anglesey, North Wales, the Swift carries the distinction of being the only RAF combat aircraft never to be used operationally in the UK.

On 31 July 1960, Vickers Armstrong Ltd (Aircraft Section) Supermarine Division became part of the British Aircraft Corporation (BAC), the company having originally become a division of Vickers Armstrong in October 1938.

Vickers Ltd

Vickers Ltd, Aviation Department, began to build aeroplanes in March 1911 to licence manufacture the designs of French aviation pioneer Robert Esnault-Pelterie. Also, the company was the British manufacturer of the Maxim machine gun and its 1912 development, the rifle-calibre Vickers-Maxim gun. With the establishment of its aviation department, it was not unnatural that the company should seek to combine the two products in gun-carrying aeroplanes, despite the official specifications for the British Military Aeroplane Competition of 1912 failing to include requirements for the inclusion of any weaponry, whether offensive or defensive; however, the military wing of the Royal Flying Corp and the Royal Aircraft Factory at Farnborough had taken a more farsighted view of the potential of armed military aircraft in any future conflicts. The Royal Aircraft Factory had already flown an Fe.2 on 24 July

Shell-sponsored Vickers Vimy (replica) at Farnborough undergoing pre-flight inspection prior to taking-off on its flight to Australia. (*Author*)

1912, a full week before the Military Aircraft Competition. Believed to have been armed with a Maxim, it is suggested that the RFC's Military Wing had flown some air-firing trials with a machine gun on an unidentified Be. type.

In 1912, the Naval Wing of the RFC indicated it was interested in 'gun-carrying' aeroplanes and Vickers was asked by the Admiralty to build an experimental fighting biplane capable of carrying and firing a machine gun (Contract No. 003330/12/53661 dated 19/11/1912). Vickers built a two-seat pusher biplane armed with a belt-fed Vickers gun installed in the nose of the nacelle. It was intended to be fired by the passenger and carried no less than 1,500 rounds of ammunition. It was designated as the EFB.1 Experimental Fighting Biplane, although the aircraft never flew having been destroyed on take-off. The successive EFB.2 and EFB.3 that followed were fitted with similar gun installations to the EFB.1 and only served to demonstrate that the gun fitment was quite unsatisfactory and brought in to question whether the Vickers machine gun was suitable for aircraft use. In 1914, the Admiralty placed an order for twelve EFB.3s, which at the outbreak of war were taken over by the War Office, while development of a new experimental model, the EFB.4 evolved. The latter was fitted with a drum-fed Lewis gun mounted on a spigot forward of the gunner's cockpit. However, this could only be regarded as an interim design as the ammunition drum's ninety-seven round capacity meant frequent changes and this led to a radically redesigned nose of an EFB.5 (a redesignated EFB.5 or prototype FB.5).

Convinced that war was imminent, Vickers decided to proceed with the production of fifty FB.5 'Gunbus' aircraft without waiting for service orders which eventually materialised with forty-six ordered for the RFC and four for the Admiralty.

In late 1915, two rather ungainly FB.7 two-seat, tractor gun-carriers were produced, having been designed under contract by R. L. Flanders, the founder of a small aircraft company at Brooklands. However, a production order for twelve FB.7As fitted with an alternative 80-hp Renault engine in place of the original 100-hp Gnôme was cancelled due to the Renault not developing sufficient power. Also in late 1915, a development of the FB.5 was designed with new wings of reduced span and all horizontal flight surfaces with rounded wing tips and a longer nose to give the observer more room. In RFC service, the FB.9 was known as the Vickers Streamline Fighting Biplane or more briefly as the Streamline Vickers. Initial FB.9s were built by Darracq in France, but later Vickers-built aircraft were produced as dual-control trainers with a lengthened nose. After a number of experimental scouts, the next Vickers type to enter series production was the FB.14 single-engined, fighter-reconnaissance biplane of which only 100 were built from an original 252 ordered. Only half of these were completed with engines and the remainder were held in storage in Islington until scrapped with three prototype FB.19s and twelve FB.19 Mk II fighting scouts completed.

Throughout the First World War, the Vickers London factories at Brooklands, Weybridge, Surrey, Crayford, Bexley Heath and Erith, Kent, were busy building large numbers of RAF Be.2s, Se.5As and Sopwith 1½ Strutters as well as several of its own prototype designs. It was not until July 1917 that the RFC changed its policy with regards to deploying heavy bombers and Air Board Specification A.3 (B) was issued for a bomber capable of carrying a 3,000-lb bomb, later reduced to 2,200 lbs, at 90 mph with a 400 mile range. This gave rise to the Vickers FB.27 or the famous Vickers Vimy of which some 239 were built, the type remaining in RAF service until 1933.

The Vimy gained notoriety as the first aircraft to cross the Atlantic nonstop on 14-15 June 1919 and its two RAF pilots, Flt Lts Jon 'Jack' Alcock (1892–1989) and Arthur Whitten Brown (1886–1948), were both knighted by King George V for their epic flight. When test flown at Martlesham Heath in January 1918, the FB.27 surprised everyone by lifting a greater load than the Handley Page O/400, a result of which orders for over 1,000 were received by Vickers. Production variants were powered by two Rolls-Royce Eagle VIII engines, although prototypes used a variety of makes. With the war's end, orders were reduced substantially but around 300 Vimy aircraft were built, equipping eight RAF bomber squadrons in the 1920s, the aircraft finishing its career as a parachute trainer. In addition to the Alcock and Brown aircraft, other modified variants of the Vimy were used on other transcontinental record breaking flights such as the first flight from Britain to Australia by Ross and

RAF Coastal Command No. 179 Squadron Vickers Warwick GR Vs carried an under-nose radar and Leigh-Light under the rear fuselage and were equipped with ADF. (*Warplane Collection*)

Keith Smith in November to December 1919. This flight was re-enacted in the 1990s with a replica Vimy and Ryneveld and Brand's flight from Britain to South Africa between February and March 1920 was also replicated.

Derivatives of the Vimy were the Vimy Commercial with a large bulbous front fuselage, forty of which were supplied to China, one to Russia and five were built for the RAF as air ambulances. These were followed by military bomber-transports: the Vernon, Victoria, Valentia and the larger Virginia bomber built as a Vimy replacement. When fully developed, although 70 per cent heavier, the Virginia could carry a bomb load three times that of the Vimy over the same range. Having entered RAF service in 1923, four were still in use when war was declared in September 1939. The Virginia was subjected to continued modification and no less than fifty-three of the 124 built were brought up to Mk X standard. As the mainstay of the RAF's bomber fleet throughout the late 1920s, the Virginia equipped nine squadrons and the Parachute School at RAF Henlow in Bedfordshire. There was a plethora of production variants including the Mk III, IV, V, VI, VII, IX and X. The Mk VII was a complete redesign to incorporate all the aerodynamic and operational improvements found necessary in operation of earlier marks. It was the embodiment of these improvements in a single airframe that turned the Mk VII Virginia into a superb aeroplane. One hundred and five Mk

Although operated by BOAC in standard Second World War RAF desert camouflage, the Vickers C.1 four-crew transports in the North African and Mediterranean theatres carried large civil registrations underlined in red, white and blue to emphasise their civil use. (*Warplane Collection*)

Xs were built, making it the most prolific variant although a number were conversions of earlier builds. The Mk X was basically a Mk VII, but with an all-metal airframe and redesigned tail unit. All other marks were of wooden construction. The Mk IX and X variants, on the recommendation of Vickers designer R. K. Pierson, had the rear gunner's position located behind the tail, the first of British-designed bombers to embody this feature.

The Vernon, which replaced by the Victoria, departed from the original Vimy design concept by having wings of an increased span, a much longer fuselage and a completely redesigned tail unit. The Victoria was produced in a number of small batches and introduced into service with No. 70 Squadron in 1928. The squadron's aircraft were involved in an unusual run of incidents or accidents on the ground. On 21 April, serial J8229 caught fire and was destroyed. In May, a gale destroyed J7924. On 7 June, as a result of a petrol cock being left on, a fire started on the line setting light to serials J7923, J7927, J8226 and J8227, all being parked close together. Also, later in the year, serial J8915 had been lost in a refuelling accident. However, the aircraft proved extremely reliable with each one flying more than 2,000 hours. Progressive updates to the Victoria by the introduction of more metal fuselage parts and fitment of Bristol Pegasus engines together with other refinements led to the renaming of the Victoria to Valentia. Fifty-four Valentias were converted Victoria Vs. In 1922, Vickers were

This Vickers Valetta was a Marconi Avionics (Elliot Rochester) trials airplane. (*Author*)

Vickers Varsity transports were used by the RAF as navigator trainers and by the Meteorological Research Flight. (*Wings*)

Despite being grounded and withdrawn from use due to airframe fatigue, the Vickers Valiant was a splendid V-bomber that served RAF Bomber Command with distinction. (*Wings*)

anxious to expand its knowledge of metal construction and this led to French designer Michel Wibault being invited to act as a consultant engineer. Wibault's pioneering work on metal construction ran in parallel with that of Claude Dornier and Prof. Ing Hugo Junkers. Although a structural duplication of the French Wibault 7C.1 scout, the Vickers-Wibault Type 121/7C.1 can generally be considered as the first all-metal fighter produced in Britain. Twenty-six Type 121 scouts were built for Chile.

The mid-1920s saw the industries preoccupied on two paths of development: the all-metal aircraft and the other towards greater speed. The Vickers Type 123/141 Scout was a private venture development returning a maximum speed of 149 mph at 10,000 feet. To demonstrate the benefits of the Vickers-Wibault liaison, the company produced an all-metal monoplane lightweight naval fighter to meet Air Ministry Specification 17/25. In the event, the Vickers Type 125 Vireo served to prove that the drag caused by Wibault's corrugated skinning was unacceptable for interceptor and fighter types, and future designs followed more orthodox structural designs. In 1923, Vickers ventured into the field of the light general-purpose bomber with its two-seat Valparaiso and Type 126 Vixen fighter/reconnaissance biplanes which appeared in 1924-1925. The Vixen II's performance in February 1924 led to the Directorate of Research awarding Vickers a contract for six army co-operation development aircraft: the Vickers Type 94 Venture. Although none of Vickers light-bomber designs entered series production, neither did its general purpose Type 131 Valiant. The aircraft was offered to Chile in 1928, but mainly in respect of the problems experienced with the wooden-winged Vixen, the offer was declined. However, in 1929, the Bolivian Government engaged in a war with Paraguay and placed an order for six Vickers Type 143s as the Bolivian Scout. While engaged in the production of the six Bolivian Scouts, Vickers decided to produce a seventh aircraft as a naval interceptor fighter, the Vickers Type 177. Once again, no series orders were received.

Delays with the introduction of the more modern Bristol Beaufort led to the Vickers Vildebeest, a 1928 design introduced into RAF service in 1932. This was followed by the Vincent, a three-seat general purpose aircraft similar to the Vildebeest, but carrying a long-range fuel tank where the torpedo had previously been fitted. The long-range tank extended the Vincent's range to 1,250 miles. Since their formation in 1908 along with their proliferation of aircraft, Vickers also designed and built airships that culminated with the R101. After its loss at Beauvais, the programme was abandoned and R100 scrapped. The airships had been designed by B. N. (later Sir) Barnes Wallis and N. S. Norway, the latter who became the novelist Neville Shute. Barnes Wallis, CBE FRS RDI BSc M Inst CE FRAeS, was to become Chief of Aeronautical Research and Development.

Vickers (Aviation) Ltd was formed in July 1928 when Vickers Ltd formed their Aviation Department into a separate subsidiary company to take over the manufacture of aircraft, aircraft accessories and subsidiary equipment.

In November 1928, Vickers (Aviation) Ltd took over control of the Supermarine Aviation Works Ltd, although the latter company did retain its autonomy.

In October 1938, Vickers (Aviation) Ltd and Supermarine Aviation Works (Vickers) Ltd were taken over by Vickers Armstrong Ltd. Barnes Wallis was not only famous for the 'Dam Busters' bouncing bomb, but also the geodetic system form of construction used in airships to obtain great strength to weight ratios as used in the Vickers Wellesley and Wellington bombers.

An order for seventy-nine monoplane Wellesleys led to its entry into RAF Bomber Command service in the spring of 1937. The type almost attained immediate notoriety in 1938 when five aircraft were allotted to the Long-Range Development Flight of the RAF for participation in an England-Australia flight. Two aircraft, serials L2638 and L2680, by successfully flying the 7,159 miles from Ismailia, Egypt, to Darwin, Northern Australia, set a up a new world long-distance record. A Wellesley Mk II variant introduced a single continuous canopy instead of two separate ones. One aircraft, serial K7736, was modified to carry torpedoes and K7722 was experimentally fitted with a Bristol Hercules engine in place of the standard Bristol Pegasus. Of the 176 Vickers Wellesleys built from 1938, much of the Vickers production was delivered directly to the RAF Packing Depot at RAF Sealand for the aircraft to be prepared for dispatch to the Middle East where it would replace the ageing Vickers Vincent and Fairey Gordon biplanes. Aircraft in operation at home with Bomber Command were also withdrawn in 1939 and despatched to the Middle East, although six were lost in the Bay of Biscay three days after

The contract for twin-engined, high-altitude Westland Welkin fighters was cancelled after sixty-seven airplanes had been delivered. The type was never used operationally as the Germans failed to pose any high-altitude threat. (*Warplane Collection*)

war was declared. In the Middle East, two Wellesleys were transferred to the Egyptian Air Force, the type grounded by the RAF in August 1943 on receipt of a Vickers Vincent sent to replace it.

The twin-engined 'Wimpy' Wellington first flew on 15 June 1936 and by the end of 1945, a total of 11,461 had been built (one aircraft every 24 hours) and continued in service until 1953 as a trainer. The Wellington was one of aviation's classic designs. It was a truly great aeroplane and confounded critics with its revolutionary geodetic construction, a shape that was easily assembled by semi-skilled labour. Also, it was easy to repair under operational conditions and could absorb a lot of punishment in battle. The aircraft served Bomber, Coastal and Transport Commands, and existed in many 'special variants' and trainers. Eventually, Wallis' geodetic construction was rendered obsolete by the metal monocoque techniques that superseded it. One hundred and eighty-three Vickers Wellington 1As with two 1,000-hp Bristol Pegasus XVIII engines were built at Weybridge.

Originally intended as a Wellington replacement, only sixteen Warwicks were completed as bombers and these did not see action, but were used for experimental purposes. Other variants such as the GR Mk V were used in the air-sea rescue role and fourteen Mk 1s were converted by BOAC as transports (the aircraft were eventually transferred to RAF Transport Command in 1944).

Post-war designs included the Vickers Viking airliner and the Valetta, a military derivative that replaced the RAF's Douglas Dakota. The Vickers Varsity that followed was extensively used as a crew trainer and like the

Valetta developed with a tricycle undercarriage. Vickers also produced the Viscount, the world's first turboprop-engined airliner and was Britain's most successful airliner to date with 445 built. It was flown by more than sixty operators worldwide and acquired new by more than forty countries while others acquired many second-hand.

Vickers Viscount sixty-five-seat regional transports built for BEA was the world's first turboprop airliner to enter route service with 356 of the total 445 built exported. Many were exported to the US for regional airline route service and series aircraft were equipped with four 1,540-hp Rolls-Royce Dart 505 engines.

The ninety-three seat Vickers Vanguard that followed did not achieve the same success although of the forty-three produced, twenty for BEA and twenty-three for Trans-Canada Airlines served the companies well with a number converted to freighters.

Production of the Vickers VC 10, of whom its origins lay in the V1000 project of the mid-1950s, was undertaken by BAC when Vickers Armstrong (Aircraft) Ltd (so named after its reorganisation in December 1954) became a 40 per cent shareholder in February 1960.

In 1963, Vickers was absorbed into the British Aircraft Corporation (BAC) at its Weybridge Division. The first of the famous V-bombers was the Vickers Valiant and the bomber variants were followed into service by a long-range strategic-reconnaissance version and refuelling tankers. The Vickers Type 106 Valiant was the first of Britain's V-bombers to enter service. Following three prototypes and four pre-production aircraft, ninety-eight series aircraft were built with four 10,050-lb static thrust Rolls-Royce Avon engines.

The Valiant – following a role change from high-level to low-level bombing to avoid Soviet radar – was a victim of its own success. After ten years of it entering RAF service in May 1965, all Valiants were grounded, later withdrawn and scrapped as a result of metal fatigue discovered during routine 'After Flight' checks by RAF ground crews in August 1964. The low-level flying operations had dramatically shortened their useful in-service lives.

Valiant B.2, serial WJ954, which was built for high-speed, low-level operations at night, was first flown by G. R. Bryce and E. B. Trubshaw on 4 September 1953. Arguably the finest British Cold War bomber, the Valiant B.2, like so many other promising British aircraft industry designs, fells victim to defence cuts.

Westland (Petters) – Westland Aircraft – GKN Westland AgustaWestland

Westland, at the Westland Aircraft Works, began building aircraft at their

West Hendford site at Yeovil as a subsidiary of engine manufacturers Petters Ltd in 1915. Initially under subcontract to Short Brothers, it was not long before they were producing designs of their own. For two years, the factory built seaplanes for Short, the Type 184 and twenty Type 166, as well as Sopwith 1½ Strutters under the management of Robert Arthur Bruce who had joined Westland from Sopwith. In 1917, Bruce and Arthur Davenport set about developing three designs of their own: the N.1B Scout seaplane, the small single-seat Wagtail fighter and two-seat Weasel. Two prototypes of the N.1B were built with the serials N16 and N17. Both performed well, but the Admiralty at this time were losing interest in seaplanes in preference to ship-borne types such as the Sopwith Pup. Westland was therefore unlucky not to receive a contract. Six prototype private venture Wagtails were ordered by the Air Board to be used as engine test-beds for the new 170-hp ABC Wasp seventeen-cylinder radial engine that was already displaying serious mechanical defects.

Westland Aircraft Ltd was formed in July 1935 to take over the aircraft branch of Petters Ltd. In July 1938, Petters Works was acquired and at the same time, John Brown & Co. Ltd, a well-known shipbuilding firm, purchased the greater part of Petter's holding in Westland Aircraft Ltd, the remainder acquired at a later date by Associated Electrical Industries Ltd.

Mr E. Petter became managing director and his son 'Teddy' became technical director. At the same time, a new main assembly building was built. Between the wars, and as with most companies, Westland turned to the civil market. The company's first commercial aircraft was the three-seat enclosed cabin Limousine followed by production of the two-seat Woodpigeon biplane and the similar size Widgeon parasol monoplane. Two other civil models were the Westland IV and Wessex four-seat, high-wing feeder-liner that entered airline service in 1929-1930. (The Wessex name was later used for the company's licensed-built S.58 Sikorsky helicopter.)

Military designs at this time comprised of the Walrus, a three-seat, carrier-borne spotter-reconnaissance aircraft. The Walrus was a heavily-modified DH.9A brought about by an Air Ministry requirement to save costs in the lean 1920s by adapting the DH.9A as a deck-landing aircraft. The result was probably one of the ugliest aircraft of all times and reportedly handled extremely badly. The Walrus was followed by the Wizard, a single-seat parasol monoplane interceptor that started life as an all-wooden aircraft. However, as the original aircraft was badly damaged in a forced landing on returning to Yeovil from Martlesham Heath, it was rebuilt as the all-metal Mk I. This later emerged as the Mk II when it was fitted with a supercharged 500-hp Rolls-Royce F.XIS Kestrel engine. The Wizard and the Westbury, a three-seat, twin-engined biplane fighter that followed, did not see service production. An Air Ministry Specification for a two-seat day-bomber resulted in the Westland

The Westland Dragonfly HC.4 played an important part in the Far East Air Force until June 1956 in support of the British Army against communist insurgents in Malaya. Civil-registered Bristow helicopters were fitted with weather radar. (*Author*)

Westland Wessex HC.2 tactical transport and assault helicopters were fitted with two 1,550-hp Bristol Siddeley Gnome Mk 110/111 turbo-shaft engines. (*Warplane Collection*)

RAF Westland SA330 Puma HC.1 tactical assault and troop-transport helicopters first entered service with No. 33 Squadron at RAF Odiham in 1971 and remain in use having operated in Northern Ireland and Iraq. The helicopters are to be upgraded for use well into the second decade of the 21st century. (*Author*)

The two-seat Westland Gazelle can carry three passengers and was used by the RAF and FAA on communications and liaison duties. The Gazelle was also used by the Army Air Corps at Middle Wallop as rotary-winged trainers. (*Author*)

Yeovil, the first prototype, serial J7508, flying at the company's airfield on 3 April 1925. The Westland Yeovil was in competition with Handley Page and Bristol designs. On arrival at Martlesham Heath for acceptance trials, the aircraft attracted a great deal of criticism and lost out to other designs. The two-seat Westland Wapiti general-purpose aircraft was much more successful with 516 being built for the Air Ministry and eighteen exported to Canada, six to Australia and over sixty converted to Westland Wallaces that succeeded it. The Wapiti, designed as a DH.9A replacement, was another Westland design of which it was requested that as many DH.9A parts as possible should be used, hence its resemblance to it. The Wallace was an improved Wapiti fitted with a Bristol Pegasus engine.

In the 1920-1930s, Westland experimented with a series of Pterodactyl designs by Capt. G. T. R. Hill. The three-seat Mark III flew in March 1931 and was followed by the Mark IV, essentially a technology demonstrator. The Pterodactyl Mark V was the most radical fighter aircraft ever built. It had an exceptionally narrow nacelle, some 17 feet 4 inches long, into which was packed a 600-hp Rolls-Royce Goshawk 1 engine, the pilot and gunner, a steam condenser, semi-enclosed fixed tandem-wheel undercarriage, guns and fuel tank. Problems with the Goshawk engine eventually resulted in the project being abandoned in 1935. One of the company's other early all-metal designs was a private venture, two-seat, army co-operation biplane: the PV.3. Its Achilles' heel was the Bristol Jupiter XFA supercharged engine as the Air Ministry overruled its use in army co-operation aircraft types. The PV.4, which featured a gull upper wing, was another unsuccessful type as was the PV.7, another general-purpose design.

During the Second World War, Westland Aircraft Ltd built Lysanders, Whirlwinds and Welkins as well as 2,200 Supermarine Spitfires and Seafires. The Lysander gained fame in the Second World War when it was adapted as a Special Duties aircraft fitted with a 150-gallon, long-range drop tank giving it eight hours' endurance at a cruising speed of 165 mph. In this variant, the Lysander was used by the SOE to fly Allied agents in and out of enemy-occupied territory. Other wartime types were the heavily-armed, single-seat, twin-engined Whirlwind fighter, Fairey Barracuda and the single-seat, high-altitude fighter, the Westland Welkin. The Welkin was plagued with problems that mostly involved engine fires and propeller failures. Of the 100 Welkins placed in series production, only sixty-seven were delivered to the RAF. None were used operationally and the remaining thirty-three were never fitted with engines or taken on RAF charge.

In the immediate post-war period, the Wyvern naval strike fighter was to be Westland's last fixed-wing design to be produced at Yeovil, and as in 1947, the company decided to specialise in rotorcraft. The Wyvern was the first Westland aircraft to enter service with the Fleet Air Arm. From the outset, it was

Twin-rotor Westland (Bristol) Belvedere helicopters were used in Singapore, Malaya and the Middle East in Aden on resupply duties. (*Aviation News*)

Royal Navy and RAF HAR.3A long-range, all-weather SAR helicopters carry a crew of four (two pilots, radar operator and winch man) and are powered by two 1,795-hp Rolls-Royce Gnome gas turbines. (*Author*)

Westland 30 Company demonstration helicopter. (*Author*)

Opposite top: The Westland HC.4 Commando all-weather support and heavy-lift helicopter has a crew of three in the commando role with two pilots, one crewman and twenty-seven fully-equipped troops. (*Author*)

Opposite middle: Westland Lynx AH.7 DRA BERP test and evaluation helicopter. (*Author*)

Opposite bottom: Westland Lynx 3 company demonstration helicopter. (*Author*)

intended that the Wyvern should be powered by a turboprop engine, but as the engines were not available until 1948, the W.34 prototype and five W35s were powered by the Rolls-Royce Eagle 22 inline liquid-cooled engine. Thirteen TF2s were the first turboprop variants fitted with the Armstrong Siddeley Clyde RC1 engine. TF.4/S.4s and series S.4s were fitted with the Armstrong Siddeley Python 3 engine with eight-bladed Rotol contra-rotating propellers. In 1947, Westland signed a licence agreement in the US to build Sikorsky S-51 helicopters named Dragonfly. Westland licensed-production of the Sikorsky S-51 gave the company the experience it needed in the design, development and production of rotary-winged aircraft. Westland later developed the S.51 into the five-seat Widgeon. Subsequent agreements involved production of the S-55 Whirlwind, S-58 Wessex and Sea King, each developed to meet British requirements and specifications with UK engines and components. In addition, the company designed and developed its own Wasp, Scout and Lynx as well as the Anglo-French Puma and Gazelle and the Agusta-Bell 47G Sioux.

Development of the forty-passenger or six-tonne payload Westminster, which flew in prototype form on 15 June 1958, was abandoned two years later. The 1957 Defence White Paper, which signalled the reorganisation of the UK's aviation industry, saw Westland acquire Saunders-Roe Ltd in 1959 followed by the Bristol Helicopter Division on 23 March 1960 and the UK interests of Fairey Aviation. With the acquisitions came factories at East Cowes,

Series Westland Lynx AH.7 attack and troop-transport helicopters have been upgraded to AH.9 standard and equip three regiments of 16 Air Assault Brigade. (*Author*)

The four-crew sea and land-based ASW Agusta EH101 Merlin prototype first flew in October 1987 with three 2,314-hp Rolls-Royce/Turbomeca RTM332-01 engines. (*Warplane Collection*)

Eastleigh, Hayes and Weston-super-Mare. From Bristol, Westland acquired the twin-rotor Belvedere, a nineteen-troop transport, general-purpose helicopter. Westland also received the Rotodyne from Fairey (abandoned in 1962) as well as the Fairey Gannet fixed-wing, naval strike and anti-submarine aircraft and P.531 five-seat general purpose helicopter from Saunders-Roe. The latter was developed into the Scout for the British Army and Wasp for the Royal Navy.

After re-establishing itself in 1952, the Italian Agusta Co. negotiated a licence agreement with Bell for production of its Model 47 Bell-47G. The first Agusta-built B-47G flew in 1954. Westland subsequently developed an association with Agusta to licence-produce fifty B-47Gs for the British Army. This initial batch was followed by 250 licensed-built by Westland in the UK. The Westland Sea King family was developed from the Sikorsky SH-3D. The first production variant flew on 7 May 1969 since when more than 250 have been built including the HC.4 Commando, a tactical variant first flown on 12 September 1973. The twin Rolls-Royce Gem-powered, medium, multi-purpose Lynx was based on the Westland WG-13 design, a product of the 1968 Anglo-French helicopter agreement.

Westland are the design authority for the Lynx and subsequently converted forty-four HAS 3s to ASV HAS 8s: twelve by Westland and thirty-two at RNAY

The Westland Sea King HAS.5 anti-submarine warfare helicopter has a crew of four including two pilots and is powered by two 1,500-hp Rolls-Royce Gnome H 1400-1 shaft turbine engines. (*Author*)

The first series AgustaWestland Merlin to leave the Italian production line was delivered to the MMI. (*Author*)

Fleetlands depot. The conversion involved the fitment of a nose-mounted thermal imager and with BERP rotors, as used on the record-breaking Lynx, the aircraft was of a similar build standard as the export Super Lynx.

The company's twin-engined, nineteen-seat WG 30/Westland 30, first flown on 10 April 1979, was less successful and only forty-one were built. Twenty-one were exported to India, where, after three fatal accidents, the whole fleet was grounded.

Due to difficulties in 1986, the British Government were forced to intervene to save the company and a minority shareholding was acquired by United Technologies and Fiat.

In 1988, Fiat sold its shareholdings to GKN who eventually gained overall control in 1994. GKN Westland then began work on what must truly be the world's most advanced helicopter at the time: the large, three-engined EH 101 Merlin military and commercial helicopter. The EH 101 matured into another joint venture with Agusta of Italy. Designed as a multi-role helicopter, the first EH 101 prototype flew at Yeovil on 9 October 1987. The aircraft (serials RN01-RN04 plus PP5) was powered by three 2,312-hp Rolls-Royce Turbomeca RTM 322 turbo-shaft engines and underwent extensive service trials with the Royal Navy in conjunction with DERA Boscombe Down.

Extensive flight trials using the RN05-08 at the Royal Navy's Intensive Flying Trials Unit at RNAS Culdrose, Cornwall, were held throughout 1998 and 1999. After the trials, up to forty-four aircraft were introduced into Royal Navy service to be deployed aboard their Type 23 destroyers, helicopter carriers and support ships. Twenty-two Merlin HC.3s were delivered to the RAF by the end of 2001. No. 28 Squadron at RAF Benson, Oxfordshire, formerly based in Hong Kong with Westland Wessex HC.2s, were the first RAF recipients.

Two civil variant prototypes, PP8 and PP9, underwent an extensive 6,000-hour operational flying programme in Italy and the UK. In addition, an RAF Merlin had been to the US on a demonstration tour in 2001 in a view to licence-produce the type. It was eventually chosen to replace the aging Sikorsky SH.3D aircraft of the US 'Marine One' Corps as used by the US President. Seven helicopters were assembled in the US by Lockheed-Martin and designated as the VH-71A (AgustaWestland US101). AgustaWestland EH101 Merlins in service with the Royal Navy and RAF have seen operational service in Iraq and Afghanistan and proved highly successful. However, in spite of the EH 101s success, on 10 January 2002, AgustaWestland announced a total of 950 redundancies at two plants at Yeovil and Weston-super-Mare due to a fall-off of orders for military helicopters.

Meanwhile, the company received an order to assemble and equip sixty-seven Boeing AH-64D Apache 'Longbow' attack helicopters for the British Army Air Corp. These aircraft designated WAH-64D were delivered in the early 2000s with a possible upgrade programme to the Boeing 'Digital' AH-64E Apache. This upgrade (pending in 2010) is currently awaiting coalition government funding.

Chapter 2

British Aero-Engine Manufacturers' Mergers and Takeovers

Napier Company – D. Napier & Son Ltd
Gwynnes Co.
Rolls-Royce Ltd (1915)
Wolseley
Royal Aircraft Factory – RAE Farnborough
Armstrong Siddeley Motors Ltd
Aero Engine Division – Bristol Aeroplane Co. Ltd
Aircraft Disposal (Air Disco)
De Havilland Aircraft Co. – de Havilland Engine Co. Ltd
Cirrus Aero Engines Ltd – Cirrus Hermes Engineering Co.
Blackburn Aeroplane & Motor Co.
Blackburn Engines Ltd Brasil-Straker – Cosmos Engineering Co. Ltd
Metropolitan-Vickers – MetroVick (MV)
English Electric
Rover Car Co. (1944)
Humber Motor Works
Bristol Siddeley Engines Ltd
BS Small Engine Division
BS Aero Division
Rolls-Royce Ltd Aero Division
Rolls-Royce Ltd - Small Engine Division
Rolls-Royce Ltd – Bristol Engine Division
Rolls-Royce (1971) Ltd – Large Engine Division (Derby)
Rolls-Royce (1971) Ltd – Small Engine Division (Leavesden, Watford)
Rolls-Royce (1971) Ltd – Bristol Engine Division
Rolls-Royce Ltd Military Engine Group (Bristol and Leavesden)
Rolls-Royce Ltd Civil Engine Group (Derby and East Kilbride)

Although the Wright Brothers have the distinction of making the first-powered flight in 1903 with an engine designed specifically for the purpose, there had

Rolls-Royce Merlin *c.* 1936 was developed from the engine that was first produced for Schneider Cup racing. More than 150,000 engines were built, and they powered all the most importatn British Aircraft during the Second World War. (*V. Consentino*)

been such an engine in existence. The engine was built by Stephen M. Blazer of New York in 1898 and later modified by Charles Manley after his own unsuccessful attempt at producing an aero-engine. Derived from a car engine that he produced in 1894 (albeit a five-cylinder, air-cooled, rotary engine), it was a complete failure and unable of sustaining an output of little more than 8 hp for a few minutes. Having failed with his own design, Manley turned his attention to Blazer's engine. First, he tried to modify it to produce the required output; however, when this proved impractical, there was no option other than a complete redesign. In January 1902, Manley tested his five-cylinder, radial water-cooled engine on a dynamometer in his workshop and found it to give a remarkable 50-hp output with a weight ratio of 3.96 lbs per hp. It was a remarkably advanced engine for the time, but unfortunately for Manley, the engine was subsequently fitted to an aeroplane that was destined to fail: the 'Aerodrome', Samuel Langley's personally-designed tandem monoplane. When launched twice from a houseboat on the River Potomac, the aircraft fouled the catapult mechanism both times and finished up in the river. The 'Aerodrome' was finally abandoned, leaving the Wright Brothers to make their move into powered flight.

When Samuel Cody made his first British-powered flight in the British Army Plane No. 1, the aircraft was powered by a 50-hp Antoinette designed by Frenchman Léon Levasseur. Despite the Antoinette having a number of advanced features such as steam cooling and direct petrol injection over the valve ports, it was inherently unreliable and cost £480. However, it paved the way in 1907 for another Frenchman, Laurant Sequin and his brother Louis, to establish what was to be the most outstanding aero-engine of the pioneering days of aviation: the Gnôme. The idea for this excellent engine came from an Australian, Lawrence Hargrave (1850–1915), in 1887. Hargrave's engine functioned on compressed air and was of a radial design where the crankshaft remained stationary while the cylinder and crankcase revolved round it, thereby turning the propeller. The radial gave more to the advancement of aviation at this time than any other factor and 70 per cent of aircraft at the 1913 Paris Aero Salon were powered by such an engine. The original Gnôme design dates back to 1892 and was a five-cylinder unit rated at 50 hp, weighing 135 lbs for a power/weight ratio of 2.71 lbs per hp. Unfortunately, the design suffered from malfunctions associated with the valves in the head of the piston and this led the company in 1911 to introduce the single-valve Monosoupape engine. This proved to be extremely popular and reliable, and inevitably led to a number of copies appearing with the makers using various means to get round patents filed on the Gnôme. As many as fifteen different Monosoupape types were available from 1913 to 1926.

In England, the Gwynnes Co., a well-known marine engine manufacturer, were granted a licence to build the French Clerget. At the time, the Clerget was far ahead of any home-produced engine and was essential to the growing impetus of air power in the First World War. However, the radial engine was not without its problems and an inherent defect was caused by heat that was generated through combustion if it was not evenly distributed. Air rushing over the engine while in flight served only to cool the front of the engine and not the rear, resulting in the cylinder walls distorting. Although the fitment of 'Oburator' piston rings went some way to providing a cure, engines had to be replaced at fairly frequent intervals. It was not until W. O. Bentley of Bentley Cars applied himself to the problem that a lasting solution evolved. After carrying out exhaustive tests, Bentley's solution was to incorporate aluminium pistons into the engine. He submitted his ideas to the Admiralty who were impressed with his idea and awarded Bentley with a commission as a lieutenant in the Royal Naval Reserve. He was then assigned as a liaison officer to the Gwynnes Co. and was unable to convince them of the advantages of fitting a new aluminium piston or lined cylinder. As a result, Bentley moved to the Humber Motor Works at Coventry with a brief to develop a new rotary engine embodying all the features he had put forward. The first engine that Bentley produced was the 200-hp BR.2 and the initial Admiralty reaction was one of horror. It was even suggested that as a newcomer, Bentley should perhaps address himself to something more modest. This he did and produced a 130-hp rotary engine that was the same size as the Clerget, but developed far more power. Having proved his capabilities, Bentley was given permission to proceed with the development of the 200-hp BR.2, an engine that has often been described by the aero-engine fraternity as an 'engineering piece of art'.

15,000 lb thrust Bristol Siddeley Pegasus Pg.5 vectored-thrust turbofan as fitted to the Hawker P.1127, later named Kestrel F(GA) Mk.1. (*Wings*).

In 1843, British inventor William Samuel Henson (1812–1888) patented plans for the first aeroplane with an engine, propellers and fixed cambered wings. However, after building one unsuccessful steam-powered aircraft in 1847 at Chard, Somerset, he gave up on the project.

In 1848, his friend, John Stringfellow (1799–1883), built a small model aeroplane using Henson's design, but it could only stay in the air for a short time due to another unsuccessful engine. Disillusioned by the public reaction to his efforts, Henson immigrated to the US in the same year. Nonetheless in the UK, from these faltering beginnings led to the new petrol-fuelled engine to be adapted to power aircraft development. From the mid-1880s until 1944, it was the petrol engine that was used almost exclusively for powered flight. In 1885, the first petrol engine had been built in Germany. Initially, Gottlieb Daimler and Karl Benz had experimented separately developing successful petrol engines for land vehicles. The adoption of their use for aeroplanes was not a problem despite in their early form the engines needed considerable redesign to propel a heavier than air machine such as the aeroplane. Even the Wright Brothers had to design their own engine for the Wright Flyer...

The original Wright engine was a four-cylinder unit with a 4-inch bore and a 4.25-inch stroke attached to an aluminium crankcase arranged so that it should be mounted in the horizontal position. The cylinders were water-cooled with low tension ignition and surface carburetion used. It was thought to have developed 15 hp for a total weight of 240 lbs. It had a flywheel and two chain sprockets for driving a right-hand and left-hand airscrew respectively. Other features of the engine were water-cooling by pump circulation, automatic inlet and overhead valves, and positively operated exhaust valves arranged over the inlet valves. In 1910, Renault produced an 80-hp, V8 engine with air-cooled cylinders that inspired a similar design from the Royal Aircraft Establishment at Farnborough. Copying was rife and even the Admiralty presented the 1914 TT-winning Mercedes car to Rolls-Royce for examination. Eventually, its engine formed the basis of the Rolls-Royce Hawk and Falcon V12, which was to power the famous Bristol Fighter. One of the most important of all engines developed during the First World War was the American Liberty V12 designed by a team of car manufacturers within three months of the US entering the conflict. The Liberty went on to form the basis of the American aero-engine industry of the future.

The evolution of British aero-engine manufacturers is not particularly straightforward. By the cessation of hostilities in 1918, the main players had evolved such as Rolls-Royce who formed in 1916, but did not produce their first engine, a V12 inline assembly, until 1915.

In the early 1930s, its most famous engine was the Rolls-Royce Kestrel that powered the Hawker Fury and Hawker Hart aircraft. A total of 1,882 Rolls-Royce aero-engines were produced from 1930 until 1934 showing a gross profit of £597,000. A total of 4,778 Kestrel engines were built in twenty-seven different variants from 1928 to 1938. Arguably, Rolls-Royce's most famous engine was its PV12 Merlin whose development started in 1932 and was to power many British Second World War fighters and bombers. By August 1936, under Air Ministry Expansion Scheme F, the company had orders for 2,854 Merlin engines. However, in order to meet wartime demand for the Merlin under the Scheme L Expansion Programme, a new factory was built at Crewe and in 1939, under the 'war potential' plan, two additional plants were sanctioned. The 1940 Rolls-Royce production organisation was as shown.

In the late 1920s, the most widely used aero-engine in the world was the Bristol Jupiter with a total of 7,100 produced (eight times as many Bristol-designed aero-engines were produced than any other).

Licensed manufacture of the Jupiter designed by Sir Roy Fedden (1885–1973) was undertaken by no less than seventeen different countries. The Jupiter engine was succeeded by the Pegasus and Mercury with 1,000 produced between 1932 and 1934, many for export. Later, Fedden turned his attentions to sleeve valve aero-engines and after many years wrestling with many technical problems, he produced the Bristol Hercules and Centaurus. These sleeve-valve engines, of which over 100,000 were made during the Second World War, were fitted to many famous British aircraft types such as the Handley Page Halifax, Bristol Beaufighter and Vickers Wellington. A number of engines were also used in post-war airliners and remained in use until the early 1990s and achieved an aviation record of some 3,000 miles before servicing.

In 1966, with the acquisition of Bristol Siddeley Engines, Rolls-Royce became the sole British aero-engine manufacturer. In 1971, after getting into difficulties developing its RB 211 engine for the Lockheed Tristar L1011 airliner, the company went into voluntary liquidation reforming once again as Rolls-Royce (1971) Ltd, the company now known as Rolls-Royce Ltd.

The Napier Co. (later D. Napier & Son Ltd) was set up by David Napier (an engineer) in 1808 making printing machinery. Napier's entry into the aero-engine business started with the production of the Royal Aircraft Factory RAF 3a engine and the Sunbeam Arab. It then concentrated its efforts on its own designs producing the famous Lion that was renowned for its reliability and performance by all those associated with aviation. In 1927, a new series of inline double-crank engines, the Rapier and Dagger, appeared. Unfortunately, the Sabre that followed was less successful proving to be a costly and unrewarding project. In 1961, after almost fifty years in aero-engine design and production, Napier merged with Rolls-Royce.

Armstrong Siddeley Motors Ltd entered into the field of aero-engine production in 1917 when they were invited to take over the manufacture of Royal Aircraft Factory designs. The first engine produced was the Royal Aircraft Factory's RAF 8, later named Jaguar. In the Second World War, over 35,000 of the extremely reliable (1,200 hours between overhauls), Armstrong Siddeley Cheetah, mainly used in training aircraft, were built with its power output increased over the years from 375 hp to 475 hp. In 1949, Armstrong Siddeley acquired Metropolitan-Vickers and in 1958, merged with Bristol Aero-Engines to form Bristol Siddeley Engines Ltd. In 1966, Bristol Siddeley was taken over by Rolls-Royce.

Wolseley started building aero-engines as early as 1909 at its Adderley Works in Birmingham. The first aero-engine to be produced by the company was the Viper based on the Hispano-Suiza engine, but with the drawdown of business after the First World War, Wolseley decided to pull out of aero-engine production. However, in 1933, having been taken over by Morris Motors, the company did make a series of small air-cooled radials, but this brief sojourn into the field of aero-engine production once again amounted to nothing.

The Bristol Aeroplane Co. Ltd Aero-Engine Division of the Bristol Aeroplane Company was not formed until 1921, but its origins go back to 1904 when Roy Fedden was apprenticed to the Bristol Motor Co. On completing his apprenticeship, Fedden joined forces with John Brasil to design a small two-seater car. Fedden later secured a position with a motor engineering company that specialised in omnibus production, The Straker Squire Co.

Later, Fedden and Brasil joined forces to produce a number of new motor cars and the Brasil-Straker Co. was formed with Fedden appointed as chief engineer. In 1915, the Brasil-Straker factory was commandeered by the Admiralty and put to work making Rolls-Royce Hawk and Falcon engines, and components for the Eagle that followed.

In 1936, in contrast to Rolls-Royce who were still developing its famous liquid-cooled Merlin, Bristol had unprecedented demand for its air-cooled Mercury and Pegasus engines used in a variety of different aircraft such as the Bristol Blenheim, Vickers Wellesley, Vickers Wellington I, Handley Page Harrow and Hampden bombers, Gloster Gauntlet and Gladiator fighters, Fairey Swordfish torpedo-bombers and the Short, Supermarine and Saunders-Roe flying boats. In order to meet Air Ministry demands that their engines be delivered by April 1939, it was necessary for the first MAP aero-engine shadow production to be implemented.

The first Bristol Blenheims entered service with the RAF in 1937 and by the outbreak of war, the air force had some 1,000 Mercury engine-powered Blenheims in use – more than any other aircraft type at this time. Many new world altitude records were also established by aircraft fitted with Bristol Mercury and Pegasus engines. Following the Mercury, Bristol introduced the nine-cylinder, sleeve-valve engine: the Perseus. This was new technology and Bristol was the only aero-engine manufacturer to successfully produce an engine of this type. The first Perseus engine flew in a Bristol Bulldog fighter in 1933 and it went on to power aircraft such as the Westland Lysander, Blackburn Botha, Roc and Skua, and the Short Empire flying boat. The Perseus was closely followed by the Taurus and the double-row, fourteen-cylinder, sleeve-valve Bristol Hercules. Pre-war, the department was reorganised and became the Aero Engine Division of the Bristol Aeroplane Co. During the Second World War, more than 50 per cent of the Bristol Hercules engine (100,000 were produced) were fitted to RAF 'heavies' such as the Bristol Beaufighter, Handley Page Halifax, Short Stirling and a number of Avro Lancaster Mk IIs as an insurance against failure of the Rolls-Royce produced Merlin. Production of the Hercules continued after 1945 with the engine fitted to the Bristol Company's first post-war project, the Bristol Freighter. The final Bristol-produced piston-engine was the eighteen-cylinder, sleeve-valve Centaurus that was used in both civil and military types such as the Hawker Tempest, Vickers Warwick, Bristol Brigand, Buckingham and Hawker Sea Fury as well as the mighty but short-lived Bristol Brabazon civil airliner prototype.

In 1955, the Aero Engine Division of Bristol Aeroplane Co. became Bristol Aero-Engines Ltd. In 1958, it merged with Armstrong Siddeley Motors to form Bristol Siddeley Engines Ltd and in 1966, Bristol Siddeley was taken over by Rolls-Royce. The last of the 66,000 Hercules engines produced left the Bristol production lines in 1965 by which time a total of 137,000 engines bearing the Bristol nameplate had been made. The engine was also licence-built by five other British companies and twenty-four foreign companies. Involvement in jet engine technology began at Bristol in 1941 shortly before Sir Roy Fedden left the company when a survey revealed that in the field of gas/prop turbine design and development, no work was being undertaken. Bristol decided to pursue this field resulting in the appearance of its Theseus turboprop that made its first run in 1945 and became the first turboprop engine to complete an official 100-hour type test.

Cirrus Aero Engines Ltd was formed in 1927 from the Aircraft Disposal Co. The Cirrus Hermes Engineering Co. had produced the light four-cylinder, in-line, air-cooled engines for the 'light aeroplane' market since 1925. In 1934, the manufacture of these engines was taken over by Blackburn Aeroplane and Motor Co. Ltd. A new series of engines were produced maintaining the company's hold on the light aeroplane engine market with such types as the 90-hp Cirrus 1 as used in the Taylorcraft Auster 1 army observation plane. In 1959, the company was renamed Blackburn Engines Ltd and became part of Bristol Siddeley Engines Ltd in 1961. In 1920, Cosmos Engineering Co. Ltd (formerly Brasil-Straker) who specialised in aero-engines was, after some considerable persuasion by the Air Ministry, taken over by the Bristol Aeroplane Co. so it could produce its own aero-engines. Taking over the designs, assets and some Cosmos staff, Bristol established its aero-engine department at Filton, Bristol, which was known as Bottom Works to distinguish it from the aircraft factory at the top of the hill. Established as the Aero Engine Division of the Bristol Aeroplane Co., it was not long before Bristol was as famous for its aero-engines as it was for its aircraft. Before its demise, Cosmos had been working on the design of three indigenous radial engines, all of which had been run on the test-bed: the fourteen-cylinder Mercury, the nine-cylinder Jupiter, and by modification of the basic Jupiter leaving six cylinders off, the three-cylinder Lucifer. The first Jupiter engine had been flown in a Bristol Badger aircraft in 1919. Also in 1919, Cosmos had set up what is believed to be the world's first engine air test centre at Filton. The first aircraft to use the facility was an Avro 504K, registration G- EADL, testing the three-cylinder Cosmos Lucifer engine. The new works completed the development of the Jupiter and the designated Jupiter II – this became the first air-cooled radial to pass the new and stringent Air Ministry Type Test.

In 1925, a Jupiter-powered Hawker Woodcock became the first Bristol-powered aircraft to enter service with the RAF. Production of the Jupiter continued at Bristol until 1935 and such was its success that it set a record for aero-engine usage by way of installation in over 280 different aircraft types and totally dominated European military and civil business in the 1920s and 1930s. The Jupiter was also built under licence in large numbers in sixteen countries.

In 1930 with the Jupiter still in production, another air-cooled radial, the Bristol Pegasus, was introduced. Developing more than twice the power of the Jupiter, the Pegasus was fitted to many famous Second World War airframes including the Vickers Wellington, Handley Page Hampden, Fairey Swordfish and Short Sunderland flying boat.

The de Havilland organisation entered the aero-engine industry in 1926. It produced the first of the Gipsy light aeroplane engine series a year later, primarily for fitment to the company's Moth series of light planes. The Gipsy range of engines was designed by Maj. Frank Halford who worked in close collaboration with the aircraft design department of the de Havilland Co. In 1948, the de Havilland Engine Co. Ltd was established at Stonegrove, Edgware, Middlesex, although most engine production was carried out at Leavesden, near Watford, Hertfordshire. De Havilland entered the aero-engine market as most of the powerplants available from the established companies at the time were either too large or expensive for the small de Havilland aircraft. Therefore, in the late 1920s, de Havilland invested £155,000 on erecting new buildings, the purchase of new plant, machinery and high-precision machine tools to enable them to produce the aero-engines needed to power their aircraft. In 1928, de Havilland reached an agreement with the Wright Corporation for the production of its aero-engines in the US. Most engine production in the UK at the time was in the hands of Bristol and Rolls-Royce along with Armstrong Siddeley and Napier. (Due to their lack of investment in research and development, Armstrong Siddeley engines were rarely selected for frontline aircraft throughout the 1930s.) Napier also made a similar mistake. They became complacent having, between 1923 and 1930, grossed earnings totalling £5.4 million for their excellent Napier Lion engine. Unfortunately, they were never able to find or produce a suitable replacement unlike Bristol and Rolls-Royce who produced a succession of successful designs such as the Pegasus and Kestrel by maintaining a high level of investment in research and development. By the time of the rearmament push, Napier had run out of work and nearly all frontline RAF aircraft were powered by Rolls-Royce or Bristol engines with both companies having a number of new designs such as the infamous Merlin and Hercules.

After the First World War, rotary engines were replaced by inline types. The radial had its cylinders arranged similar to the rotary, but with the crankshaft revolving. In the interwar years, there was much controversy over which type to use. Up until the mid-1920s, the inline water-cooled engine was the most advanced and most used. Radials were the newcomers, but gradually with production of the American Pratt & Whitney Wasp and Bristol Jupiter, it was the radial that became the most popular. An obvious disadvantage of the water-cooled inline when fitted to a military aircraft was the radiator and its vulnerability to enemy fire. Also, 'flush fit' radiators used for streamlining were troublesome. However, when used in civil aircraft such as racing aeroplanes and Schneider Trophy entrants, water-cooled 'V' engines were often used. Rolls-Royce produced a water-cooled 'V' engine for British Schneider Trophy entrants which won the trophy three times. It was this engine that formed the basis of the Merlin, Britain's most famous Second World War engine that powered the Hurricane, Spitfire, Lancaster and the North American P-51

Mustang with its 'Packard Bell' Merlin. However, the radial was not dead and buried as proved by Focke-Wulf and its Fw 190 'Butcher Bird', the most successful German fighter of the period. In fact, the radial engine was developed for both civil and military aircraft until the advent of the jet engine.

In 1930, RAF Flt-Lt (later Sir) Frank Whittle (1907–1996) filed a patent for a turbojet power unit. However, to bring his prodigy to fruition, Whittle needed financial backing, which neither the Air Ministry nor private companies were prepared to risk. Most aero-engineers agreed the design might work, but the Under Secretary of State for Air was far less enthusiastic stating '...scientific investigation into possibilities that the jet engine could be a competitor to the propeller-driven engine as a means of propulsion for the aeroplane indicate the invention does not warrant serious consideration'. Undaunted, Whittle carried on his research and two years later with a revised design, again filed a patent. The Air Ministry were still unimpressed, but this time Whittle managed to secure financial backing for his project from the Investment Banking Co. of O. T. Falk and Partners who provided Whittle with sufficient capital of £2,000 to set up Power Jets Ltd. A further £725 was subscribed later. However, due to the need for secrecy, Power Jets were not able disclose the nature of the project to investors and it was necessary for the Government to ensure sufficient funds were available to allow research to continue.

In March 1941, de Havilland had been invited to design a jet fighter and its engine. Design of the engine began in April 1941 and within a year the prototype was running on the Hatfield test-beds. The engine was designated as the H (Halford) 1, later named the Goblin, and had its first flight on 5 March 1943 in a Gloster Meteor. By the end of 20 September 1943 – like the DH.100 Vampire aircraft and Whittle's engine before it – a de Havilland H-1 was supplied to the US in July 1943. The engine was turned over by the US Air Technical Service Command to the Lockheed Aircraft Corporation to form the initial power unit for the Lockheed XP-80 Shooting Star single-seat fighter. This airplane, being America's first true jet fighter, was designed, built and flown in 145 days. A de Havilland H-1 engine was also installed in a Curtiss XF15C-1 single-seat naval fighter, a dual-powered aircraft with a normal Pratt & Whitney R-2800 radial piston-engine driving a tractor airscrew and a turbojet exhausting beneath the tail unit. The DH Goblin I engine was the first British jet engine to pass the official type test in the new gas turbine category holding the official Approval Certificate No. 1.

In 1944, the de Havilland Engine Co. Ltd was formed. There then followed further jet engine developments by way of the Ghost, Gyron and Gyron Junior as fitted to the Blackburn Buccaneer strike bomber. In 1961, DH Engines became part of Bristol Siddeley Engines Ltd. Production of the British Halford H-1 engine was assumed in the US by the Allis-Chalmers Manufacturing Co., Milwaukee, Wisconsin. The US Navy monitored production of the new engines, which were plagued by endless maintenance difficulties. In the event, the USAAF received only three Allis-Chalmer H-1 engines and turned them over to the US Navy in January 1947. Consequently, the Lockheed P-80 (F-80) Shooting Star airframe was fitted with the more powerful General Electric I-40, later followed by the 4,600-lb static thrust Allison J33-11 engine of 12,000 were built.

Sir Frank Whittle can be rightly acclaimed as the 'father of the jet engine' in Britain as can A. A. Griffiths of the Royal Aircraft Establishment as the 'grandfather of the single-stage axial compressor/turbine and free vortex blading'. Whittle's design was a refinement of Griffiths' simpler unit with a shrouded engine and efflux emerging as a high-velocity jet. Or, put another way, Whittle was the 'father of the jet' and Griffith the 'father of the gas turbine'. The first Whittle jet engine was built by the British Thomas-Houston Co. at Rugby under contract to Whittle's state-owned development company Power Jets (Research and Development) Ltd. The engine first ran in April 1937 and was intended to be fitted to a small transatlantic mail-plane. From April 1937 to October 1938, a number of modifications were made and the engine known as the WU was produced, which until December 1940 was the only one in existence and providing the test-bed for all W1X development work. In fact, this W1X engine that was not officially airworthy was the first jet in Britain to become airborne when an 'unofficial' occurrence arose during taxiing trials of the Gloster E.28/39 aircraft in April 1941. The official engine cleared for flight was the W1 that was flown for the first time in the E28/39 by Flt Lt P. E. G. Sayer at RAF Cranwell on 14 May 1941 (thereafter, only routine maintenance was allowed as the engine was restricted for no more than ten hours of use). It is worth mentioning that the highly experimental engine and aircraft completed their proving trials without modification and that not one minute of scheduled flying time was lost to an engine or airframe defect. Within forty-six days, the engine had completed a twenty-five-hour special test programme when it was installed and operated in the aircraft for a further ten hours with only routine maintenance necessary.

In October 1941, a Whittle engine, a complete set of manufacturing drawings and a number of engineers from Power Jets Ltd, were flown to the US to assist General Electric to commence manufacture of the engine in the US. Within a year, the Bell XP-59A aircraft fitted with two General Electric (Whittle W type) engines became the second Allied jet-propelled aircraft to take to the air within two years. Events in the European theatre dictated that the use of the new jet engines should be for jet fighter propulsion, the opposite of the original intention. Whittle and Power Jets continued with further developments and evolved a number of new projects that were restricted by wartime contingencies and very limited resources available.

In 1944, the Ministry of Aircraft Production nationalised the financially troubled Power Jets Ltd with its assets valued at £320,000. Production of Power Jets' W2 engine was undertaken by Rover Car Co. who very wisely subcontracted combustion system responsibilities to Lucas. Power Jets were eventually sidelined to an advisory role. Whittle engines only came into their own when Rolls-Royce assumed responsibility for production and developed the Welland from Whittle's W2 design. It was in a way fortuitous for Rolls-Royce who until this time had been working on its own first jet engine, the WR1. The engine was designed for experimental purposes with low turbine blade stresses i.e., it was a comparatively large engine for a given thrust of 2,000 lbs (910 kg). Two WR1s were built of which the first ran for some thirty-five hours; however, trouble was experienced with the combustion equipment. Extensive development work on combustion chambers and turbine blades was carried out, the restricting factor being the construction of the turbine blades due to limitations of temperatures and rpm.

Fortunately, firms such as Rolls-Royce and de Havilland with far greater facilities and resources were able to explore various avenues of development to greater depth resulting in both companies producing their own jet engines. Rolls-Royce had converted a Vickers Wellington into a flying engine test-bed for the W2B/23 Whittle engine that was mounted in the tail in place of the gun turret. The related instrument panel was mounted forwards in the aircraft with remote control to the engine. A total of twenty-five flying hours took place with the first engine giving 1,250 lbs (565 kg) static thrust and a second Wellington airplane adapted to investigate high-altitude operation at 10,675 metres (35,000 feet). The first production Rolls-Royce version of the Whittle W2B/23 engine passed its 100-hour type test in April 1943. It was 1,098 mm (43 inches) in diameter and gave a thrust of 1,700 lbs (772 kg) for a weight of 850 lb (386 kg). It was named Welland after Rolls-Royce designated their new class of jet propulsion units after British rivers (the name was chosen to represent the idea of 'flow' associated with jet propulsion). Production deliveries of the Welland to the RAF began in May 1944 when it had passed its 500-hour type test and went into service with 180 hours between maintenance overhauls. Rolls-Royce's first important innovation to Whittle's design was to straighten the reverse airflow of the Welland giving rise to a greatly improved new engine: the Derwent I.

Development of the Derwent I had been pursued by the Rover Co. until Rolls-Royce took over the Rover plant at Barnoldswick in April 1943. The W2B/26 served as the prototype Derwent I and was the first Rolls-Royce engine of this type. The engine was completed in three and a half months and entered tests in July 1943. It passed its 100-hour type test at 2,000 lbs (910 kg) static thrust in November 1943 and in April 1944 completed its first air test. The Derwent was subsequently chosen for fitment to the twin-jet Gloster Meteor F.1 of which over 500 were eventually built and first flew in March

1944. Rolls-Royce continued with the development of the Derwent producing the Derwent 4 rated at 2,350 lbs of static thrust followed by the Derwent 5 at 3,500 lbs of static thrust and powered some 3,000 post-war Meteors.

It would be true to say that at the end of the war, Britain led the world in jet engine technology. Also, it would be true to say that the Rolls-Royce Nene that developed 5,000 lbs of thrust was at the time the world's most powerful jet engine. Unfortunately, the Nene was never to realise its full potential for want of a suitable airframe. In the axial class, the Avon (originally Rolls-Royce Tay two-shaft turbofan) started production at 6,500 lbs of thrust as the AJ-65. This was followed by the AJ-85 and AJ-105 developing 10,500 lbs of thrust followed by the redesigned RA-14, etc. The Rolls-Royce Sapphire was developed in parallel with the Avon and this proved to have been quite expedient when the Avon engines displayed compressor problems (rectified by adapting solutions embodied in the design of the Sapphire). The larger 10,000-lb thrust engines such as the Bristol Olympus and Rolls-Royce Conway underwent considerable development, eventually producing increases in thrust levels to almost double their original output. The Bristol Olympus was used in the famous Vulcan V-bomber and in a modified up-rated form in the BAC/Aerospatiale *Concorde* SST.

In the small-sized turboprops, the axial Armstrong Siddeley Mamba together with the centrifugal Rolls-Royce Dart were the main exponents. Among larger turboprops, the Theseus, Proteus and smaller Naiad reigned supreme. There were also a number of coupled engines like the Double Mamba as used in aircraft such as the Fleet Air Arm's Fairey Gannet and naval patrol aircraft.

With a background in producing gas turbines for power stations, Metropolitan-Vickers started work on gas turbines for aircraft propulsion and in 1938 to 1940, designed the F2 jet propulsion engine with axial-flow compressor. The first engine was run on the test bench in 1941 and after modifications, passed a special category test for flight in 1942.

Early flights with the engines took place in an Avro Lancaster flying test-bed on 29 June 1943 and in the fourth Gloster Meteor F.9/40 prototype, serial DG204/G (MetroVick MFV.2), on 13 November 1943. The first engine had a thrust rating of 1,800 lbs (817 kg) on a weight of 1,525 lbs (692 kg). This was followed by an engine of a new design that ran in 1945 known as the F2/4 with a maximum thrust rating of 3,500 lbs (1,590 kg). The company also designed the first ducted fan augmenter which when combined with an F2 engine gave rise to the F3 of which bench tests began in August 1945.

By 1948, Dr David Smith at MetroVick had developed the F9 Sapphire, at the time the world's most advanced axial-flow gas turbine engine. Unfortunately, MetroVick did not pursue production of the F9 and under pressure from the British Government, the engine and associated research data was handed over to Armstrong Siddeley Motors who had taken over the work of MetroVick. This gave rise to the Sapphire development which was ordered by Air Cdr Banks as a backup for the Avon. In 1949, MetroVick was acquired by Armstrong Siddeley Motors. Later series production Armstrong Siddeley Sapphires were used to power various marks of Hawker Hunter and Gloster Javelin jet fighters, and the supersonic English Electric P.1A prototype, serial WG763. Dr Smith's research work was used to resolve problems with the Rolls-Royce Avon Series 100 gas turbine engines with solutions already adopted and embodied in the Sapphire.

The Rolls-Royce Avon started life as the AJ-65 axial jet developing 6,500-lbs static thrust (The 'AJ' designation indicated that the forward compressor element of the engine was axial (inline) rather than centrifugal as pioneered by Whittle.) The prototype that was tested in 1946 gave disappointing results. It refused to accelerate and broke its first-stage compressor blades, but these were early days and many problems needed to be overcome. It was discovered that blade design was critical and at the exhaust end, the power turbine had to cope with flame temperatures in the region of 1,830 degrees Centigrade. At one time, Lord Hives, Managing Director of Rolls-Royce, had hoped the Avon would be the Merlin of jet engine production, but with only 10,433 compared to a total of around 160,000 Merlins produced, this was not to be. Following further development, series production engines began in 1950, the units designated RA-3. By 1952, following much redesign and further development – which included new compressor aerodynamics – the Avon was a competitive engine. An unexpected problem arose with its fitment to the Hawker Hunter fighter as the engine stalled when the guns were fired. The cause of the problem when discovered was quite unexpected as it was found that the fuel pressure to the Avon's burners was simultaneously reduced when the 30-mm Aden cannon button was depressed. However, by 1953, these problems had been overcome and the engine was at the foremost of jet engine technology in the UK. In the same year, a specially-prepared Avon-engine Hawker Hunter F.5 fitted with a custom nose radome piloted by Sqdn Ldr Neville Duke set a new world record attaining a speed of 727.48 mph. This record was later broken by an Avon-powered Supermarine Swift F.4 attaining 735.1 mph and flown by Supermarine test pilot Lt Cdr Lithgow on 25 September 1953 over Libya, North Africa. On March 1956, the record was once again broken by a Fairey Delta 2 experimental aircraft fitted with an Avon RA.5 and piloted by Lt Peter Twiss recording a maximum speed of 1,131.76 mph. The Avon had been planned to power the English Electric Canberra B.2 light-bomber, one of which set a new world altitude record of 65,889 feet piloted by W. F. Gibb on 29 August 1955. By this time, the Avon was also the preferred powerplant for the Vickers Valiant, de Havilland Sea Vixen and English Electric Lightning as well as a number of Canadair F-86 Sabres used by the RAF. In service as the Sabre F.4, they equipped 2 EAF Squadrons in West Germany pending delivery of the indigenous Hawker Hunter.

In the civil field, the Avon powered the DH Comet airliner and the French Caravelle. As if three air-speed records and an altitude record were not enough, the Rolls-Royce Avon can lay claim to be the first jet engine to make the first polar intercontinental flight powering an EE Canberra bomber as well as making the first non-stop flight across the Atlantic. Some fifty years later, licensed-built Swedish Flygmotor Avons were still in operational service with the Austrian Air Force powering their Saab J35OE Draken interceptors. (Powered by the Swedish-built Series 300 12,790-lb static thrust Avon known as the RM6C with afterburner, this was a very different Avon engine from that which first emerged from Rolls-Royce in 1946.) A turbofan development of the Avon, the Rolls-Royce Conway, powered the third of the V-bomber trio, the Handley Page Victor, which was renowned for its in-flight refuelling exploits during the Falklands conflict in 1982 and the first Gulf War in 1991.

A major mistake made by British aero-engine companies was to not apply sufficient resources to small engine development and production. This resulted in a loss of orders for the extremely lucrative trainer aircraft market in which the French were eventually to specialise where they produced 10,000 engines over a twenty-year period with projected sales in the following twenty years estimated at around 50,000 units. A second problem was the inability of securing a marriage between a specific engine and suitable airframe, diminishing Britain's competitiveness in the aero-engine market considerably in the two decades immediately following the Second World War. Unfortunately again for British aero-engine manufacturers, they were unable to secure volume series production orders in the larger sector for units to power such aircraft as the Boeing B-52 Stratofortress, Lockheed C-141 Starlifter and C-5 Galaxy. As an example, if we take engines such as the GE J57 and the Bristol Olympus in the 13,000-lb thrust region, some 16,500 GE units were delivered compared to just 1,000 Olympus units produced to meet Avro Vulcan bomber requirements. Another intrinsic problem that severely handicapped British aero-engine manufacturers and airframe makers was that with initial marks of new designs, the correct powerplants for the airframes was not always available. In many instances, early engine variants for initial aircraft batches were somewhat underpowered. An example of this occurred with the Handley Page Victor that should have all been fitted with Rolls-Royce Conways. Also, this may have helped Rolls-Royce maintain a larger share of the civil airliner jet aero-engine market in the mid-1960s.

The Bristol Siddeley Olympus was a twin-spool turbojet, which in effect was two engines in one, since it had two independent compressors each linked to its own turbine. The Olympus 593 had evolved from a design that had commenced twenty-five years earlier to meet the requirement for an engine for the Avro Vulcan bomber that entered RAF service in 1956. As stated, the first

Olympus engines powered an English Electric Canberra light-bomber that broke the world altitude record as long ago as 1953. The original Olympus 100 that powered the Vulcan B.1 was rated at 9,140-lbs static thrust, the 101 was rated at 11,000 lbs and the 104 13,400 lbs. The 201 or 301 at 20,000 lbs were fitted to the Vulcan B.2, but there was plenty more development to exploit in the Olympus. The Olympus 320 was developed for the cancelled BAC TSR.2 bomber where for the first time new materials were introduced to cope with higher operating temperatures. While the TSR.2 project was cancelled in April 1965, a prototype aircraft fitted with Olympus 320s had been flown on a number of occasions from Boscombe Down. In addition, the 320 had undergone considerable test-bed hours running and prior to fitment to the TSR.2 had been test flown in a Vulcan bomber test-bed. It was a giant step for the 38,050-lbs static thrust (tested to 40,000-lbs static thrust) Olympus 593 Mk 601 with 17 per cent afterburning. Also, it was realised that test and development work conducted on the engine for the TSR.2 aircraft was invaluable and it was for this reason the Bristol Olympus was the engine selected to power the Anglo-French *Concorde* SST.

Two major problems had to be overcome in the development of the up-rated Olympus engines. The first was exhibited by the early Olympus 593B variant as fitted to the first two prototype *Concordes* with an unusual amount of arid black smoke that was emitted on take-off and landing. In order to overcome the problem, Rolls-Royce and Snecma decided to develop a combustion chamber of the type already used in the Rolls-Royce Viper, Sapphire and Pegasus engines where similar smoke issues had been encountered. The introduction of the 'annular' combustion chamber as it was called, in conjunction with a new vaporising fuel injector system, made *Concorde's* engines virtually smoke free. The second most pressing problem associated with the up-rated engine was how to cope with the higher operating temperatures encountered in producing the higher thrust required for supersonic flight. At Mach 2.0, air that enters the intake at -60 degrees Centigrade or so will be compressed and be in the region of 130 degrees Centigrade when it reaches the face of the engine. Once the air leaves the compressor, it will reach a temperature of around 550 degrees Centigrade. In order to cope with the extremely high temperatures, it was necessary to reassess the materials used in the subsonic engine. The low-pressure compressor intake and the first stages of the high-pressure compressor are now made of titanium. This means the components are lightweight but robust enough to withstand ice, bird strikes and other foreign objects that may get sucked in the engine. To cope with the high temperatures further back in the engine, nickel-based alloys are used for the final stage of the high-pressure compressor, the combustion chambers, the turbine blades and reheat assembly. Having ensured the up-rated Olympus engines were 'man enough' for the job, comprehensive testing was carried out and by the time the first *Concorde* SST entered airline service, the engine had been test-bed/flight tested for some 46,000 hours.

If the post-war period is split into three ten-year periods, the first from 1945 to 1955 is when aviation was new to jet engines and of experimentation and development with many refinements in materials and gas dynamics. The second ten-year period of 1955-1965 saw a marked improvement of gas dynamics with split compressors, multi-stage arrangements and fans of all kinds with mechanical and novel gas connections. The third period, 1965-1975, straddles a period of change to the use of new materials. Following the lighter, stronger and stiffer aluminium of the 1930s, 1940s and 1950s, came titanium and stainless steel. These new materials led to three categories of super materials such as oxide-dispersed alloys, laminated composites and polymers-organic and non-organic synthetics. With these new materials, the aim of the aero-engine designer is to achieve 10,000 hours between an engine overhaul. The new materials permitted twice the power-to-weight ratio and thus a considerable reduction in fuel consumption by about 5-10 per cent to values below half the typical 1950s and 1960s figures.

Rationalisation and mergers over the fifty years since the Second World War left Britain with just one aero-engine manufacturer: Rolls-Royce Ltd. With two groups, the Civil Engine Group and the Military Engine Group, Rolls-Royce has also acquired Allison Engines of the US. The company now claims to have the largest 'thrust range' from the diminutive Williams Rolls FJ 44 used in the Cessna Citation Jet to the Trent Series, currently the most powerful range of aero-engines in the world. New engines available include the AE2100 for the Lockheed C-130J Hercules II, Saab 2000 regional airliner and ITPN's N250 transport as well as the AE3007 for the Citation X and Embraer EMB-145 regional jet. Also, the BMW/Rolls-Royce BR715 was designed for the MD-95 and the BR710 powers the Canadair Global Express (it was also to be the powerplant of the cancelled BAe Nimrod 2000 (MRA 4)). The company is also working with GE on the F120 powerplant for the Joint Strike Fighter (JSF) aka Lockheed Martin F-35 (Lightning II). The company currently employs 40,700 people and produces civil and military gas turbine engines for more than 320 airlines, 120 armed forces and 640 executive customers. The company's aero gas-turbine activities are based at Derby, Glasgow, Bristol and Coventry. Rolls-Royce is also involved in a number of collaborative joint ventures with other aero-engine firms such as BMW/Rolls-Royce, Rolls-Royce Turbomeca MTR, Eurojet (Eurofighter Typhoon) IAE, Turbo Union and Williams Rolls Inc. in the US. On 24 March 1995, Rolls-Royce Plc completed the £331 million ($525 million) acquisition of the Allison Engine Company in Indianapolis, Indiana. At the same time, Rolls-Royce announced its intention to continue and expand Allison without changing in name, programmes or workforce.

Research into aero-engines continues both in the US and the former Soviet

Union. In the UK, Rolls-Royce is locked into a technology demonstrator programme which should see a new combat aircraft engine produced with some 40 to 60 per cent improvement in thrust-to-weight ratio over the Eurofighter's EJ 200 powerplant. Also, improvements are always being sought in other areas of engine development such as fuel burn, life cycle and acquisition costs. However, enhancements to the jet engine as we know it are definitely finite. Endeavouring to double the power-to-weight ratio of existing designs by 2020 may not be worth the effort or cost. It should be borne in mind that an essential requirement of a modern day powerplant is like its airframe: it needs to be 'stealthy'. Gone are the days of the 'smoke generators' as fitted to the MDC F-4 Phantom II and other aircraft of the era. The way forward might well be the Integrated High-Performance Turbine Engine Technology (IHPTET) programme currently under development in the US. By 2005, IHPTET was planned to be delivering 100 per cent thrust-to-weight improvements over current fighter-type jet engines.

Chapter 3

British Aero-Engines 1915–1945 and the New Jet Propulsion

In the early years of the Second World War, the average radial inline or engine built in Great Britain generated around 700 hp, although special racing engines such as those developed for the Schneider Trophy floatplanes were a different case. The first Rolls-Royce Merlin, the 1934 model, generated 700 hp. Two years later, this engine provided 900 hp. This period led to the last stage in the evolution of the piston aero-engine. Once the inline engine had reached the end of its development, design and production, engineers focussed on the large radial types that powered the heavy bombers. These engines were necessary for aircraft making long intercontinental and transoceanic flights. Also, they were undoubtedly best suited for the long-range heavy bombers, even though they were extremely noisy and caused a lot of vibration. It was in Germany and the UK that the reciprocating aero-engine reached its upper limits and finally gave way to its successor, the jet engine, where Germany and the UK led the world in this development.

The 1915 Rolls-Royce Eagle liquid-cooled V12 was developed in unison with the Falcon and marked the beginning of a long line of famous Rolls-Royce engines. Developed in several versions, the Eagle ended with the 1917 375-hp Mk VII version. It was the engine that powered the famous Vickers

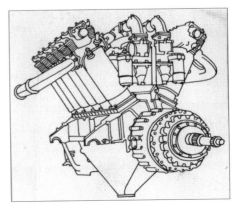

Rolls-Royce Eagle c. 1915, the Mk VII developing 375-hp introduced in 1917 powered the Vomy that Alcock and Brown flew across the Atlnatic in June 1919. (V. Cosentino)

Napier Lion *c.* 1918 developed towards the end of the First World War and was one of themost important British Aerooengines of the era. A 12-cylinder W engine designed by A. J. Rowledge it could generate 450-hp. A racing version could generate 1,329-hp. (*Wings*)

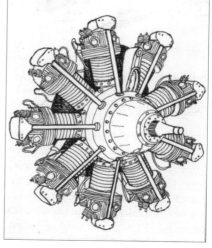

Left: Bristol Jupiter *c.* 1920. Designed by Roy Fedden, this was one of the most popular engines of the 1920s. It could generate 375–400-hp and 500-hp versions were developed. *Right:* Bristol Mercury *c.* 1927. This was the second engine that Bristol built after the Jupiter, a 9-cylinder radial power output 725–905-hp. (*V. Cosentino*)

Vimy that Alcock and Brown flew across the North Atlantic in June 1919.

The Napier Lion generated 450 hp at 1,925 rpm and was a liquid-cooled engine developed towards the end of the Second World War. Also, it was one of the most important British aero-engines of the era. Designed by A. J. Rowledge, it was a twelve-cylinder W-engine having three banks of four engines set at sixty degrees. Several versions of the engine were built with ever greater power generated. A racing version produced 1,320 hp at 3,600 rpm.

The Bristol Jupiter 375–400-500-hp nine-cylinder radial was one of the most popular engines of the 1920s and was license-produced in no less than sixteen countries. It was a nine-cylinder radial engine that could generate from 375 to 400 hp in its original form, but over the years as the design improved it could provide up to 500 hp.

The Bristol Mercury 725–905-hp nine-cylinder radial was the second engine that Bristol built in 1927 after the 1920s Jupiter, although it had the same general structure as its predecessor. It was a nine-cylinder radial engine with a reduction gear. Power output varied between 725 hp and 906 hp. Although the Mercury design was an old one, the engine was used in several airplanes during the Second World War with a total of 20,700 built between 1939 and 1945 alone.

Produced initially in 1927, the DH Gipsy Major 1 130-hp inline engine was to be the start of a long line of world famous Gipsy engines. However, almost all Gipsy Majors were used in de Havilland light Moth aircraft during the 1930s and made a significant contribution to post-First World War civil aviation in the UK. Among the 27,654 de Havilland Gipsy series built from 1932 to 1947 were the Gipsy Minor, Major, Six, Queen and King.

This Rolls-Royce liquid-cooled V12 engine started life in 1929 and when fitted to Reginald Mitchell's Supermarine S.6 floatplane racer won the Schneider Trophy for the UK. However, the engine only reached its pinnacle in 1931 by way of the Rolls-Royce R that generated 2,350 hp. Unbeknown at the time, it was to be the progenitor of the famous Rolls-Royce Merlin as was the S.6 to give rise to Mitchell's equally famous Supermarine Spitfire.

In 1932, Bristol produced the 450-1,000-hp Pegasus radial and the Perseus nine-cylinder, sleeve-valve radial which were followed in 1936 by the Taurus fourteen-cylinder, sleeve-valve, two-row radial.

The famous 1936 Rolls-Royce Merlin 990-2,000-hp, liquid-cooled V12 – around 160,000 were built with 55,235 produced in the US by Packard and Ford – was developed from the engine that powered the Supermarine racing airplanes. The Merlin also powered one of the most important British monoplane designs of the Second World War: the legendary Spitfire. A twelve-cylinder V-engine, its power increased from 990 hp of the prototypes to almost 2,000 hp of the final models.

The Bristol Hercules 1,375-1,800-hp, twelve-cylinder radial (57,400

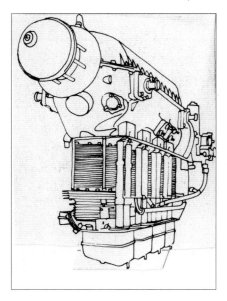

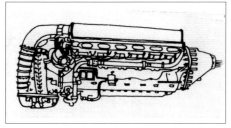

Above: Rolls-Royce R *c.* 1931. The engine that won the Schneider Trophy for Great britain was built in 1929; a 12-cylinder Vee could generate 2,300-hp. (*V. Consentino*)

Left: de Havilland Gipsy Major I *c.* 1927; an air-cooled 4-cylinder inline engine that generated 130-hp. (*V. Consentino*)

built) was one of the most powerful engines of the Second World War and it powered many of the famous heavy bombers such as the Lancaster, Halifax and Stirling. It first appeared in 1936 and 57,400 were produced during the war.

The Rolls-Royce Griffon was the successor to the Merlin and retained its basic design of twelve cylinders in a V formation. It was water-cooled and supercharged by means of a compressor of one or two stages and two speeds. Extensive use was made of the Griffon during the latter stages of the war to power the late and post-war Supermarine Spitfire designs with power increasing from 1,730 hp to 2,300 hp in the final version.

After the successful Hercules engine in 1943, Bristol produced the Centaurus, a 2,500-3,000-hp, sleeve-valve radial (wartime production: 2,500) and this engine reached the upper limits for power output in its category. The Centaurus in its original form was derived from the Hercules, a typical feature being the adoption of valves situated in the cylinders and not in the cylinder head. However, it was a considerably bigger and heavier engine with eighteen cylinders in two rows instead of fourteen. The Bristol Centaurus was used mainly to power military airplanes, but in the immediate post-war period, some of the numerous versions available were also put to civil use.

Developed from 1947 onwards, the Bristol Proteus turboprop engine was used in numerous civil and military airplanes, in particular the Britannia airliner. During its lengthy process of development, the engine's power was increased to a massive 4,400 hp from the meagre 760 hp when it first appeared in the early 1940s. When compared with the Rolls-Royce Dart, the

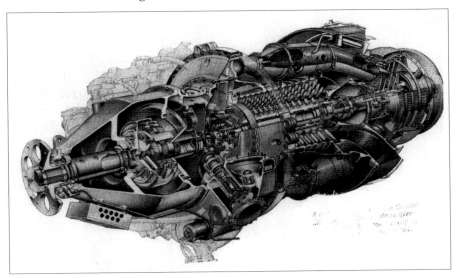

Above: Bristol Hercules *c.* 1936 power 1,375 to 1,800-hp. (*V. Consentino*)

Right: Bristol Perseus *c.* 1932 9-cylinder air-cooled sleeve-valve engine 24.9 litres was the first mass-produced sleeve-valve engine in the world. (*V. Consentino*)

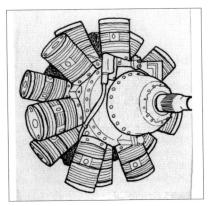

Below: Rolls-Royce Griffon *c.* 1942. Successor to Merlin, retaining its basic 12-cylinders in a V-formation. Water-cooled and super-chargesd power increased from 1,730 to 2,300-hp in the final version. (*V. Consentino*)

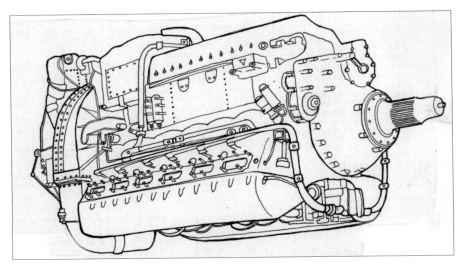

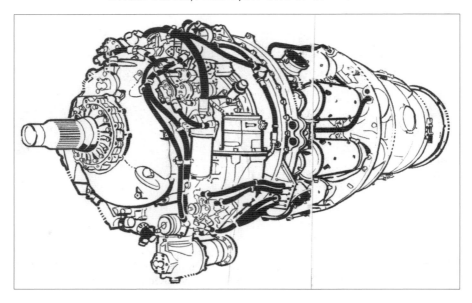

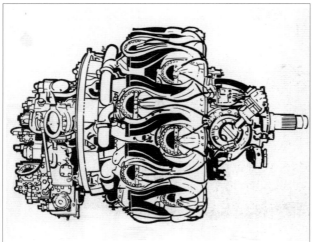

Above: Bristol Proteus
c. 1947 turbo-prop
750 series used in
the Britannia, 1960s
760 4,400-shp. (*V.
Consentino*)

Left: Bristol Centuras
c. 1943 derived from
the Hercules upper limit
3,000-hp.

Proteus was somewhat more complex. The compressor comprised of twelve axial stages and a centrifugal stage. There were eight combustion chambers and the turbine consisted of two separate units, each with two stages. The first unit drove the compressor and the second powered the reduction gear of the propeller shaft. It was also rather heavy for its size. The Proteus 705 as fitted to series production Bristol Britannias in the initial series had a dry weight of 2,807 lbs (1,273 kg).

Also during the post-war years, Rolls-Royce produced the Dart turboprop engine that was fitted to the world's first turboprop passenger plane: the

Rolls-Royce Dart *c.* 1945 was fitted to the first passenger turbo-prop to operate regular route services in the world: the Vickers Viscount. The project for the engine started in 1945 but with constant updating the power of the engine increased by over 150 per cent over the years. (*Wings*)

Rolls-Royce Avon was the turbojet which earned great credit for British aero-engineering in the 1950s. It was installed in numerous military aircraft but was also developed for civil use as the R.A.29. The initial thrust of 4,763 kg (10,500 lb) was increased to 5,675 kg (12,500 lb) in the last version as installed in the DH Comet airliner. (*Wings*)

Vickers Viscount. The project for this engine first began in 1945, but the basic design was developed by a constant process of updating which saw the power of the Dart increased by more than 150 per cent.

The Rolls-Royce Avon was the jet engine that earned great renown for the British aero-engine industry in the 1950s. Unlike the Derwent, the Avon was not only installed in numerous military aircraft, but was also developed specifically for civil use as the RA.29. The initial thrust of 10,500 lbs (4,763 kg) of the version installed in the infamous DH Comet increased to 12,500 lbs (5,675 kg) in the final versions. The civil Avon had a sixteen-stage axial compressor, eight combustion chambers and a three-stage turbine.

Aero-engine designer and mathematician Sir Stanley Hooker (1907-1984) came to the fore in the industry by greatly improving the performance of Rolls-Royce Merlin superchargers. His work made a major improvement to the amount of power generated by the engines, thereby greatly increasing the speed at which British Second World War combat planes flew. When Rolls-Royce took over early W.2B jet engine work from Rover Car Co., managing director Ernest Hives placed Hooker in charge at Rover's former works at Barnoldswick. Hooker supervised production of the Derwent and developed the Nene, the latter entering licensed-production in France, Australia, Canada and the US (as well as Russia and China where it was reversed engineered). However, after a falling out with Hives, Hooker moved to Bristol Engines Ltd to sort out their troublesome Proteus turboprop and developed the Olympus and highly successful Orpheus. In the 1960s, Hooker worked with Sidney Camm, Hawker's chief designer, to design the vectored-thrust Pegasus that in various upgrades and ratings powered the various marks of military Harrier I and II V/STOL Jump Jets. Though not often mentioned, it should be noted that the Bristol (Rolls-Royce) Pegasus engine design concept received some input from French aero-engine designer Michel Wibault.

Sir Stanley Hooker retired in 1967 or so he thought. However, in 1970, he returned to Rolls-Royce Derby to resolve issues that had plagued the production of the massive RB 211 engine that Lockheed had on order for its L1011 TriStar, the project having gone awry following the death of chief designer Adrian Lombard. Hooker succeeded in curing the engine of its problems, but not before Rolls-Royce was forced into insolvency, an act that very nearly crippled Lockheed too. Nevertheless, Rolls-Royce resurrected itself as Rolls-Royce (1970) Derby Ltd and with the RB 211 problem solved, the company went from strength to strength continuing development of the powerplant that became one of the most reliable and efficient in airline service. Rolls-Royce secured many worldwide orders and the engine continues to be a major export earner for Britain securing the company as a cutting edge specialist in engine technology, especially in the military field in collaboration with other American and European aero-engine concerns.

Sources and Bibliography

Sources

The British Library, Great Russell Street, London
Dancey, Peter G., Milton Keynes, Buckinghamshire (author personal archives)
Imperial War Museum, Lambeth Road, London (library and archives)
Public Record Office, Kew, Surrey (Air Ministry and Ministry of Aircraft Production Files)
The Royal Aeronautical Society, 4 Hamilton Place, London (library and archive material)
Royal Aircraft Establishment, Main Library, Q4 Building, Farnborough, Hampshire
Royal Air Force Museum, Hendon, London (manufacturers' archives)

Books

British Aerospace: The Facts (BAe, London: several editions)
Bristol Aircraft, Westland Aircraft, Aircraft of the Fighting Powers, Vols I to VII (Harborough Books, Hayward)
British Aircraft Industry, The (Manchester University Press, 1989)
Following the Standards of Henry Royce (Rolls-Royce, London, 1989)
Gunston, Bill, *World Encyclopaedia of Aircraft Manufacturers* (PSL, London, 1993)
Günter, Endres, *British Aircraft Manufacturers Since 1908* (Ian Allan Ltd, London, 1995)
Jane's All the World's Aircraft, 1919, 1930, 1938, 1945-46, 1960-61, 1970-71, 1980-81, 1992-93, 1995-96
Longyard, William, *Who's Who in Aviation Military History* (Airlife, Shrewsbury, England, 1994)

Mason, Francis K. *British Fighters and British Bombers*

Military Registers from J1 to VZ999 (Air Britain Books: twenty-two volumes)

Morgan, Eric B. and Edward Shacklady, *Spitfire – The History* (Key Publishing Ltd, 1987/2000)

Plowden Report on the Aircraft Industry (1966)

Production 1935-1941 (Frank Cass, London, 1997)

Robertson, Bruce, *British Military Aircraft Serials 1912-1966* (Ian Allan Ltd, London, 1967)

Rolls-Royce: SBAC (The Society of British Aerospace Companies) (Britain in Aerospace, London, 1985)

Sebastian, Richie, *Industry and Air Power: The Expansion of the British Aircraft* (Frank Cass, London, 1997)

Shorts Bombardier (company publication, Belfast, 1990)

Thetford, Owen, *Aircraft of the Royal Air Force & British Naval Aircraft Planemakers*

Magazines and Periodicals

Aviation magazine and periodicals (various)

Flight Special (October 1956 issue on the British aircraft industry)

Wings Part Work (Orbis Publishing)

Take-off Part Work (Orbis Publishing)